LIVING
ISLAM

From Samarkand to Stornoway

LIVING ISLAM

AKBAR S. AHMED

AN INFOBASE HOLDINGS COMPANY

Only connect

In the hope that this book will help
to connect different peoples and different faiths
and thereby encourage understanding between them.

Published by arrangement with BBC Books,
a division of BBC Enterprises Ltd.

Copyright © 1994 by Akbar S. Ahmed

Facts On File, Inc.
460 Park Avenue South
New York NY 10016

Library of Congress Cataloging-in-Publication Data

Ahmed, Akbar S.
    Living Islam: from Samarkand to Stornoway/Akbar S. Ahmed.
      p. cm.
    Includes bibliographical references (p.) and index.
    ISBN 0–8160–3103–7: (alk. paper)
    1. Islam.   2. Islamic countries.   I. Title.
BP161.2.A443   1994
909'.097671—dc20   93–38378

A British CIP catalogue record for this book is available from the British Library

Facts On File books are available at special discounts when purchased in
bulk quantities for businesses, associations, institutions or sales
promotions. Please call our Special Sales Department in New York at
212/683–2244 or 800/322–8755.

Manufactured by Butler & Tanner Ltd
Printed in Great Britain

10 9 8 7 6 5 4 3 2 1

This book is printed on acid-free paper.

Contents

Preface

In our world, Islam is a challenge, a mystery and an enigma. The subtitle of this book, *From Samarkand to Stornoway*, reflects this. It encapsulates a journey in time and space; but it is also a journey in imagination. Samarkand in the past was famous as a great and glittering Muslim capital. The Golden Road to Samarkand was as much a figment of the literary imagination evoking the romance of the East as the symbol of a period in history. What is generally not known is that there is also a small, thriving and integrated Muslim community in Stornoway in the Outer Hebrides. The subtitle therefore suggests that Muslims are truly a global community. I hope to convey what it feels like to be a Muslim today, what are the main problems that Muslims face, how history colours their perception of the present, why they feel strongly on certain issues which are often in the news, and what are the essential features of their religion, Islam.

Consider how many different ways Islam is viewed. Islam is not only attractive mystical poetry, superbly symmetrical architecture and esoteric Sufi thought; Islam is also mobs in the street, young men attacking embassies and images of self-flagellation on the television screen. Islam has become all things to all people. It is not only theology; it is also polemics, debate, media images, conflict and a point of view.

This book arose out of a BBC television series with the same title. The aim of both projects is to help explain the other, the strange, the foreign, the distant. Underlying this attempt is the hope that explanation will engender understanding. This is desperately needed in a world so increasingly full of hatred based on ignorance of other people. The spirit in which I shall examine Muslim societies, customs and attitudes will emphasize that looking at the other is not to look at the exotic, the strange or the bizarre. It is simply to look at the different. My aim will be not to minimize the differences but to explain them.

Writing this book posed a dilemma. The television series derived from, and was in part based on, two of my recent books – *Discovering Islam: Making Sense of History and Society* (1988) and *Postmodernism and Islam: Predicament and Promise* (1992). The challenge was thus to write a book which was completely new but which reflected some of the earlier arguments; the material was to be fresh yet in a sense familiar. This I have tried to do.

The journeys I made during the course of this project were fraught with uncertainty. There was the nightmare of travel and life under the remnants of the Soviet system. At Dushanbe airport for the flight to Samarkand we were told the plane had not arrived. No one knew why. It could be shortage of fuel. It could have been a change of schedule. It could have been political problems between the two recently independent Central Asian states. We were advised to take the road to Samarkand. It was a journey that would take ten hours.

There were also real dangers. We were filming in Tajikistan in the summer of 1992 with a civil war raging in the background. At night from the hotel in Dushanbe I could hear gunfire. To interview an Islamic leader I travelled a hundred kilometres into the mountains where he was avoiding the authorities. The president fell a few days later. In Moscow I was attacked by a gang of young gypsies outside the Kremlin in broad daylight. In Qum, Iran's holy city, I, along with the BBC television crew, experienced some nervous moments when an excitable crowd surrounded us until the arrival of the local gendarmerie.

In the following pages we will travel to and fro in time and space; the reader must bear with me. The book is not academic. I am not propounding and defending a thesis. It is not a chronological history; for that there are other admirable books. The book is impressionistic – part travelogue, part history.

I write and record and analyse the reality of Islam today. I cannot invent or create something that does not exist. So even if I do not like or approve of something I must record it, for the sake of authenticity and accuracy. Some of what I write may displease Muslims, some will displease non-Muslims. Scholars may criticize me for not being scholarly enough; others for being too scholarly. Some Muslims may criticize me for not being Islamic enough, others for being too Islamic. This is expected. I am dealing with a subject that is over a thousand years old and has always been at the centre of debate and controversy. It is not an easy subject to write about, especially today.

There are many important Muslim countries, such as Nigeria in the western part of the Muslim world and Indonesia in the eastern, which have been left out owing to considerations of space. And although about a third of the total Muslim population live in South Asia some may still regard my South Asian references as excessive.

What repeatedly emerged throughout the Muslim world was the unity of Muslim belief and yet the diversity of Muslim societies. So while prayers, values, emotions and even architecture reflect unity, their expression often changes within a different cultural and political environment.

The reader must be prepared to have old assumptions challenged and prejudices overturned. We will challenge many assumptions and look afresh at stereotypes: that Muslims are fanatic, that they destroyed Christian churches and Hindu temples; that Christians have been tolerant; that Muslim civilization is worthless; that Muslims spread Islam with sword in one hand and Quran in the other; and that Muslim women are mistreated and subjugated.

Throughout the filming of the series I faced questions of my own identity. When pressed I will say that I am a Sunni with Pukhtun ancestry and also that of the Sayyed, the descendants of the Prophet. But I do not feel especially spiritual or religious on account of family background. Rather, I come to Islam from the conviction that in it I find the best way to grasp the complexity and pain of living in a world with so many religions and races, each insisting on its superiority. Islam gives me security and stability, a sense of identity, a coherent world-view in a world constantly in flux.

I do not pretend I have all the answers; I am not even sure I have raised all the right questions. For me, this has been a journey of discovery, a journey that promises to be unending.

Far too many people have given of their generous support to the television series and this book to be named in acknowledgement. I must, however, express my gratitude to the executive producers of the television series: to my friends Hugh Purcell, for his unfailing support, good cheer and understanding, and Paul Kriwaczek; also to John Percival, Jonathan Drori and all the other producers, researchers, assistants, camera and sound technicians who contributed so enthusiastically to the series.

Suzanne Webber, Linden Stafford, Khadija Manjlai and Martha Caute have been ideal editors: wise, helpful and enthusiastic. Peter Avery, Dr Abdul Mabud, Professor Francis Robinson and Dr Chris Rojek have supported both the book and the series with characteristic generosity from the start, and I am most grateful. I warmly acknowledge the Faculty of Oriental Studies and Selwyn College, University of Cambridge, for their marvellous hospitality and for providing an academic atmosphere conducive to creative work. Finally, my deepest gratitude, as always, to my wife Zeenat for her support for the series and the book. She also typed the drafts of the book and in a heroic burst completed over 800 pages of the first draft in August 1992 when she should have been enjoying the brief English summer and our baby daughter, Nafees.

Akbar S. Ahmed
December 1992, Cambridge

ONE

INTRODUCTION: RAISING QUESTIONS

●

On the threshold of the next millennium two global civilizations appear to be poised in a complex confrontation on various levels of human activity. One is based in Muslim countries and the other in the West (mainly North America and western Europe). For the sake of simplification we will use the shorthand terms Islam and the West, although they are unsatisfactory and do not express the diversity and complexity of either Islam or the West. The central ideas of both are expressed through the processes of globalization and radicalization that swirl and eddy around the world like an atmospheric storm. Commentators are already seeing the confrontation in apocalyptic terms and calling it the last crusade.

ISLAM AND THE WEST

It is well to remember that there are about a billion Muslims in the world today. Significantly, about ten million of them live in the West and are shared about equally between the USA and Europe. There are about fifty Muslim nations, the number having been inflated by the six recently independent former Soviet republics.

In the next decades the planet will continue to shrink at a breathtaking pace because of the rapid technological changes in the media, transport, communications and so on. It is therefore clear that few exercises will be more worthwhile than helping to increase understanding between Islam and the West, with a view to easing the tension between them. Confrontation is neither necessary nor desirable; besides, there is much in common both in ideas and in human societies. It is this which needs to be increasingly explored. We need to be able to see the other and say: 'We understand you are different but we also understand your difference.'

Despite the many superficial differences, deeper and more permanent values are similar: the respect for knowledge, for justice, for compassion towards the less privileged, for a healthy family life, the need to improve the here and now. The last is significant. Islam, unlike some other religions, does not reject the world. The Muslim ideal balances matters of the world (*dunya*) with ideas of religion (*din*); a good Muslim must participate in both. This goes a long way towards explaining the power and popularity of Islam in today's world.

Although there is a genuine desire in the West to understand Islam, people do have a problem in understanding it, perhaps because of the mutually hostile experiences of the last thousand years. False images and ideas are thus perpetuated. For example, it is an almost unshakeable article of belief in the West that Muslims treat their women badly and that Muslim priests – in the form of mullahs – tyrannize Muslim society. We will show that these assumptions are not correct. None the less, Europeans will instinctively refer to their own medieval times, recalling the long and tortuous struggle to free themselves of the church's domination. Confronting the images they themselves created and imposed on to Muslims, they are really looking at their own history. In order to appreciate Islam, therefore, Europe must come to terms with its own past. An exercise like this is crucial not only for building bridges with the alien other, but also for exorcizing the ghosts within.

Muslims complain of being colonized by the West twice over: politically in the last century and then culturally in this one. But Europe also has its memory of Islamic conquest in the first centuries after Islam. Spain and Sicily were under Muslim domination for centuries, and Muslim armies were stopped from conquering France by Charles Martel in the eighth century. Vienna was almost conquered twice, the second attempt being made in the seventeenth century. It is time, then, to stop scoring points against each other and start looking at the new realities and the future.

Only a few decades ago it appeared possible for Islam and the West to be compartmentalized into separate geographical areas; indeed they seemed destined to live on different continents. This is no longer true. By the 1980s we had become aware of how interlinked and interwoven the modern world actually is. Not only are millions of Muslims living in Europe and the USA but there are thousands from the West working in Muslim countries. Besides, there are large Muslim groups like those in former Yugoslavia, who are European by race, culture and location. Furthermore, scholars and students, diplomats and politicians, economists and entrepreneurs continue to travel to and fro between the two. In any case videos, television, fax and satellite communications ensure that everyone on the planet has access to common ideas and programmes; it is no longer possible to isolate one from the other.

Although Western ideologies seem mainly to be rooted in a vision of the world as secular, democratic and ordered by the need to acquire material goods for a satisfactory life, whereas those of Islam are motivated primarily by religious belief, the picture in practice is not so simple or clear. It is further confused by elements of both philosophies in each camp. Many living in secular material societies openly challenge them; many look back to traditional beliefs and seek answers in religion or ethnicity or the tribal group. Similarly, many of those who live in Muslim societies pay only lip-service to the notions of piety and faith, and often disguise materialist greed with religious rhetoric.

In the Gulf War of 1991 we saw how America's attempts to maintain global hegemony, to ensure continuing supplies of oil so that the high material lifestyles of the West could be maintained, were also a chance to show who was boss or, as the American soldiers put it, to 'kick ass'. For many Arabs who opposed Saddam Hussein and his policies their paradoxical support of Iraq was a gesture of defiance against the West. What began as an unpopular invasion by a larger neighbour ended up with huge processions in Morocco, Egypt, Jordan, Pakistan and even India supporting Saddam. Somehow his standing up to the West had tapped deep reservoirs of resentment in many parts of Africa and Asia. Those people who still clung to tradition and religious belief were depressed by world developments for which they blamed the West, in particular the USA, which symbolized the West. Support for Saddam allowed them to express their disgust and anger at forces they felt were enveloping them but which they could not fully comprehend or control. Their support had little to do with the merits of Saddam or his policies – both roundly condemned by the very same Muslims before the war.

Later in the year, many Muslims with funds in the Bank of Credit and Commerce International (BCCI) were financially devastated by its collapse. None the less, throughout the Muslim world there was a perception that the hostile media attacks on the BCCI were motivated by hatred for Muslims. Imam Khomeini's *fatwa* condemning Salman Rushdie to death in 1989 had kept these attacks on the boil (see chapter 4). Indeed, Western commentators were freely talking of a 'criminal culture'.

The confrontation between Islam and the West is widely seen in the Muslim world as a straightforward clash between greed and faith, between a way of life that encourages violence and anarchy and one that stresses balance and order. Yet these images are completely reversed in the Western viewpoint, which tends to see Muslims as a source of violence and anarchy threatening a stable and prosperous West. It is truly a topsy-turvy world, but perhaps by simplifying difficult and complex issues we can hope to make some sense of it.

LOCATING THE KEY TO UNLOCK MUSLIM SOCIETY

Anyone acquainted with the work of the great Persian poets (Hafiz, Sadi, Firdausi), the travelling scholars writing in Arabic (Al-Beruni, Ibn Battuta, Ibn Khaldun) or the Mughal rulers (Babar, Jahangir) will have discovered something of the richness and complexity of Islamic culture. We will try to locate the key to unlock the mysteries of Muslim civilization. The Islamic tradition is rooted in thought and debate, a tradition going back to the Prophet himself. The history of Islam is the history of ideas and their power to affect people's actions. Today there is a bewildering range of theories and trends which form the intellectual baggage confronting the young at the end of the century. Many of these are fads and fashions which rise and fall with different generations.

When Islam first appeared, it came with a big idea. The idea was that you could believe in the divine directly and yet live in the here and now; this reflected the central principles of balance (*adl*) and compassion (*ihsan*) in all walks of life. Today, in sharp contrast, Muslims are often stuck with small ideas. Some are locked in battles raging around political parties, others in conflicts regarding ethnic identity. The idea of a single integrated unity that explains the universe is reduced to the notion of the clan or lineage; from the universe to the village is as dramatic a jump as one can make and highlights the dilemmas of contemporary Muslims.

Although Islam emphasizes balance and order, many Muslim societies show signs of internal warfare and confrontation. The issues are not Islamic but often tribal or ethnic. Many societies are witnessing a breakdown of law and order as people lose faith in the administrative and political systems. These societies have moved away from the Islamic ideal which is based in the Quran and the life of the Prophet. It does not help them but further worsens the situation, since Muslims are always aware of how far they are moving from the ideal. So the further they move the greater the dissatisfaction in society and the stronger the need to move back towards the ideal. However, although Muslim society and Islam in the ideal are fused, in reality many

Muslims do not live by the ideal. It is the attempt to live, as far as possible, according to the custom and laws of Islam that provides one of the most crucial dynamics of Muslim society.

My attempt, therefore, is to explain the processes at work among Muslims, not to whitewash them. So if a husband mistreats his wife or if a political figure is corrupt or a religious one a hypocrite I cannot condone their actions simply on account of their being Muslim. Muslimness in itself, the label of Muslim, is no guarantee of good behaviour. This is what the Quran tells us – that each individual is responsible for his or her own actions. I shall point out where Muslims are able to live by the ideal and where they are not. By not concealing what is wrong I will indicate how Muslims interpret their own social reality.

This simple model of society should help us understand events throughout the Muslim world. From Algeria to Pakistan similar tensions are evident in society. Those who sympathize with Islam wish to be given a chance to explain and implement their vision of society. They stress that what exists is not Islamic and has clearly failed to deliver the goods. They point to the anarchy, corruption, nepotism and general dissatisfaction among the people.

Islam constantly points to the interlinking of everything, the unity of the universe. It is in this context that the notion of *tauhid*, or the oneness of God and the unity of existence that it reflects, is so critical in understanding the Muslim attitude to life. The Quran constantly emphasizes that we must walk softly on the earth and that we are tenants and not owners of the earth; we are here for a short while only. It is this sense of transience that creates not only humility but the knowledge that we must leave things behind, if not better, certainly not worse than we found them. The Quranic injunction to look at the stars and wonder, to look at different peoples and races and wonder, to acquire knowledge and wonder, is in itself wonderful. It evokes the essential spirit of humanity in facing the challenge of existence.

Some Western scholars of Islam talk of many Islams, a 'Moroccan Islam', an 'Indian Islam' and so on. This is inaccurate and misleading. There is one Islam only. Throughout the world Muslims accept that it is rooted in the Quran and the *sunnah*, the life of the Prophet. Together they point to the *shariah*, the Islamic path. However, culture, history and ecology have affected how Muslims live their lives.

It is well to recall that Islam not only caused Islamic civilization to develop but also enabled the European Renaissance to take root and grow. The time when Islam was most strongly established was also the time when art, culture and literature flourished, whether in Spain or, later, under the

Ottomans, the Safavids and the Mughals. Christian Europe was enveloped in darkness until Islam came to the Iberian peninsula. For centuries Islam fed Greek, Sanskrit and Chinese ideas into Europe. Slowly and steadily Europe began to absorb these ideas. In England, France, Germany and Italy society began to explore literature and art with a new perspective; thus the seeds of the Renaissance were sown.

Yet centuries later Hollywood, one of the most powerful image-makers of history, glibly created its own early images of the Orient and Muslims (the two were equated). Half-naked faqirs lying on beds of nails, and rope-tricks and magic carpets defying gravity, depicted a mysterious, half-understood Orient. Whether or not these images were also vaguely associated with Islam (Hollywood was never particular about anthropological accuracy), they conveyed the message that in some ways the people of the Orient were different from other human beings, that they possessed some secret powers that were not available in the West. Obviously nails puncture the skin and gravity has the same force for an American as for an Indian. What makes people different is the way the civilization within which they live conditions them to respond to reality. While not being able to defy nature or gravity, a Muslim can certainly express an understanding of reality through Islamic concepts that seem strange, mysterious and even threatening to the West.

How, then, are Muslims different? The answer is that they are not. What is different is the emphasis each culture places on universal aspects of life. It is emphasized in Islam that life must be one of balance; that a person must pray but also find time for the family; that one must eat in moderation and take regular physical exercise; that personal hygiene and cleanliness are necessary; that sex is natural but should be restricted to the legal bounds of marriage, and so on.

Thus Islam is not only about angels and divine revelations. As a theology it generates particular social practices in culture, manners, food and language, and in this respect Islam is also sociology. The Prophet's sayings encourage Muslims to greet one another warmly, to avoid gossip and slander, to accept invitations to visit one another, to call on those who are sick, to join funeral processions. It is also about children respecting parents, and parents giving love and affection to children. Islam encourages social activity, a sense of community, a sense of belonging, a sense of place. It explains the remarkable resilience of Muslim communities through the ups and downs of history and in their changing situation in different non-Muslim societies. Islam is an entire civilization; it is a philosophy of life.

All this does not, of course, mean that every Muslim is a saintly character who never thinks of wrongdoing. Muslims have the same drives and desires as people everywhere. But if they violate Islamic laws and customs they are no longer behaving according to Islam.

Islamic custom is largely derived from the five pillars based on the Quran and the life of the Prophet (see chapter 2). This is called *riwaj* (Afghanistan and Pakistan) or *adab* (Persia, South Asia and Arabia). It includes culture, food, clothes, language and various aspects of behaviour. It is *adab* that defines a Muslim: one can be a bad Muslim from the orthodox point of view and yet a good one because of *adab*, and vice versa. A convert to Islam may master Arabic and be an orthodox Muslim yet be weak on *adab*.

The need for non-Muslims is not to look at Muslim practice and say, 'My, how exotic', but to look at it and say, 'Yes, *we* don't do this but we can appreciate why *you* do'.

MISUNDERSTANDING MUSLIMS

There are certain essential terms deriving from Islam that need to be explained. Some are rooted in Islam and are authentic in their usage. Others are used loosely in the Western media, often incorrectly. As we shall come across them in the following pages, it will be useful to acquaint ourselves with them.

The concept of the *ummah*, community or brotherhood, may be intangible and even amorphous but it is powerful. It allows ideas to be carried across national borders and can generate emotions wherever Muslims live. It is the notion of the *ummah* that triggers a response when Muslims see or hear scenes of other Muslims being denied their rights or being brutally suppressed when voicing them.

Another concept that is widely known but usually incorrectly applied is that of *jihad*. The concept in Western literature and usage has come to mean the idea of holy war, of Muslim fanaticism. In fact *jihad* means struggle, and there are various forms of it; physical confrontation is just one. The holy Prophet identified the greatest *jihad* as the struggle to master our passions and instincts. It is therefore a much more complex and sophisticated concept than that bandied about in the media.

Fatwa is another Islamic word that has become current in the West because of its pronouncement against Salman Rushdie, the author of *The Satanic Verses* (1988). The term simply means a formal opinion or decision on a point of Islamic law. A *fatwa* can be delivered by any religious leader on a variety of topics. It does not have the status of law and, indeed, must be ratified in a proper court if it is to carry legal status. Its authority is also generally restricted to the cultural or geographical boundaries within which the Muslim divine who delivers the *fatwa* functions.

Islam is seen in the West as an evangelical religion, wishing to spread the message and encourage conversion. This is correct. Muslims are enthusiastic about *dawah*, the call to Islam. This *dawah* is usually carried out not by government but by private organizations, by the hard work and dedication of scholars and ordinary people. The conversions are based on low-key and ordinary humdrum activity. They are usually conducted in the local mosque by the local Imam. Muslim conversion is a simple affair. It rests on the declaration of faith – the *shahada*. Once a person becomes a Muslim the other aspects of Muslim life must then be cultivated. But a great deal depends on the enthusiasm of the Muslim. He or she must acquire the information which is available through the local mosque and through helpful and dedicated Muslims.

There is also confusion regarding Muslim titles – mullah, sheikh, Imam, ayatollah – which are often used interchangeably. Although all these refer to religious figures, the *ulema* (from *alim* or scholar), their gradation and roles differ. A mullah (more respectful terms are *maulvi* or *maulana*) is in charge of a local mosque and he usually teaches children the Quran and prayers. A sheikh has higher status and more learning. Sufi leaders are also called sheikh. An Imam is a senior figure often in charge of a large mosque. The title of Imam is also given to the highly respected spiritual figures directly descended from the Prophet who are the basis for twelve Imam Shiism which dominates Iran (see chapter 2). An ayatollah (or ayatullah), which means 'sign of God', is in the senior-most category of *alim* in Iran. From the ayatollahs is selected the Ayatollah al-Uzma, the chief ayatollah (a position which Khomeini held; it explains the immense respect for him and his many titles). The equivalent outside Iran among Sunnis would be the Sheikh al-Azhar, the head of the Al-Azhar university in Cairo.

Pir and *faqir* are terms used by Sufis; the former is a master, the latter a beggar who has embraced poverty. *Wali* is a Sufi saint. Caliph, sultan and shah are the equivalent of king or ruler. The caliph was originally the successor of the Prophet and therefore also a religious figure. Shah among Muslims can also denote a descendant of the Prophet.

Western commentators often use – or misuse – terms taken from Christianity and apply them to Islam. One of the most commonly used is fundamentalism. As we know, in its original application it means someone who believes in the fundamentals of religion, that is the Bible and the scriptures. In that sense every Muslim is a fundamentalist believing in the Quran and the Prophet. However, in the manner that it is used in the media, to mean a fanatic or extremist, it does not illuminate either Muslim thought or Muslim society. In the Christian context it is a useful concept. In the Muslim context it simply confuses because by definition every Muslim believes in the fundamentals of Islam. But even Muslims differ in their ideas about how, and to what extent, to apply Islamic ideas to the modern world. These differences are noted from age to age, country to country, indeed individual to individual. Yet a Muslim even talking of Islam will be quickly slapped with the label fundamentalist in the Western media.

QUESTIONS FOR OUR AGE

Language, religion and culture are important markers of our identity. Today groups which had long been thought to have forsaken their original identity reassert their ethnicity, often with guns and violence (as in the former communist states). Can Muslims accommodate to the modern world without giving up central aspects of their faith? If not, then how much change must come within Muslim society itself? If change must come who will order it? And where will it stop? These questions open up a whole host of sensitive theological issues which touch on the essential features of Islam.

The key question, of course, is whether watertight boundaries can be drawn in the present age. Where do Muslims set those boundaries when videos and televisions in living rooms bring in a flood of foreign images to the younger generation? Is a clash between Islam and the West inevitable? How can Muslims learn to understand and respect the values of Western society without compromising their own central beliefs and practices? What do they have to contribute to non-Muslim societies? How will young Muslims adapt to Western values which are so obviously foreign to their own culture and yet because of repeated exposure make an impression on their minds? Will Islam be swayed by the West?

One response is seen in the fact that many Muslim girls living in the West are consciously wearing the *hijab*, the covering of the head. But what comes next? Will the *hijab* form the substance or simply the external symbolism of the Islamic response? For the response to be valid and long-term it must be more sophisticated than just wearing the *hijab*; it must also be books, libraries, thought, ideas and behaviour. Muslims need to debate these issues honestly and seriously. Important questions of this kind pose a challenge for both Muslims and non-Muslims. In searching for answers we are promised a time of excitement and vitality.

In the following pages we shall try to discover some of the answers. We will examine the basic features of Islam itself. We will learn of the Quran, the divine word of God, and the Prophet to whom it was revealed; we will explore the history of the heyday of Islam when its empires were the superpowers of the age, providing stability and order, creating great architecture, art and science; we will examine issues of modernity, democracy and identity, including the core unit of Muslim society, the family, and appreciate why Muslims attach so much importance to a stable family; we will look at Muslims living in non-Muslim countries and discuss the dilemmas and problems they face; and we will also consider the age of the Western media and technological developments, which challenge traditional Islamic values and beliefs.

So we shall approach Islam not as an exotic other, something foreign and strange, but as a system seriously involved in suggesting a way of living in the late twentieth century and prepared to tackle the difficult questions that will face us in the coming century. In order to learn about Islam, we need to look at its history and society, and we turn to this in the next chapter.

TWO

WHAT IS ISLAM?

─────── ● ───────

To understand Islam it is crucial to understand the nature of its Prophet and holy book, the Quran. For that it is necessary to journey to what is now Saudi Arabia.

THE MESSENGER: THE PROPHET OF ISLAM

A few miles from Makkah (Mecca) is a bleak and forbidding mountain called Hira which rises abruptly from the earth. It has a steep and jagged face pointing towards Makkah. On top, precariously perched, is a cave. It was here that one of the most remarkable events of history took place in the seventh century. The event centred on Muhammad ibn Abdullah (son of Abdullah), who was in the habit of retreating to Hira to meditate during the month of Ramadan. In AD 610, when he was aged about forty, he heard the voice of the angel Gabriel. It ordered him to recite some of the divine verses of the Quran. The Quran was thus revealed; the world would henceforth know Muhammad as the Prophet of Islam. (Whenever Muslims speak or write the Prophet's name, they usually add, 'May the peace and blessings of Allah be upon him', sometimes written as 'pbuh', short for 'peace be upon him', or its Arabic translation 'salla Allahu alayhi wasallam', which is abbreviated to 'saw'. Many even make a gesture of kissing their fingers and touching them to their eyes and lips as a further sign of respect.)

The Prophet's retreat to Hira – known as 'the mountain of light' after the revelations – tells us many interesting things about him. It confirms for us his contemplative nature and his desire to search for answers to the eternal problems that face human beings. It suggests a man prepared to undergo sacrifice and physical hardship in his quest (Hira is a formidable climb; and the Prophet was no longer a young man when he used to go there). It also echoes a pattern established by the earlier prophetic figures – Jesus, Moses,

Abraham – who retreated from the hurly-burly of the world to caves and mountains for spiritual renewal.

As the Prophet is central to the understanding of Islam, many questions relating to him are raised. What sort of a man was he? What kind of society did he live in? What was his message? What impact did it have on history? And how is it relevant to us in our times?

The Prophet's early life

More than any earlier religious figure – such as Jesus, Moses or Abraham – the Prophet lived his life in the full glare of history. He is neither a mythological nor a semi-divine figure but lived like other people. His triumphs, joys, pain, sorrow and anger are documented. His gentleness, compassion, piety – his 'humanness' – would help explain why for Muslims he is simply *insan-i-kamil*, the perfect person. But his human nature would allow critics to mock him.

The Prophet belonged to the Banu Hashim (sons of Hashim), one of the clans of the powerful Quraish tribe that dominated Makkah, the chief trading centre on the Arabian peninsula. It was a vast land, one million square miles in size, consisting largely of deserts and mountains, where nomadic and pastoral Bedouin tribes led a precarious existence. Their social habits reflected the ecology which, in a sociological sense, helped to form them. The extended family or clan was at the core of society. Several clans formed a tribe. Each tribe was led by a chief who was *primus inter pares*, first among equals. He was usually selected by a consensus among his peers. The tribal code permeated society.

In the time of the Prophet's youth, religion meant numerous gods and goddesses, often worshipped through trees and stones. While the tribal code encouraged the notion of *muruwwa*, manhood, which was the glorification of tribal chivalry, the treatment of women was abominable. Female infanticide was common. Society was on the verge of anarchy and disorder. This period before the coming of Islam would be known subsequently as *Jahiliyya* or the age of ignorance.

The Prophet was born about the year AD 570 in Makkah. His father had died a few weeks earlier. Since it was the custom for new-born babies to be fed by a foster-mother, at first the Prophet was cared for by a Bedouin woman, Halimah. This relationship has ensured a special place for Halimah in Muslim affection and folklore.

The Prophet's mother died when he was six and he went to live with his grandfather, Abdul Muttalib. Just two years later his grandfather also died, and he was then cared for by his uncle, Abu Talib, a merchant. The sense of loss at such an early age made him a pensive and sensitive person. He would always emphasize the need to be especially kind to orphans, women, the weak in society. As a boy, he looked after sheep in the desert. Later he would look back with quiet satisfaction. 'Allah', he would say, 'sent no prophet who was not a shepherd.'

An incident in his early life reveals his manner of dealing with disputes. Pilgrims gathered in Makkah to marvel at the black stone that was kept in the Kabah, the designated holy site which was guarded by the Quraish. The Arabs believed the black stone came from heaven and was a divine sign. After the coming of Islam, the Kabah, which is a simple cube-shaped building now covered with black and gold cloth, would be regarded by Muslims as God's first house on earth, built by Adam and later rebuilt by the prophet Abraham and his son Ismail. But during the time when the Arabs were pagans the Kabah housed hundreds of idols.

One year, heavy rain had damaged the walls of the Kabah. Extensive repairs were needed, and the four major tribes of Makkah were to share the work. The work proceeded without a hitch until the time came to replace the black stone. Then an argument began which reflected typical tribal society and its notions of esteem. Which tribe would have the honour of actually putting the stone in place?

If the matter was not resolved amicably it could start a tribal war. To prevent this from happening an old man made a suggestion. They would let the gods help: the first person to walk through the temple gates next day would be asked to solve the dispute. The first person turned out to be the Prophet. While still a young man the Prophet was well known and respected for his honesty – he was widely called *al-Amin*, 'the honest one'. His solution to the dispute was simple. Taking a cloak, he spread it on the ground. The black stone was placed on it and leaders from each tribe took hold of the four corners of the cloak. Holding tight, they lifted the stone and then the Prophet slid it into place.

The Prophet's marriage

Among the Quraish there was a respected and wealthy widow named Khadijah, who was involved in trade. On hearing of the Prophet's reputation, she sent for him and asked him to take her goods and trade them in Syria. He agreed, and left for Syria with one of Khadijah's caravans. Accompanying the caravan was Khadijah's slave, Maysarah.

Long journeys are when you get to know your companions; nothing can be hidden for long. So as Maysarah came to know the Prophet he grew to admire him. He was not like any other man he had met.

Two events took place during this journey which greatly puzzled Maysarah and are now part of history, recounted by millions of Muslims. The first happened when the caravan stopped for a break near the lonely home of Bahira, a Christian monk. The Prophet sat under a tree while Maysarah was busy with some work. The monk came up to Maysarah and asked, 'Who is the man resting under the tree?' 'One of the Quraish, the people who guard the Kabah,' replied Maysarah. The monk shook his head in wonder, saying, 'No one but a Prophet is sitting beneath this tree.'

The second event occurred on the return journey. As they crossed the desert, Maysarah, who was riding behind the Prophet, felt the heat of noon, and when the sun was at its hottest he saw two angels appear above the Prophet and shield him from the sun's harmful rays.

On their return Maysarah told Khadijah everything about the trip, including his observations about the Prophet's character and behaviour. The trip was declared a success: the Prophet had made more profit for Khadijah than she had ever received before.

Khadijah was intrigued. Wealthy and attractive, she had declined many marriage offers. Now she was interested. She sent a friend to ask the Prophet why he was not married. The reply was that he had no money to support a family. The friend then asked: 'Supposing a rich, beautiful and noble lady agreed to marry you?' The Prophet was curious about her identity. The friend told him it was Khadijah. He went with his uncles, Abu Talib and Hamzah, to see Khadijah's uncle, and asked his permission to marry her. The uncle agreed and soon after the Prophet and Khadijah were married.

Although there was an age difference (Khadijah was some fifteen years older), the marriage was a happy one and they were well suited to each other. Khadijah would play a critical role in the coming of Islam, standing like a pillar beside her husband when the first revelations came; indeed she would have the singular honour of being the first Muslim in history.

They had six children, two sons and four daughters. There was domestic sorrow: their first-born, a son called Qasim, died shortly before his second birthday, and their last child, also a son, lived only a short time. But their four daughters – Zainab, Ruqayyah, Umm Kalthum and Fatimah – all survived, and played important roles in Islamic history.

The first words of the message

The message of Islam was first revealed to the Prophet in 610, when he was engaged in one of his periods of retreat to the cave on Hira. One night, during the month of Ramadan, an angel appeared to him. 'Read,' he said. But the Prophet was unlettered and could neither read nor write. Three times the Prophet said he could not read and three times the angel insisted. It was as if someone was squeezing his heart. Then the angel taught him this verse:

> *Read in the name of thy Lord who created,*
> *Created man, out of a clot of congealed blood.*
> *Read! And thy Lord is most Bountiful,*
> *He who taught (the use of) the Pen,*
> *Taught man that which he knew not.*
> (*The Quran*, Surah 96: verses 1 – 5)

When he returned home he was assailed by many questions and emotions. But Khadijah had little doubt that something very special was happening in their lives. One of her Christian relatives, the saintly priest Waraqah, explained to the Prophet that he had seen God's messenger, the angel Gabriel. Khadijah reassured him that it was a sign that he had been chosen as a prophet. A short while later, he had another vision of the angel Gabriel on Hira. This frightened him and he came hurrying home. Once again, Khadijah was a rock of comfort. It now dawned on him: God had chosen him for a special purpose, as the Messenger.

After those momentous revelations in the month of Ramadan, others came regularly to the Prophet. Islam was now proclaimed to the world (the word itself means submission to the will of God). The Prophet knew what he had to do and prepared himself for what was to come. Khadijah was the first to accept Islam. Then one day the Prophet's young cousin, Ali, found the Prophet and Khadijah praying. He was curious and asked what they were doing. The Prophet explained the nature of Islam. That night Ali could not sleep. He was thinking about what the Prophet had said. He had great admiration and respect for his cousin and his words had made a deep impression. By dawn he had come to a decision: he too would accept Islam. Thus, as Khadijah is the first female to embrace Islam, Ali is the first male.

Now the Prophet began to preach Islam openly; but few people took him seriously. The Quraish were increasingly hostile. They had good reason. The idols of Makkah which symbolized degradation and ignorance had become the focus of the Prophet's preaching. When the Prophet told them not to pray to these idols the people of Makkah were furious. Pilgrims came to visit their pagan shrines and brought business. The Prophet's talk would destroy it; the merchants were outraged. So they called him a liar and a madman. Some of the early Muslims were beaten up and tortured. The attacks grew worse.

What the Quraish did made no impression on the Prophet. He would not be deterred from spreading his message. When the Quraish offered him a blank cheque – untold wealth, leadership, anything – if he gave up his ideas, he replied: 'I would not do so even if you placed the sun in my right hand and the moon in my left hand.'

The journey across the desert: the *hijra*

However, a crisis point was approaching. There was talk of assassination, and plots were being hatched. At this stage, pilgrims from the city of Yathrib – or Madinah – heard the Prophet preach and were impressed. They invited him to come and live with them, over 400 kilometres away across the Arabian desert, and the Prophet accepted their invitation.

The journey in 622 across the desert is a crucial event for Muslims. It is called the *hijra*, which means departure. Even today, the Muslim system of dating years starts with the Prophet's journey; AD 622 is the first year of the Muslim calendar. On another level, the *hijra* suggests that Muslims must not live under tyranny, that they must remake their lives elsewhere if necessary in order to practise their faith. So deep would be the Prophet's attachment to Madinah that he would be buried there, thus providing the second most holy place for Muslims after the Kabah in Makkah.

In Madinah, the Prophet started the first Muslim community. Rules and regulations which govern a society were formulated – and these still influence Muslims today. The first mosque was built next to the Prophet's house. The Prophet himself helped to build the mosque. He taught that everyone was equal in the eyes of God. 'None of you can be a believer unless he loves for his brother what he loves for himself,' said the Prophet. To set an example he mended his own clothes and did his own shopping. The Prophet's compassion extended to all creation, not just human beings. After all the Quran has said: 'No creature is there crawling on the earth, no bird flying with its wings, but they are nations like yourselves' (Surah 6: verse 38).

Many stories are told of the Prophet's humility and kindness. Here is one example. Abu Hurayrah went to the market with the Prophet to buy some clothes. The seller stood up and kissed the hand of the Prophet. The Prophet withdrew his hand and stopped the man from kissing his hand, saying, 'This is the practice of the Persians with their kings. I am not a king. I am only a man from among you.' The garments were purchased and Abu Hurayrah wanted to carry them for the Prophet. The Prophet did not allow him and said: 'The owner of something has more right to carry it.'

So great is the respect and affection the Prophet commands that his very sayings, *hadith*, are the source of wisdom and social practice in the Muslim world. These cover the entire range of human activity. Since there was always the danger of people incorrectly attributing things to the Prophet, scholars collected and authenticated 'genuine' *hadith*. Intensive research was involved as each *hadith* was rejected or accepted depending on its traceable links to the Prophet. The integrity of those who formed the links needed to be unimpeachable. Thus each *hadith* required a chain of those who had actually heard the saying and could trace it to the Prophet. The exercise is an Islamic science. Centuries ago Imam Bukhari, who is generally considered the authority, selected about 7300 from 600 000 in ninety-seven books.

Respect for the Prophet is reflected in the high status his descendants have always enjoyed. Called Sayyeds or Sharif or Shah, they are expected to behave with dignity and decorum. Although some who claim to be the Prophet's descendants have little evidence of their ancestry, many support their claims with genealogical charters.

The marriages of the Prophet
The Prophet's marriages have led to colourful innuendoes by critics of Islam. They were often cited in the Middle Ages to prove the voluptuous sensuality of the Prophet. In medieval Europe they helped create a powerful image which contrasted with the spiritual and ascetic Jesus who never married. But even a cursory examination of the marriages will dispel the charge. The Prophet married Khadijah, older, as we know, by fifteen years, and led a happily monogamous life by all accounts until her death in 619. There are no hints of improper behaviour during this period.

Once Islam spread, the wars produced many widows. They would come to the Prophet in desperate straits. Many were daughters or wives of close companions. Sauda, the first wife he married after Khadijah's death, was a widow of forty, and one of the Muslims who had migrated to Abyssinia to escape persecution. She had a son by her previous husband. Rather than leave Sauda and her son destitute to fend for themselves in a society still used to treating women with cruelty, the Prophet asked her to share his home in honourable marriage.

The Prophet contracted twelve marriages in all after Khadijah. Most of his wives were between forty and fifty, divorced, often more than once, and had offspring by previous spouses when the Prophet married them. In the harsh terrain of Arabia, and in the difficult circumstances of those days, people aged rapidly, and these women would have been elderly. If the Prophet had wished for sensual pleasure there would have been no dearth of any kind of women available to him.

The marriages provided the women with pious and sheltered lives in the simple household of the Prophet. It is the Prophet's treatment of his wives – with fairness, gentleness and respect – that has laid the basis for the treatment of women in Islam. It must be understood that these marriages were only allowed to the Prophet. A Muslim is encouraged to marry once only but in extraordinary circumstances he may marry up to four wives (see also chapter 4).

If there had been sensuality or depravity in the Prophet's household the women themselves would have talked – as they often did, commenting critically on his austerity and attempts to be scrupulously fair between them. But they did not. On the contrary he inspired deep love in them, as the following story illustrates.

The Prophet is lying ill on his death-bed. His family and friends are around him, all deeply concerned. His beloved daughter, Fatimah, does not leave his bedside; she is dignified in her grief. He beckons to her and whispers in her ear. She begins to cry. A little while later he again says something to her. This time she smiles. Later, those close to her would ask the meaning of what transpired between father and daughter. 'I cried', she said, 'because my father said he did not have much time to live. But then he told me I would follow him soon. I was happy, as I would be with him again.' This story is widely known among Muslims. It reveals the deep affection between a father and daughter. On another level it reflects on the brevity of life, the concept of death, its inevitability as part of the natural cycle of life, and the need to put it into perspective. The story also points to the idea of an afterlife. Above all, it shows the love that the man in the story inspired.

The last address

The Prophet's last address at Arafat on his final pilgrimage, just before his death in 632, sums up the essence of Islam. It clearly identifies the five pillars upon which to rest Islamic belief and practice (which we shall discuss in detail below):

O people, indeed your lives, your properties and your honour are sacred and inviolable to you till you appear before your Lord. O people! Be conscious of God. And even if a mangled Abyssinian slave becomes your leader hearken to him and obey him as long as he establishes and institutes the Book of God.

Worship your Lord and Sustainer. Perform your five daily salat *[prayers]. Fast your month [of Ramadan]. Make pilgrimage to your House [the Kabah and Makkah]. Pay the* zakat *on your property willingly and obey whatever I command you. Then will you enter the Paradise of your Lord and Sustainer.*

The address ends with the clearest statement possible of equality, of the need to abolish barriers created by race and colour. It is a message of the greatest relevance to our world with its ethnic and racial prejudices:

*All of you descend from Adam and Adam was made of earth. There is no superiority for an Arab over a non-Arab nor for a non-Arab over an Arab, neither for a white man over a black man nor a black man over a white man except the superiority gained through consciousness of God [*taqwa*]. Indeed the noblest among you is the one who is most deeply conscious of God.*

The role of the Prophet in Muslim social custom

The immense reverence for the Prophet explains why Muslims often do ordinary everyday things which are associated with him; this is called *sunnah*. Some Muslims do so consciously, others almost without knowing their association. Many personal habits and social customs – for example, in matters of personal appearance, the naming of children, diet and hygiene – can be explained by reference to actions of the Prophet or by association with his personal history (see Ahmed 1980).

The opening of the fast during Ramadan by eating a date is *sunnah*. Muslims all over the world, and through the centuries, have opened the fast in this way. This is true whether the Muslim is rich or poor, male or female, young or old. There are all kinds of sensible dietary arguments claimed on behalf of the date. It is a whole meal in itself; it grows virtually on its own and requires minimum care; it is easily available; it stores well; it is cheap. Most important, it is the main fruit of the Arabian peninsula where the Prophet lived. In his habit of retreating to a mountain cave to pray and meditate, the Prophet would have found the date a convenient food. The fact is that Muslims eat dates because of their reverence for the Prophet. For those too poor to afford dates, the fast is opened with simple salt. No one is too poor to afford salt. That, too, derives from the custom of the Prophet.

Another custom derives from the Prophet's use of the early Islamic toothbrush called *siwak* or *miswak*. It was a twig which, when rubbed, secreted juices that cleansed the mouth. It is often mentioned as a symbol of the importance given to dental health by Islam. Although not mentioned in the Quran, the *siwak* gained popularity because it was attributed to the daily practice of the Prophet whose understanding of preventive dentistry is lauded as being part of his general concern with hygiene and health. Even on his death-bed he is said not to have given up the use of *siwak*. 'Purify your mouths, for they are the channels through which utterances of praise to God *subhana allah* travel,' he had said.

Recently some Swiss pharmaceutical companies, after researching the Islamic *siwak*, concluded that it contained chemicals active against oral bacteria that caused inflammation and caries. The *siwak* possessed other medical qualities also. Consequently a yellowish toothpaste from the *siwak* extract was produced (Rispler-chaim 1992).

Images of the Prophet

Muslims do not allow images or representations of the Prophet. The reason is rooted in the history of Islam. As Islam rejected any form of idol worship, Muslims feared that images of the Prophet would soon become objects of worship: nothing must detract from the worship of God. Many Muslims even object to those who wish to treat the Prophet's burial place in Madinah – or the cave at Hira – with special reverence. Pictures of the Prophet that do exist usually show his face veiled, with a large, flame-shaped light behind it. This is not dissimilar to the halo of light denoting a particularly spiritual or holy person in Christian artistic tradition.

It is important to recall that early this century the Christian church still had a great say in how Jesus was to be portrayed. In early films, for example, Jesus does not appear. Either we see only his shadow or the camera records the response of people who talk to him. Until the 1930s British censors did not allow two things on the screen – nudity or Jesus. As late as the 1960s Jesus was not supposed to sweat or show signs of physical exertion (as in *King of Kings*). But then Martin Scorsese made *The Last Temptation of Christ* (1987), which was offensive to everyone who respected Jesus in the traditional manner. We have come a long way from the position early in the century.

Muslims object on religious grounds to pictorial representation of the Prophet but not to verbal descriptions. The following contemporary accounts are from the literature:

Hind says that the Prophet was grand, in fact he was grandeur itself. His face shone like the full moon. He was of middle height, inclined to tallness but was shorter than very tall people. . . . He walked softly and firmly with a rapid pace and a slightly forward bend, as if he were descending from a higher to a lower level. Whenever he looked at anything he would look straight into it; his eyes were always downcast, directed more towards the earth than towards the sky. Jabir ibn Samurah says, 'The Prophet of Allah had a wide mouth. The eyes were of light brown hue. . . .' Abu Hurayrah says that the Prophet 'had a white complexion as if he were made of silver. There was a moderate wave in his hair.'

(Azzam and Gouverneur 1985: 124)

The Prophet of Islam and the people of the Book

There is a close ideological and theological relationship between Christianity, Judaism and Islam. All three believe in the notion of the one divine God; they also believe that we are mortals temporarily put here on earth and that there is accountability for our actions, an afterlife. The Quran repeatedly points out that both Jews and Christians are 'people of the Book', that their original Books came from God. Indeed, for Islam the prophets of Judaism and Christianity are also prophets of Islam. The prophets of Islam begin with Adam, and include Nuh (Noah), Ibrahim (Abraham), Ismail (Ishmael), Ishaq (Isaac), Loot (Lot), Yaqub (Jacob), Yusuf (Joseph), Musa (Moses) and Ayyub (Job). There is even a genealogical link with Jews: Jews claim descent from Abraham through his son Isaac while the Arabs claim descent from his son Ismail.

The Prophet of Islam would always display a special affection for Jesus. It was Bahira, the Christian monk, who predicted he would be a prophet and Waraqah, the Christian relative of Khadijah, the Prophet's wife, who encouraged him to believe in his call to prophecy. When persecution drove some of the early Muslims from Makkah it was to Christian lands that they fled. The Quran says: 'You will find the most affectionate among them towards those who believe are those who say "we are Christians"' (Surah 5: verse 82).

It is important to point out that the Prophet is seen not as the founder of Islam, merely as the messenger. Muslims regard their religion as the natural way of life. Therefore God is seen as the originator of this religion and Adam, the first person on earth, is the first Muslim. The great prophet Abraham, who lived about 2500 years before the Prophet, is called a Muslim in the Quran (Surah 3: verse 60). The Quran asks Muslims to recite: 'We believe in the revelation made by Allah to Abraham, Ismail, Isaac, Jacob,

Moses and Jesus and all Prophets and we make no distinction between any of them' (Surah 11: verse 136). Clearly, these spiritual figures were carrying the same message from God – the message of Islam, of peace and piety. For Muslims, therefore, the Prophet is one in a long series of prophets.

What about those good and saintly people not mentioned in the Quran by name? While there is a direct relationship with prophets who preached monotheistic religion, others elsewhere are not overlooked. Indeed, Muslims believe that there have been over 124 000 'prophets' who spread the message of God, whether directly or indirectly. Such figures, some Muslim scholars have suggested, include people like Plato and Buddha, although the matter remains debated as to who precisely was a prophet. Sayings of the Prophet support the essential universalism of Islam: 'Truly I am the brother of every pious man even if he is a slave from Abyssinia; and opposed to every villain even if he is a noble Quraishi'. When Muslims encounter conflict the Quran has also said: 'To you your religion and to me mine' (Surah 109: verse 6) and 'Let there be no compulsion in religion' (Surah 2: verse 256).

What, then, makes the Prophet of Islam different? The explanation given by one of the most influential Muslim scholar-activists of the twentieth century, the founder of the Jamaat-i-Islami party, is representative of broad Muslim opinion throughout the world:

> He was the last Prophet of God. God revived through him the same genuine faith which had been conveyed by all the former prophets. This original message had been corrupted, and split into various religions by people of different ages, who indulged in interpolations and admixture. These alien elements were eliminated by God, and Islam in its pure and original form was transmitted to mankind through Muhammad. Since there was to be no messenger after Muhammad, the Book revealed to him was preserved word for word so that it should be a source of guidance for all times.
> (Maududi 1978:3)

While Islam continues and incorporates Christianity and Judaism, Muslims believe that over time these religious systems wandered from the straight path and eventually needed further divine instruction. Islam came at the end, filling in all the gaps, correcting all the errors, dotting the 'i's and crossing the 't's. Muslims believe prophethood itself comes to an end with the Prophet, who is Allah's last prophet, the 'seal of the prophets' (Surah 33: verse 40). The implication is that there is no longer a need for further revelation, all that needs to be revealed is revealed, and humanity has come of age.

Muslims feel a sense of affinity and continuity with the earlier religions.

The prophets, many traditions and rituals and, above all, the belief in one divine, transcendent, omnipotent God are common. There are numerous points of conflict in ritual and even in doctrinal matters, but these are all secondary to the one central connecting feature which is belief in the one God. Thus Muslims believe that there are many paths to God, and, although theirs is the last and final path, there are others which may also be valid. Indeed the Quran goes out of its way to emphasize that Christians and Jews – the people of the Book – are to be treated with special respect.

Although for Muslims the Prophet is *insan-i-kamil*, the perfect person, he is not divine. The religion is not 'Muhammadanism', as it was incorrectly called in the West until recently. The idea of 'Muhammadanism' for the West corresponded to the fact that Christianity was named after Christ and Buddhism after Buddha – both figures seen as divine or semi-divine by their followers. As the name of Islam is not linked to the founder of the religion, it is also not linked to a geographical area. This is unlike Hinduism, which derives its name from Hind or the river Indus, or Judaism, which derives its name from the land of Judaea.

There are important differences, however, between the three monotheistic religions. It therefore appears to be easier to deal with stereotypes and reject the other, in the way in which a cousin may feel contempt for another cousin yet be able to deal comfortably with a total stranger. The differences need to be clarified so as to overcome problems of stereotyping and misunderstanding.

First of all, there are no priests in Islam, no rabbis, no padres. This has implications for society and politics. Muslims are granted equal access to the one divine supreme being. However, those in charge of the mosque or religious teaching sometimes assume powers that are not delegated to them in the Quran. Indeed in certain sects there are men who act as priests and assume authority. The Shias believe that Imams, who are descended from the Prophet, assist them as religious leaders and guides. Thus social hierarchies are more developed in Iran and in South Asia – influenced culturally by Iran – than in the Arab world.

There is another theological difference between Christianity and Islam. Christianity sees men and women as embodying Original Sin and in need of redemption; they are by nature not to be trusted. The Muslim view is diametrically opposed to this. A human being represents the highest form of God's creation; acknowledged by God as 'a vicegerent on earth' (Surah 2: verse 30). This status is confirmed in the fine qualities humans embody – piety, generosity, compassion, the love of learning. A Muslim's perception of the world is thus an attempt to live up to this noble idea of humanity.

Another difference lies in the relationship between human beings and God. Both Judaism and Christianity emphasize that their people are special to God; a covenant was made and they were the 'chosen ones'. Islam widens the relationship beyond Muslims. Islam may talk of the *ummah* or community of Islam but it also underlines the affinity with the people of the Book and indeed *all* creation. Yes, Islam is the last of the series of messages sent by God but it covers all humanity and even the smallest of living creatures. Included for the message is not only our planet but the universe – indeed universes (the Quran uses the plural). This is a far cry from tribal or parochial notions of God.

The universalism of Islam is reflected in its attitude towards matters of statehood. Throughout history Muslim rulers have been tolerant of other religions when their empires have been secure and stable – Ottomans, Mughals, the Umayyads in Spain. One reason for Islam's tolerance is that, in contrast to both Christianity and Judaism, from its early days Islam emerged as the dominant ruling religion of the area. This gave Muslims confidence in their religion, allowing them to act with generosity and wisdom. Within a few decades of the Prophet's death, Muslims were racing across North Africa towards Spain and through the Middle East towards India; they soon began to found great dynasties. In contrast, the other two religions took much longer to gain any kind of political equilibrium. Christianity and Judaism have memories of persecution, their followers hounded by the established systems. The former took centuries to establish itself; the latter was driven from its ancestral lands and forced to roam the world until this century.

Many people, thinking of the situation in the Middle East and the bitter contest between Israel and its Arab neighbours, assume incorrectly that Islam is against Judaism (see also chapter 4). The relations between Muslims and Jews were reflected in the treaty the Prophet made with them in Madinah. The first of its kind, it allowed them free trade, free travel, and freedom of thought and expression. The Jews insisted that the Prophet must not sign the treaty as the prophet of God. He complied and signed the treaty as the son of Abdullah. It was a breach of this contract that led to the defensive *jihad* against the Jews. Later, much was made of the breakdown as symptomatic of the animosity between the two religions.

The Prophet's critics

Western critics often complain that the Prophet was too worldly, too involved in affairs of the here and now, and that this disqualifies him from being a truly spiritual person. This view is rooted in the Christian tradition whereby religious figures must forsake the world and lead a life of austerity. The perfect figure is Jesus Christ. In the ideal this is both attractive and even possible; in practice it is difficult. Islam thus aims for a more middle position, a greater balance.

A good Muslim must balance the world (*dunya*) with the principles of religion (*din*). He or she must live in the real world but be guided by the principles of religion, by the idea of the afterworld. The ideal Muslim is the Prophet himself, leading the prayer in the mosque, the army in the battlefield, the council of elders as they discussed matters of state. His successors, the caliphs – and indeed all Muslim rulers – have tried to follow this model. The balance between *dunya* and *din* is crucial for a Muslim.

The Prophet had to face critics in his lifetime and continues to do so until today. His enemies in Makkah had said that he was 'a man possessed', 'a soothsayer' and 'a poet'. They condemned the Quran as 'a forgery' or 'sorcery' containing old stories stolen by him. Medieval Christian priests rightly saw the Prophet as central to Islam and attacked him with religious frenzy. For them he was the Antichrist. Stories circulated by the church projected him as a debauch, a charlatan and the ultimate enemy of Christ. They served to rally people, especially in the face of a seemingly unstoppable Islam. If he did not exist he would have had to be invented by the church.

Dante placed the Prophet in the inferno in his *Divine Comedy* (see discussion in chapter 4). For Luther there were 'two arch-enemies of Christ': the Prophet and the Pope. Voltaire's play *Mahomet*, written in 1742, was another grotesque misrepresentation. The Prophet thus became the lightning rod for all kinds of social, political and religious ills of Islam as seen by the Christian West over the centuries.

THE MESSAGE: THE HOLY QURAN

As the Prophet is the messenger, the Quran is the message of God. Together they provide the basis for the ideal type of Muslim behaviour and thought (Ahmed 1988). The Quran is divided into thirty sections – which makes it easy to recite right through the month. In the holy month of Ramadan, Muslims try to finish reading the Quran in this manner. They believe that the Quran is divine, the last revelation of God's truth to humanity (Surah 5: verse 5 and Surah 2: verse 2). The Prophet himself had said in his last sermon: 'I leave behind me two things, the Quran and my example the *sunnah*, and if you follow these you will never go astray.'

The thirty sections of the Quran are further divided into 114 chapters called Surahs, arranged roughly in order of length. The short and popular prayer which constitutes Surah 1, *Al-Fatiha*, the opening, is the first. Surah 2, *Al-Baqarah*, the cow, has 286 verses; Surah 3, *Ali Imran*, the family of Imran, has 200; Surah 4, *An-Nisa*, women, has 177, and so on down to the final Surahs which have only three to six short verses. Those revealed later in Madinah are generally longer than the earlier ones in Makkah and the order is not chronological.

The Quran is not a structured book or an academic set of arguments in a recognizable sequence. It is like a vibrant, powerful outpouring of divine messages. At one place it warns, at another it encourages, at one place it advises, at another reflects. The messages cover all aspects of life. Its language, Arabic, is marvellous, its imagery awesome. For a Muslim the Quran is a miracle; even Christian Arabs consider its language to be perfection.

In the Quran, God has ninety-nine names which help us understand the nature of God. If we divide the names into those with positive attributes – truth, justice, mercy and compassion – and those with negative ones – suggesting anger and retribution – we would have only four or five in the latter category. The names of God are beautiful and they describe God's divine qualities: *Ar-Rahman*, the Beneficent, *Ar-Rahim*, the Merciful (these two are the most often repeated); *As-Salam*, the Peace, *Al-Khaliq*, the Creator, *Al-Hakam*, the Judge, *Al-Halim*, the Patient, *Al-Karim*, the Generous, *As-Samad*, the Perfect, *An-Nur*, the Light, *Ar-Rashid*, the Guide.

Above all, Allah is *Ar-Rahman*, the Beneficent, and *Ar-Rahim*, the Merciful. These two attributes occur in the common Muslim recitation, *Bismillah ar-Rahman ar-Rahim*, in the name of Allah, the Beneficent, the Merciful. This is used throughout the day by millions of Muslims all over the world, from starting a meal to opening a major business venture. *Rahman* and *Rahim* in the Muslim recitation are the first words a baby will hear, and probably the last ones a dying person will hear. Life thus begins and ends with the two most beautiful attributes of God.

A European Muslim scholar, Frithjof Schuon, analyses these two names: 'In the names *Rahman* and *Rahim* the divine Mercy confronts human incapacity in the sense that consciousness of our incapacity is, when coupled with confidence, the moral receptacle of Mercy. The name *Rahman* is like a sky full of light; the name *Rahim* is like a warm ray coming from the sky and giving life to man' (Schuon 1976: 63).

The spirit of compassion which is reflected in the two names is crucial to Muslims, who are told: 'Be foremost in seeking forgiveness' (Surah 57: verse 21); 'Be quick in the race for forgiveness from your Lord' (Surah 3: verse 133); and, in the next verse, 'Restrain anger and pardon men' (Surah 3: verse 134). 'When they are angry, even then forgive', advises the Quran (Surah 42: verse 37).

Human beings are God's finest reflection, the culmination of creation. The title of vicegerent is an extraordinary vote of confidence and bestowed on the species because of its capacity to think and reason. It is to fulfil this destiny that *ilm*, knowledge, is so emphasized; *ilm* is the second most-used word in the Quran after the name of God. Human beings are told to use their mind and think in at least 300 places. Numerous sayings support this. The Prophet said, 'The first thing created by God was the Intellect.' Ali is quoted as saying: 'God did not distribute to His servants anything more to be esteemed than Intelligence.'

The universal nature of humanity is underlined in the Quran. God's purview and compassion take in everyone, 'all creatures'. The world is not divided into a North and South, an East and a West. On the contrary, these divisions are obliterated: 'To Allah belongeth the East and the West. Whithersoever ye turn, there is Allah's countenance' (Surah 2: verse 115). Again and again the Quran points to the wonders of creation, the diversity of races and languages; God cannot be parochial or xenophobic.

The Quran suggests an ideal of social behaviour (as in Surah 17, 'The Children of Israel'). Be kind to parents, kin, the poor and the wayfarer, it exhorts. Do not be a spendthrift, do not kill, commit adultery or cheat, it warns. Boasting and false pride are condemned and honesty praised. But when humans err, and if they are sincere, 'God forgives those who repent' (verse 25). Corruption is discouraged: 'Seek not mischief in the land. For God loves not those who do mischief' (Surah 28: verse 77). Humility is encouraged: 'Nor walk in insolence through the earth. For God loveth not any arrogant boaster' (Surah 31: verse 18).

Understanding the Quran today
How does a modern Muslim student view the Quran? What of Darwin's theories of biological evolution and Stephen Hawking's of the universe? For a Muslim there is no clash between science and the Quran. Explaining the

nature of creation, the Quran says: 'To Him is due the Primal origin of the heavens and the earth: When He decreeth a matter, He saith to it: "Be", And it is' (Surah 2: verse 117). Is this the Big Bang theory? When the Pope met Hawking he said his church had accepted the Big Bang theory (Hawking 1988: 116). He had learnt from the mistake of Galileo. Hawking's response, however, was that the theory had already been overtaken. It is a dangerous business to match science with faith too closely.

For our times, and sceptical minds, it is important that information in the Quran does not clash with facts. The Quran does not suggest worship of the sun or moon, or any special dispensation for them, or that ours is the only heaven. If this were so critics would have said, 'Here is a seventh-century compilation when people had outdated and incorrect ideas.' On the contrary, the Quran clearly explains the balanced and predictable nature of the movements of the sun and moon (Surah 39: verse 5) and talks of the heavens in the plural (Surah 6: verses 75, 79 and others).

The Quran constantly emphasizes that God's measure is not like ours while suggesting ideas of man's creation from water and clay. While stating that creation took six days (Surah 7: verse 54), the Quran explains that one of God's days may be like a thousand years (Surah 22: verse 47) or even fifty thousand years (Surah 70: verse 4) of ours; clearly Darwin may be accommodated.

The mystery of the stars and heavens, of birth and existence, of life and death are thus contained in the Quran. It is likened to a vast ocean by Muslim sages; it can as easily absorb Darwin as Hawking. The metaphor of an ocean is apt for the Quran. It contains numerous levels of depth; its mysteries remain unresolved; its treasures are unending.

Schuon has attempted to capture the mystery of the Quran in these words: 'In order to understand the full scope of the Quran we must take three things into consideration: its doctrinal content, which we find made explicit in the great canonical treatises of Islam such as those of Abu Hanifah and Et-Tahawi; its narrative content, which depicts all the vicissitudes of the soul; and its divine magic or its mysterious and in a sense miraculous power; these sources of metaphysical and eschatological wisdom, of mystical psychology and theurgic power lie hidden under a veil of breathless utterances, often clashing in shock, of crystalline and fiery images, but also of passages majestic in rhythm, woven of every fibre of the human condition' (Schuon 1976: 48).

The Quran may therefore be understood in numerous ways. It is a comment on seventh-century Arab society, the cradle of Islam. We learn of local politics, culture and customs. We hear of the tribulations of the Prophet, the birth of Islam. The Quran may also be understood as a message for all people, at all times. Universal principles apply to societies through time and space. It is remarkable how some features in society remain unchanged: for instance, the needs of the poor and less privileged, which the Quran emphasizes, require as much attention today as they did in the seventh century. Finally the Quran is to be understood as a treasure-house of the secrets of the universe, of metaphysical and spiritual mysteries.

Western scholars, by imputing authorship of the Quran to the Prophet, who was unlettered, complain of the lack of logic and method in its arguments (see, for instance, the earlier work of Professor Montgomery Watt). However, for Muslims the power and sublimity of the Quran remains untouched over the centuries. It is, as an English convert wrote, an 'inimitable symphony, the very sounds of which move men to tears and ecstasy' (Pickthall 1988: xix).

For Muslims the Quran is a source of guidance and inspiration. They revere it as the word of God and place it, usually wrapped in clean cloth, on a high place in the room. Out of respect they will not point their feet at it or leave it lying on the floor. In traditional society it is still used to administer oaths and to be chanted as part of the cure for illness. Its recitation is therapeutic to Muslims, who derive comfort and strength from it.

Crowds pack stadiums and auditoriums throughout the world to hear contests in which the Quran is recited. It is an art form, and those with skill enjoy celebrity status in the media. Memorization of the entire Quran brings immense prestige as well as merit. Recordings of the Quran are enjoyed for their aesthetic as well as their religious value and are very popular.

Those Muslims who just learn it by rote without understanding its meaning and those who have little time for it in their daily pursuits are deprived of the true message and spirit of the Quran. Its study is both challenging and elevating.

The five pillars of Islam

The message of God is understood by Muslims through what are called the five pillars of Islam. The Prophet had underlined them in his last address at Arafat. The edifice of Islamic religious belief and social practice thus rests on these five pillars.

The first pillar is the *shahada*, a simple statement declaring belief and bearing witness in the one God and accepting Muhammad as the messenger. Muslims believe this declaration allows a person to enter Islam.

The second pillar of Islam is prayer or *salat*. Muslims must pray five times a day and each prayer takes about five to ten minutes. The day is divided neatly into five by the timing: the prayer at dawn, afternoon, late afternoon, after sunset and night. On Fridays, there are special prayers after midday in the mosque instead of the normal afternoon prayer.

Men are encouraged to pray at the mosque. If that is not possible they may pray on any spot that is clean. So the sands of the desert or an open field in the village or a corner of a room or office are equally acceptable. Women are encouraged to pray at home. This is not a form of discrimination but conforms to social practice and tradition. It is also convenient. Muslims over the age of ten are expected to pray, and children are taught to pray when they are six or seven.

The daily prayers help Muslims to remember God and prevent them from incorrect or wicked acts. By bowing their heads to the ground Muslims accept the omnipotence of God. It also encourages humility and the notion of equality. They must pray even if they are in the middle of a war or ill-health. The prayer helps them transcend the mundane and the everyday.

In most Muslim countries Muslims are able to pray freely and provision is made for a clean place even in factories, offices, and so on. Public places like airports normally reserve a specially designated place for prayer. In non-Muslim countries it is more difficult. None the less many non-Muslims employing large numbers of Muslims provide a place for prayer or give them permission to say the main Friday prayer in the local mosque. If prayer mats are not available a clean sheet or even clean spot is used for prayer.

In whatever part of the world they are, Muslims face Makkah when they perform *salat*. There is a place in the mosque wall which shows them which way to face. Outside the mosque Muslims calculate the direction by the sun. British Muslims face south-east when they pray; in Pakistan, Muslims face west, in Morocco they face east. Facing Makkah, the holiest place on earth, creates a sense of unity among Muslims by providing a spiritual and social focus.

The third pillar is *zakat* (alms). *Zakat* reflects the essential compassion of Islam. 'He is not a believer who eats his fill while his neighbour remains hungry by his side,' the Prophet had said. Muslims believe that everything belongs to God, whether it is money, possessions or even children. Muslims should use material things as God wishes them to be used. This means giving things to those who need them, especially the poor, and not keeping them for ourselves. *Zakat* is widely understood as a form of tax, a social method of redistributing wealth in the community.

Since it is one of the pillars, every able Muslim has a duty to pay *zakat*. At the end of each year Muslims must give some of their wealth away for good causes or to help the poor. The amount of *zakat* a Muslim pays varies with the individual's wealth. The rates are fixed: Muslims must give at the end of the year at least 2.5 per cent (one-fortieth) of their money/assets; farmers at least 5 per cent of their crops and a number of animals; traders at least 2.5 per cent of the value of their goods.

Some Islamic governments take the money from Muslims and share it among the needy. In countries like Pakistan *zakat* became part of what was called the process of Islamization in the 1980s. That is, it became a governmental affair rather than a private one. If a Muslim lives in a country which is not Islamic such as Britain, then Islamic organizations collect and distribute *zakat*.

Zakat can be given directly. But Muslims are encouraged to give secretly. This is in order to prevent the giver from feeling superior and the poorer person from being embarrassed. The Prophet had expressed it well: 'The best charity is that which the right hand gives and the left hand does not know of.'

The fourth pillar of Islam is *sawm* (fasting). Fasting takes place during the ninth month of the Islamic calendar which is called Ramadan. As the Islamic months are based on the moon, the fast lasts for twenty-nine or thirty days, depending on when the new moon is first seen.

Muslims must fast. As Muslims believe they need to give up some sleep, food and rest in obeying God, fasting helps them to remember this idea. There are other aspects to fasting. It assists a Muslim to appreciate how the less fortunate suffer. It is also a spiritual and physical training in self-discipline. Socially it brings Muslims together during the month because they all fast at the same time; camaraderie is encouraged and barriers of age and class are dissolved.

Fasting is not just refraining from food and drink; there must be no sexual intercourse, no tobacco, no backbiting, no lying and so on. If, however, a Muslim eats or drinks something by mistake, then the fast may be continued as before and it is not nullified. If the fast is broken intentionally it must be compensated for by keeping a number of consecutive fasts or feeding poor people. Those who are very old or sick, or on a journey, or women in menstruation are exempted from fasting. Since fasting generally begins at puberty, children are also exempt.

The family rises before daybreak to eat a light meal, the last they will eat until after sunset. There will be no drinking of water either during the day.

Children, usually eager to display their devotion, often disobey their parents by fasting secretly. In Cambridge, during Ramadan in 1992, I was surprised to be told one day that my son Umar, who had just turned twelve, was fasting. He had kept his intentions a secret by not rising for the morning meal or asking permission from me or his mother. His day at school, normally active enough, would have been a difficult one.

The fast is opened after sunset, invariably with a date and some water. This is followed by the evening prayer. It is then time to open the fast properly. The family gathers for the only full meal of the day. At both meals many cups of tea or coffee are drunk. Yoghurt and fruit juices are favoured by those who can afford them. People try to avoid salty foods in the morning meal, which would make them thirsty during the day. A great deal of water is drunk in the morning. During both meals the children learn of the meaning of the fast. It is a process of learning that never leaves them. In turn, it is passed on to the next generation.

It is a long hard month. The denial of water is especially felt during the hot summer days in Muslim lands. One African tribe calls Ramadan the 'thirst month'. During the month Muslims are on their best behaviour. And after the first few days a sombre determination descends on those who are fasting. The old and the weak begin to show signs of wear and tear. But few of the devout will even think of giving it up.

For the poor the evening meal comprises spinach or some other vegetable, lentils and onions eaten with bread, usually made of wheat or maize. Reflected in this traditional simple Muslim diet is the Islamic philosophy of austerity, self-reliance and discipline. Paradoxically, it is this diet that keeps the poor in better physical shape than the rich. Some of the wealthy spend much of the fast in a stupor watching videos. They eat the morning meal and then sleep late. In this manner they pass the difficult hours of the day. And at the evening meal they compensate by over-eating. The table groans under dishes of rice, curries, kebabs, a number of sweet dishes and a variety of fruit. 'I ended up by gaining weight in spite of the fasting,' they will complain.

But this is like Scrooge missing the spirit of Christmas. It is far from the main aim of the month, which is to revive ideas of the other-world, to heighten spirituality, to make people break the everyday routine. Abstinence is thus a physical exercise to invigorate the spiritual condition.

The atmosphere among Muslims is charged. It is easy to dream dreams, a condition heightened by the lightness of the mind. It is not surprising to see Muslims displaying greater religious fervour than usual in this month. The mosques are full and people attempt to complete the reading of the Quran. There is an air of goodwill and charity in the mosque. Meals are specially cooked for the poor, who can turn up at sunset and eat their fill.

Tempers are often frayed, however. Those who are used to tea or cigarettes will find the fasting especially difficult; their glazed eyes and irritable manner will betray withdrawal symptoms. It is not a good time to expect normal punctuality in the offices or courteous drivers on the roads in Muslim countries. Those who attempt to lead a normal life with a normal timetable soon find the fast pushing them towards a different rhythm. Introspection and meditation are inevitable. There is no other way of passing the time.

There is a marvellously evocative night in the last few days of the month called *Lailat al-Qadr*, the 'Night of Power'. This was when the Prophet received the first Quranic revelation. Muslims throughout the world try to stay up all night praying and reading the Quran. God has promised that their prayers this night will not go unheeded. The holy Quran tells us: 'The Night of Power is better than a thousand months. The angels and the Spirit descend in it by the permission of their Lord – for every affair – Peace! it is until the rising of the morning' (Surah 97: verses 3–5). The *salat al-tarawih* (the night prayer) every night during the month of Ramadan is another popular prayer and attracts young and old alike in large numbers.

The month of fasting is like no other for a Muslim. It is a time of prayer, of contemplation, of good deeds and of testing the self to the limits. It is the month when the Quran was first revealed by God to the Prophet on the mountain top. And it is the month when God looks down with special favour on humanity.

The final pillar of Islam is *haj* (pilgrimage), that annual spectacular gathering in Makkah which cannot but move the visitor. Once in a lifetime, each Muslim – male and female – is expected to travel to Makkah. The conditions are that they must pay for themselves without borrowing the money and be able to afford it. Every year, during the twelfth Islamic month, about two million Muslims from all over the world gather here.

The *haj*, like the other pillars, also reinforces basic Islamic principles; for instance, that all are equal in the eyes of God. Before entering Makkah, pilgrims change their clothes. Instead of ordinary everyday clothes, a male Muslim wears two sheets of unsewn white cloth. All other signs of everyday life such as watches and wallets are removed by the pilgrim. In this way there is no sign of worldly rank or association. A Muslim may rub shoulders with a king or president and not know it. Women may wear their everyday clothes, but must be covered from head to ankles. The white sheets are symbolic. They remind Muslims that they must be willing to give up everything for God. It is also a reminder that dead people are wrapped in similar sheets. After death, all fine clothes and wealth are of no value.

The *haj* lasts five days. On the first day, beginning at Makkah, Muslims walk seven times around the Kabah, starting at the black stone. Many non-Muslims assume that Muslims worship the black stone or pray to it. This is absolutely incorrect, since Islam expressly forbids worship of anything but God. Yet because the Prophet respected the stone most Muslims have come to regard it as special, and most pilgrims attempt to touch and kiss it – a task made difficult by the surging crowd of people milling around it at all times. The Prophet's celebrated companion (and later caliph), Umar, in his usual forthright manner, addressed the stone thus: 'I know you are only a stone but because I saw the Prophet kiss you I will do the same.'

The pilgrim then goes to two small hillocks nearby. Here God had wished to test Abraham by ordering him to leave his wife Hagar and son Ismail, a progenitor of the Arabs. When Hagar's supply of water was exhausted she ran between the hills desperately searching for water. Her search was rewarded as a spring burst forth from the earth. To this day Muslim pilgrims ritually enact her plight. The water from the spring, called *Zamzam*, is highly valued, and pilgrims take it home in bottles for their relatives.

Then, the pilgrims spend the night at Mina. At dawn they move to the valley of Arafat. Here thousands of tents have been put up to protect them from the heat. After sunset the pilgrims leave to spend the night at Muzdalifah. Part of the evening is spent hunting for small stones for the next part of the *haj*, another ritual tracing back to Abraham. On returning to Mina, they set off for the three stone pillars which mark the place where the devil attempted to make Ismail disobey Abraham. Muslims believe that Ismail drove the devil away by throwing stones at him. In memory of that incident Muslims throw their stones at the pillars. It is symbolic of rejecting evil and wishing to follow God.

The pilgrimage ends with a festival when animals are sacrificed. This custom again goes back to Abraham, who had been willing to sacrifice his son on God's command. (Muslims believe that it was Ismail, not Isaac, whom God commanded Abraham to sacrifice; according to the Jewish and Christian traditions it was Isaac.) When God spared Ismail, Abraham sacrificed a ram instead. So the pilgrims sacrifice a sheep, goat, cow or camel to commemorate the act. This is a symbol of how willing they are to give up everything they value for God. Pilgrims eat some of the meat but most of it is given to the poor. Finally, pilgrims circle the Kabah once more. Those who can afford it go on to Madinah to visit the burial place of the Prophet and pray there.

On returning home the pilgrim is given the title *haji* and in traditional societies treated with respect. Most *hajis* become conscious of their visible role as proper Islamic models on their return from the *haj*. In a book based on my anthropological fieldwork among the Pukhtuns in Pakistan, I described a typical *haji* and his attitudes: 'Haji Hassan repeatedly quoted the Prophet: "To respect a *haji* means you respect me." He would start sentences with a self-conscious "I cannot tell lies" (*darogh nasham waylay*)' (Ahmed 1980: 114). Not all Muslims are, however, impressed: 'Locally the newly achieved status of the *haji* is balanced by the status of the Pukhtun *mashar* (elder). I heard Shahzada and other *mashars* in both areas speak cynically about the entire business of *haj*: "They go to smuggle watches and cloth." They would quote a saying attributed to the Prophet: "The *haj* decides a man's course for the rest of his life: he either returns very holy or very wicked", and agree that the *hajis* they know fell into the latter category' (Ahmed 1980: 110).

The Islamic calendar
The Muslim year is based on a lunar cycle. It contains 354 days and varies annually by ten or eleven days from the Christian solar calendar. The year is divided into twelve lunar months of twenty-nine or thirty days. It begins with the month of Muharram and ends with Zul-Hijja. The names of the months, some which refer to the seasons, belong to the pre-Islamic Arab calendar, when a month was added every three years to keep the lunar calendar in harmony with the solar year.

The holy Prophet and his early followers in Arabia were desert people for whom the waxing and waning of the moon marked the passage of time. The new day started not at midnight but in the evening with the appearance of the moon. The position of the stars was used as guidance by desert people who travelled when it was cool at night and rested in the heat of the day. Stars were also used for finding the direction of Makkah, the holy city of Islam. Astronomy became an important Islamic science, with the minaret as an ideal astronomic observatory. By the tenth century the Muslims had invented the astrolabe, an instrument with which they calculated the movement of stars and planets. They were able to tell the time of night from this forerunner of the modern clock.

The Islamic calendar reflects the social and spiritual aspects of Islam and helps to keep them in harmony. There are two festivals: *Eid al-Fitr*, the Festival of Charity or the feast of breaking the Ramadan fast, and *Eid al-Adha*, the Festival of Sacrifice. *Eid* itself means 'festival' or 'time of happiness' in Arabic, and on both occasions people send each other greetings cards, like Christmas and New Year cards. *Eid al-Fitr*, which is celebrated at the end of the month of fasting, used to be the less important of the two *eids*. However, so overpowering is the joy at the end of the month of Ramadan that Muslims have come to celebrate it with much more festivity and rejoicing than *Eid al-Adha*.

Eid al-Fitr provides one of the earliest and happiest memories of a young Muslim. Special dishes are cooked to celebrate the end of fasting. It is the day for the sticky, colourful sweetmeats made of milk, almonds and pistachios. The children, in their new, bright clothes, wait for the feast, which takes place after the prayer at the nearby mosque. And somewhere on the table there will always be a plate of dates (favoured by the Prophet, as we noted earlier). Elders will give money to the poor at the mosque and to children.

To enjoy the *Eid al-Fitr* festival Muslims try to go to the largest or most central mosque. Even where they live as a minority Muslims celebrate the *eids*, congregating at the central mosque or in someone's house. In the UK the mosque near Regent's Park in London is the most popular for *eid* prayers. In 1992, in the first week of April, I went down from Cambridge with my family to pray there. The gathering was large and colourful. The administrator of the mosque said that 50 000 to 60 000 people had come that day. Of course, everyone is not present at the same time. People arrive separately for prayers, which are said in assembly every hour from daybreak to midday.

There is a festive air in the mosque as good-natured people with their families jostle and mingle. Old friends are recognized and new friends made. Children, brightly dressed, enjoy themselves. Vendors set up stalls selling kebabs, balloons and other items. The colour of the occasion is heightened by the number of national dresses that are on display – Nigerian, Malaysian, Arab, Pakistani. The variety of people reflects the diversity of Islam: there are fair-skinned Europeans, black Africans, brown Asians and distinctly Central Asian visitors in the congregation.

There is also another element increasingly visible in these gatherings. Just outside the main gate I saw groups of young, earnest, hollow-cheeked, bearded men. That they were at the gates symbolized their situation outside the mosque, since they are not quite allowed to air their views inside. Some distributed leaflets against Arab kings, others denounced Zionism, some sought funds for Kashmiris, others for the Palestinians. One vociferous group argued that any Muslim taking part in the coming election in the UK in April would be indulging in un-Islamic activity. Their logic was that the present government is one of *kafirs* (non-believers), and because it had bombed Muslims in Iraq how could Muslims participate in or be part of its nefarious system? Soon a heated argument developed, as an Algerian opposed this point of view. Quickly a large crowd gathered to hear the two sides. But it was all good-natured and within the bounds of free debate.

Underneath the diversity and colour of the congregation we note the same Islamic patterns that are present throughout the world: the unity of Islam; the men praying in the main courtyard, the women in their own enclosures; the decorum and the dignity of prayers; the sense of community and conviviality; the themes of the *khutba* (the congregational sermon) which are also increasingly similar and touch on the problems of the Muslim community, whether the suffering of the Palestinians, the Kashmiris or, recently, the Bosnians. Beyond the festivity is the deeper awareness that the hard month of Ramadan, with its fasting, is now over successfully and Muslims need to enjoy the blessing and bounty of God.

The origins of the other festival, *Eid al-Adha*, the Festival of Sacrifice, go back to the Prophet Abraham and his willingness to sacrifice his son, as we saw in the description of the *haj*. Abraham's act is commemorated in the last rite of the pilgrimage to Makkah. Muslims throughout the world celebrate this day at the same time as those in Makkah. The day begins with communal prayer, as at *Eid al-Fitr*, followed by the ritual sacrificing of a sheep, a cow or a camel.

The third *eid* widely celebrated throughout the world is known as *Milad al-Nabi* (the birthday of the Prophet), and falls on the twelfth of the month of Rabi al-Awwal. It is a social and cultural function which is enjoyed by the family and is intended to express the community's love for the Prophet. Stories from his life, devotional songs, acts of charity and prayers mark the day. This third *eid* began to be celebrated with increasing fervour from the tenth century onwards. It seems to have gained in importance as Muslims encountered Christianity, with its especial emphasis on the birthday of Jesus. For most Sufis, who have a special regard for the Prophet as *insan-i-kamil* or the perfect person, the day is particularly important, and its observance may sometimes be the culmination of celebrations which begin on the first day of Rabi al-Awwal. This *eid* is the most striking expression of love and reverence for the Prophet in Islam.

At the *Milad al-Nabi* festival I attended in Cairo on 9 September 1992 the famous song was sung that the people in Madinah recited when the Prophet arrived from Makkah on that first great migration. It is a song that has been immortalized in Arabic literature and performed by the leading singers including the legendary Umm Kulthum of Egypt: 'The full moon has arrived and grace is upon us, the messenger is with us. He came in accordance with God's order, welcome the best of messengers to Madinah.' Here Sufism and populism, private joy and public festivity, belief and custom met as thousands and thousands of people danced, sang, cheered and chanted. There was no tension in the air. Flags proclaimed and acknowledged the four caliphs, the first rulers of Islam. The procession slowly wound its way to the Hussaini mosque by the Al-Azhar. It was not government sponsored, although the government attempts to cash in on it with ministers and officials visiting late into the night.

On two other occasions the community comes together in large numbers in the mosques: *Lailat al-Baraat* (the Night of Fate) and *Lailat al-Qadr* (the Night of Power). The former is the night of the 15th of Shaaban and the latter is generally the night of the 27th of Ramadan (as we saw above).

Two other events are commemorated by Muslims throughout the world: *Ashurah* or the 10th of Muharram and *Isra wal miraj* (The Night Journey) on the 27th of Rajab. The first commemorates the martyrdom of the Prophet's grandson Hussain at Karbala (see the following section). The second commemorates the night of the *miraj* (ascension) in the tenth year of the Prophet's prophethood. On this night the angel Gabriel conducted the Prophet, mounted on the winged horse called Buraq, through the seven heavens, where he spoke with God and prayed with the other prophets including Jesus, Moses and Abraham. He returned the same night with instructions that included the institution of the five daily prayers. Sufis and religious scholars read various and deep mystical meanings into the ascent. The *miraj* is celebrated by reading from the Quran, particularly Surah 17, 'The Night Journey', and by saying extra prayers.

Such occasions in the Islamic calendar maintain the religious consciousness of the community while deepening spiritual awareness. They also communicate traditional culture from one generation to the next (for further details of Muslim practice and belief, see Ashraf 1988; Esposito 1991; Haykal 1976; Robinson 1982).

SUNNI AND SHIA DIVISIONS IN ISLAM

On the face of it there is one monolithic Islamic faith; in essence each Muslim believes in the Islamic ideal. But, in practice, political and historical factors have helped to create differences within the community. These are essentially of a social and cultural nature.

Although there are numerous Muslim sects let us stay with the two broad divisions, the Sunni and the Shia. Sunnis account for about 90 per cent of the Muslim world population, Shias about 10 per cent. The differences between the two at the core are minimal and lie in custom and practice. There are other shades of opinion within the Sunni and the Shia, often based in cultural factors with little doctrinal significance. In many cases there is an overlap between the practice of a sect within the Shia and one within the Sunni.

The Shia

The Shia concentration has been in Persia – now Iran – and South Asia. A sense of exclusiveness characterizes them. The Shia see themselves as an 'elect' (*al-khassa*) living among the generality (*al-amma*) of Muslims, according to Shia scholars (Ahmed 1988: 56).

Shia belief revolves round the figure of Ali. A cousin of the Prophet, he was, as we saw above, the first male Muslim, and he was also a son-in-law of the Prophet. He was the last of the four early caliphs who succeeded the Prophet as the rulers of Islam. Ali's charisma, comprising personal chivalry and wisdom, is undisputed. The Prophet had said of him, 'I am the city of knowledge and Ali is its gate.' Ali, his wife Fatimah, and their two martyred sons Hassan and Hussain, are the key figures in Shia tradition. They are also widely revered by Sunnis.

The Shias believe that the Prophet chose Ali as his successor and that he should therefore have been the first caliph. The only caliph that both Shias and Sunnis accept is Ali. In particular the Shias reject the first three caliphates of Abu Bakr, Umar and Uthman. (However, a small minority of the Shias, the Zaidis, do accept the first three caliphs as well as Ali.)

To a non-Muslim the causes of the Shia split with the Sunnis may appear obscure, but these are central to the parting of the ways. Shias believe that Ali should have been the first caliph of Islam after the Prophet rather than merely the fourth one – not only because he richly deserved the appointment but because he was also the Prophet's son-in-law. If Ali had been the first caliph, his son Hussain would then have been caliph in place of Yazid, the very man who ordered Hussain's death at Karbala.

The events at Karbala are of deep significance to Shias. After both his father and his elder brother Hassan had been assassinated, Hussain led his family and followers against the caliph Yazid's army at Karbala in 680, but they faced impossible odds. About seventy men were slaughtered on the battlefield by an army of thousands, and after the battle Hussain's body was beheaded.

The motif of martyrdom is crucial to Shias, who believe that, starting with Ali himself, all except one of the twelve Imams (that is, Ali and his direct descendants) were martyred. Loyalty to the *ahl al-bayt* – the house of the Prophet, or Ali and his descendants – is at the core of the sect. Indeed, the word Shia derives from 'partisans' or group of supporters of Ali.

Shias believe that each new leader of the community should be chosen by the previous Imam and they believe that he should be a descendant of the Prophet and thus of Ali. For the Sunnis the caliphs held mainly political power. For the Shias their religious authority is far more important. They could therefore regard Ali's son Hassan as their Imam even when he had no political influence.

The Shia heartlands would remain in the region where the deaths of Ali and Hussain took place – present Iraq and Iran. In particular the death, and the manner in which it took place, of Hussain and his followers at Karbala have helped shape the Shia world-view. The need to stand up against all odds on a matter of principle, the readiness for martyrdom, total passion, disregard for death and acceptance of tragedy are familiar aspects of the Shia. It is termed by scholars the 'Karbala paradigm' (Fischer 1980). Iran in the last decade has exhibited aspects of the Karbala paradigm which would help explain its actions.

Differences between Shias and Sunnis

The main historical significance of Imam Khomeini on the international Muslim stage was his stand that there are no differences in Islam, especially between Shia and Sunni. And this is a matter of fact. Many scholars believe that the historical and cultural confrontation between Arabs and Persians helps to explain the differences between Sunni and Shia.

Both Shias and Sunnis believe in the five pillars of Islam. But over the centuries an entire body of different rituals, even forms of prayer, have evolved. It must be emphasized that much of this is only marginally different from Sunni practice: Shias tend to combine the five prayers into three sessions; on journeys during Ramadan they only fast for half the day until noon, and so on.

One of the differences between Shias and Sunnis, the Shia doctrine of the imamate as distinct from the Sunni concept of the caliphate, which may seem unimportant and puzzling to a non-Muslim, has led to major political consequences. The caliph was the selected or elected successor of the Prophet. However, he succeeded to political and military leadership but not to the Prophet's religious authority. In contrast, Shia leadership of the Muslim community is vested in the Imam (leader), who, although not a prophet, is the divinely inspired, sinless, infallible, religio-political leader. His descent is traced directly from the Prophet and Ali, the first Imam, and his authority thus sanctified.

The Imam is both political leader and religious guide who is himself divinely guided. He is the final authoritative interpreter of God's will as formulated in Islamic law, and thus has almost unlimited power. This concentration of religious authority is unique to the Shia and not accepted by the Sunni. For Sunnis religious authority required to interpret Islam lies in the consensus (*ijma*) or collective judgement of the community, that is, the consensus of the *ulema*, the traditional religious scholars.

Sunnis believe that the Prophet's role in revealing God's laws in the Quran and guiding people to God in the *sunnah* ended with him. Shias believe that God would not leave them without guidance and their leaders have the right to interpret the Quran. It follows that the Imams must be sinless and unable to make mistakes because God is guiding them. To the Sunni argument that the Quran is to be interpreted literally, the Shias claim there is a hidden meaning given by the Prophet to Ali.

There is another difference between the two. Sunnis and Shias have developed divergent interpretations of history. For Sunnis, early Islamic success and power were signs of God's guidance and rewards to a faithful community as well as validation of Muslim belief and claims. For Shias, history was the enactment of the struggle and sacrifice of an oppressed and disinherited minority community endeavouring to restore God's rule on earth over the entire community. The struggle was to be led by the Imam. The Shias were to struggle in God's way, irrespective of the forces of evil personified by Satan ranged against them. The lives of the Imams were seen as embodying this struggle. Their martyrdom, especially that of Ali and Hussain, gave the Shia a model.

Another difference between Sunnis and Shias rests in their belief regarding folk or cultural practices around tombs of saints. Sunnis are ambivalent about this, and the orthodox strongly reject these practices as un–Islamic. The Shias incorporated these as part of their custom. The difference reflects a deeper philosophic position. For Sunnis, God and human beings have a direct relationship; saints and scholars cannot be intermediaries to God but are only formal interpreters of religion. Belief in shrines and saints was often viewed by the Sunni orthodox as heretical and even dangerous deviation from the true and singular worship of God (*bida*).

By contrast, the Shias believe that intercession is an integral part of the divine plan for salvation. Ali and the other main Imams were divinely inspired people who because of their spirituality were intermediaries between God and the believers. After them, it is believed, in the absence of the Imam a distinguished religious scholar can act as the supreme guide and authority on Islamic law. He thus becomes the paragon of Islamic behaviour. In a society where there is general respect for such clerics (*mujtahids* and mullahs) it is easy to exaggerate that devotion and suggest an almost super-human status. The highest rank is that of an ayatollah, and on top of the entire religious structure is the Ayatollah al-Uzma, the supreme ayatollah of the age. It is in this context that the widespread reverence for Imam Khomeini, the Ayatollah al-Uzma during the later part of his life, is to be understood in Iran.

Religious zeal provided the ayatollahs with a following prepared to make immense sacrifices, the belief in the Imam made the masses susceptible to command from the leaders, and the social structure of the Shia clergy provided, as it was transformed into, a ready-made revolutionary command structure. This prevented the revolutionary movement from disintegrating. Without Shia history and the structure of the Shia clergy the Iranian revolution would not have been possible.

In countries where both Shias and Sunnis live, conflict between them can be violent. Pakistan's Shia population constitutes about 20 per cent of the total population of about 110 million. Armed clashes can take place, especially during the month of Muharram in the ten days of Shia mourning for the events at Karbala. It is during this period that Shias mourn, flagellate themselves, bring out processions symbolic of Karbala, and recite moving poems about the tragedy at Karbala. These scenes taken from Lebanon or Iran and shown on television in Western living rooms often convey the picture of Islam today. Taken out of context they appear alien and disturbing, suggesting fanaticism and violence.

By acquainting ourselves with Shia doctrines we are able to understand the depiction of Islam in the Western media. Much of what is popularly associated with Islam originates from Shia practice. Seeing the passion of a political procession in an Iranian city and hearing its slogans is to encounter over a thousand years of Shia history: justice, struggle, sacrifice, martyr-dom. We are familiar with these through the revolutionary slogans of the Iranian revolution.

Western media commentators on Islam in the last few years made one major mistake in their analysis. Noting the fervour in Iran, they tended to ask: 'Which Muslim country will be swept by an Islamic revolution next? Will the next Ayatollah Khomeini emerge in Egypt or Pakistan?' If they had done their homework they would have come to a different conclusion. Although there is a great wave of Islamic revivalism in Muslim societies the Iranian revolution is to a large extent tied to the Shia view of history and society. It is for this reason that a similar revolution is not possible in Egypt and Pakistan, where Sunnis form the majority of the population.

The other Shia groups

The main branch of modern Shiism is the Ithna Ashari or twelve Imam Shiism. According to this sect, the line of descent from Ali ended with the twelfth Imam, who is believed to be not dead but hidden. The notion of the hidden Imam reinforces loyalty to the house of Ali through belief that the twelfth Imam will return one day as the Mahdi (the expected one). It also strengthens the role of the *ulema*. For during the absence of the Imam the community was to await his return and be guided by its religious experts. This branch of Shiism became the official state religion under the Safavids in Persia and is practised by the majority of people in modern Iran.

As the Shias split from Sunnis, in turn other sects formed within the Shia. Apart from the Ithna Ashari, the two other major divisions are the Zaidi and the Ismaili. Sunnis consider Zaidis to be the most moderate Shias; they do not abuse Abu Bakr or Umar, the first two caliphs. Again, to the outsider the reasons for the divisions seem obscure. In essence they reflect the principle of succession, which lies at the heart of Shia belief. For instance, the Zaidis claimed that Zaid ibn Ali, a grandson of Hussain, was the fifth Imam, whereas the majority of the Shia recognized Muhammad al-Baqir and his son Jafar al-Sadiq as rightful heirs to the imamate. Unlike other Shia, who restricted the imamate to the descendants of Ali by his wife Fatimah, Zaidis believed that any descendant of Ali could become Imam. The Zaidis were the first Shias to gain independence when Hassan ibn Zaid founded a Zaidi dynasty in Tabaristan, on the Caspian, in 864. Another Zaidi state was established in 893 in Yemen, where it continued to exist until 1963.

The Ismailis led by the Aga Khan (the Ismaili Imam) are also worth mentioning because of the high profile and forward-looking policies of their leader. In particular his propagation of Islamic architecture has allowed him to provide a lead and draw in Muslims all over the world. The combination of tradition and modernity has generated a global feeling of Muslim pride and identity.

The image of the Ismailis as a prosperous and peaceful merchant community belies their early turbulent history. Centuries ago they attacked and assassinated Sunni political and religious leaders. The famed Saladin, battling against the Crusaders led by Richard I of England, was one of their targets. The Ismailis at one stage ruled an area which stretched from Egypt to the province of Sind (in what is now Pakistan). Like other Shias, the Ismailis believed that the Quran was to be understood on two levels: an exoteric, literal one, that is, according to what is on the surface, and an esoteric, inner one, that is, meanings hidden from those without inner knowledge and those not part of the group. They believed that they possessed understanding of the latter kind.

Shiism in the Western media

With the Iranian revolution in the late 1970s the special friendship between Iran and the USA under the Shah was converted into one of intense mutual hatred. For Iran the USA became the Great Satan. Here was a confrontation which resonated in Shia history: the fight for a just cause against the mighty power of an evil force.

For the USA, Iran represented fanaticism and religious hatred, a throwback to the worst excesses of medieval Europe, a revolution led by crazed priests. Because of the power of the American media, the images of Iran became the images of Islam throughout the world. These images were of shouting mullahs with death in their eyes or of women veiled from head to toe or of young men with Kalashnikovs. The gap between the substance of Islam's message and its universal image was reminiscent of the time of the Crusades centuries ago. We must again emphasize how the Shias have become representative of Islam in the Western media. Sunnis who may not perhaps mention it in public will often resent this development in private. Yet there are no ayatollahs among Sunnis, for Sunnis do not believe in powerful, centralized figures of religious authority; even the black robes and turbans are specifically Shia (black is symbolic of mourning, of Karbala). The ritual of self-flagellation which has also become associated with television images of Islam is specifically related to the tragedy at Karbala and to Shia Islam. To many in the West, however, all Muslims look alike and behave in a similar fashion.

SUFISM: THE MUSLIM UNIVERSAL WAY

Sufism is Islam's tolerant, mystical and universal philosophy. Its message of *sulh-i-kul*, peace with all, has endeared it to Muslims and non-Muslims alike. It appeals to all Muslim sects and social classes. One has only to visit shrines such as that of the Sufi saint at Ajmer in India and observe the stream of Muslim and non-Muslim visitors for confirmation of this (see chapter 3). Sufis see the unity of God, *tauhid*, in everything and everyone. Although in its vulgar or more populist forms Sufism has acquired distinctly un-Islamic practices, its origin is unimpeachable, tracing back to the Prophet himself. The Sufi must first master the *shariah*, the true path of Islam, before venturing on to the *tariqah*, the Sufi way.

Sufi masters are central figures for their disciples in helping to unravel the mysteries and ideas of Sufism. The first and primary function of the Sufi master is what may be called ego-busting, that is to diminish the individual ego in order to establish the supremacy of God. To aid this, numerous exercises are devised, most of them baffling to the layman. Many stories are told of how Sufi masters instruct their disciples. There are tales of princes who, on entering the Sufi circle, are ordered to clean latrines.

As with all things Sufic, many layers of meaning lie beneath the surface. The idea is first to deconstruct and then to construct the seeker of truth before the *tariqah* can be understood. These esoteric practices allow Sufis to endure hard times, even times of persecution. One such practice is the ritual of *dhikr*, mention of the name of Allah. Each of the ninety-nine names is known to contain a special quality. Pronouncing and repeating the name in a special manner produces a spiritual state in the believer. *Dhikr* kept Islam alive in Central Asia during the harsh days of Soviet rule (see chapter 5).

The following prayer sums up the spirit of Sufism. It is from the Naqshbandi order associated with Bahauddin Naqshband, the saint of Bukhara, who lived in the fourteenth century (and whom we shall meet again in chapter 5). The universal strands of Islam are clearly visible; it could be the prayer of any religion, anywhere in the world:

Oh my God, how gentle art thou with him who has transgressed against thee: how near art thou to him who seeks thee, how tender to him who petitions thee, how kindly to him who hopes in thee.

Who is he who asks of thee and thou dost deny him or who sought refuge in thee and thou dost betray him and drew near to thee and thou dost hold him aloof? And fled unto thee and thou dost repulse him?

The all-pervading and tolerant spirit of the Sufis is not surprising when we consider their sources of inspiration. Although the Prophet is their ultimate model, other spiritual figures – which include Abraham, Moses and Jesus – also mould them. This is enunciated in 'The Eight Qualities of the Sufi' by the well-known Sufi master, Junaid of Baghdad:

> In Sufism, eight qualitities must be exercised. The Sufi has:
> Liberality such as that of Abraham;
> Acceptance of his lot, as Ismail accepted;
> Patience, as possessed by Job;
> Capacity to communicate by symbolism, as in the case of Zachariah;
> Estrangement from his own people, which was the case with John;
> Woollen garb like the shepherd's mantle of Moses;
> Journeying, like the travelling of Jesus;
> Humility, as Muhammad had humility of spirit.
> (Shah 1990: 246)

For me personally, Sufism's message of compassion, humility and universal love is attractive and inspiring. But what is a youngster, soaked in the materialist urban milieu in which television provides the greatest input, to make of Sufism? How would he or she understand the Sufi stories?

The following tale from the celebrated *Mathnawi* of the greatest of Sufi masters, Rumi, illustrates the point. A disciple seeking the Sufi path finally feels he has mastered it and arrives to announce this to his master. He knocks on the door and when asked 'Who is there?' answers 'I'. The master says, 'Go away, you have not yet acquired knowledge.' He leaves to return after he has performed more spiritual exercises, and this time when asked who is knocking says 'Thou'. 'Come in,' says the master. 'There is no room for two Is in this house.'

This Sufi story illustrates the layers of understanding that lie in Sufism: the obliteration of the ego, the need for the master who will help the quest for knowledge along the divine path, and the search for the true way, the way of God, however difficult and esoteric. These stories are allegories, metaphors, stories within stories, and like the layers of an onion they require patience to peel; they sometimes end in tears.

Sufism is not calculated to be popular or understood in an age that is dominated by the media, by the sound bite, by the simplistic analysis, by the noise and thunder of the sound-track and by a cynical irreverence (see chapter 6). Our age demands simple heroes – Superman, James Bond, Indiana Jones. Themes that remind us of the transience of our life on earth, that point to the mysteries of existence, the complexity of being, are not readily accepted.

THREE

THE CHALLENGE OF THE PAST: EMPIRES AND DYNASTIES

●

Five hundred years ago the fortress palace of Alhambra in Spain was captured by the Christians. To celebrate the final defeat of Islam in Spain the Te Deum, a hymn of thanksgiving, was sung at St Paul's Cathedral in London. It is hard for a Muslim to stand at the Alhambra without feeling a sense of loss. It is the same at the mosque at Cordoba. Nor is this feeling of regret confined to Andalusian Spain. Throughout what were the traditional heartlands of Islam in Turkey, Iran and North India great Muslim civilizations lie in ruins. I believe the past challenges Muslims today in all sorts of complex and interesting ways.

In this chapter we shall take a selective dip into Muslim history in order to come up with some principles that help us understand it better. It will be an impressionistic view, not restricted by regular chronological sequences. In order not to be completely lost in the dates, events and doings of the main historical figures, however, we shall concentrate on only three Muslim empires: the Ottomans, the Safavids and the Mughals. But first we shall go back a few centuries to the great days of the Arabs, especially their glorious period in Spain.

In the next chapter we shall see how modern Turkey, Iran and Pakistan, respectively, relate to the three empires from which they derive so much cultural inspiration. The choice of these three nations is appropriate: each is a major Muslim nation, and each represents a different geographical and cultural area.

A Muslim view of history

Contemporary Muslim society cannot be understood without reference to important events that took place centuries ago. For Muslims what happened in the past is important, since they live in the present with an acute awareness of their history. The Muslim association with their past is explained through religion. For the majority of Muslims, the ideal society is that of seventh-century Arabia. Although in our world of high technology it is difficult sometimes to relate to such different time periods, most Muslims manage to do so quite successfully in their daily lives.

Many Muslims believe that there is a strong argument for interpreting Muslim history differently from Western history. For the West, history in general means progress and evolution from societies that are labelled as 'primitive' to those that are industrialized, urbanized and 'advanced'. Undulations and cycles delay but do not stop the march of history. History is thus the triumph of the individual, the culmination of the attempt by humans to master their environment. The notions of progress, development and betterment are an integral part of this view.

We may identify the Muslim perspective on history as rooted in the early days of Islam. At the heart of this view is faith: in the early days Muslims believed with full faith and fervour; they were anxious to spread the word of God; and God provided them with triumphs rarely matched in history. History for Muslims is the attempt to live by the ideals of Islam as far as possible. It is this attempt that creates the rhythms and tensions of Muslim history and society; it also helps cause the rise and fall of dynasties. History is therefore sometimes a burden and sometimes a source of inspiration. But as history is never far from Muslim life, it allows Muslims to bear the failures of fate. It allows an in-built mechanism for optimism; for if there is a collapse today surely once Muslims live by the ideal there will be triumph tomorrow.

'Once we have comprehended the key to our universe we are able to understand its structure and organization,' I wrote in 1988, trying to explain the rhythm of Muslim history. 'Birth, rise and decline then become comprehensible. There is science and meaning beneath apparently random patterns of history and society: Islam disintegrating in one place, reviving in another, fading here, growing there; but Islam always a factor, a force providing the dynamics of society' (Ahmed 1988: 31–32).

Characteristics of the great Muslim empires
A discussion of the Ottoman, Safavid and Mughal empires is important in the context of not only Muslim history but also world history. We must bear in mind that these were the superpowers of their age in their economic, cultural and political strength and influence. For example, the Mughal empire at its peak covered about half a dozen contemporary Asian countries with a population today amounting to about one-fifth of mankind: Pakistan,

India, Bangladesh and (depending on how strong the emperor was) parts of Afghanistan, Iran and Burma.

There is also a contemporary reason for looking at these empires. Their history affects how the modern nations which claim to be their inheritor states see themselves: Turkey, Iran and Pakistan respectively. Their perception of the past and their situation in our own time offer dramatic contrasts, yet the relationship between past and present clarifies certain issues in these societies. In each case there is one major ongoing historical encounter that explains the main responses of each society: for the Turks with Christian Europe, for the Iranians with Shia belief and for the Pakistanis with Hinduism. The encounter embraces notions of religion, ideology and culture. The attempt to define themselves in relationship to this other has created a certain tension in Muslim societies which is a constant source of challenge and renewal. Sometimes harmony and sometimes confrontation have resulted, but there has always been an element of tension which affects the balance and symmetry of society.

Denied from creating human images, Muslims have poured their artistic talents into the building of mosques and tombs. We shall thus enter into these great empires not only through the conquests and the kingdoms of the mighty rulers but also through their art and architecture. In particular, mosques and tombs tell us much about the society that created them.

The Ottoman mosques are magnificent, with characteristic architecture. A major dome sitting powerfully at the centre dominates everything around it; the grey colour reinforces the impression of impregnability and solidity. Four pencil-like minarets at the four corners soar towards heaven. These Ottoman mosques are a contrast to the Safavid and Mughal mosques with their onion-shaped, seemingly lighter domes, their numerous pavilions, thicker and shorter minarets, and monumental entrance arches and, above all, the dazzling decorations: the gold and blue of the Safavids and the white marble of the Mughals. There is lightness, even magic and mystery here. The Taj Mahal is one example. The philosophy behind the architecture too has a subtle difference. The Sulaimaniye in Istanbul was made as a Muslim response to the St Sophia church, a challenge to Christian architectural achievement in the eyes of the Ottoman architect Sinan, another statement of confrontation; the Taj Mahal was a synthesis of Hindu and Muslim architecture, a monument of love.

EARLY MUSLIM HISTORY: THE GREAT ARAB DYNASTIES

Although for the Arabs their days of glory are a thousand years in the past – and there have been two major intrusions in their area, the Ottomans and the Europeans – most Arabs carry with them memories of past greatness. The Arabic language itself is a living reminder of the past.

The Arabs carry the message of Islam to the world

When the Prophet died in 632 the Arabs were trembling with energy and faith, ready to explode on to the world stage. Led by the first four 'righteous caliphs', Abu Bakr, Umar, Uthman and Ali (632–61), they raced with the exuberance of their message across most of what was then civilization. Within decades they had arrived at Spain in the west and Sind in the east. It seemed nothing could stop them.

The world had not seen anything like that early Muslim explosion. The Roman conquests had been slow and steady. Alexander the Great had effected a spectacular entry into Asia, but Alexander was like a meteor and immediately after he died his Greek empire fell apart. The Muslims brought with them a fresh civilization, a new way of looking at and living life; they had come to stay.

In order to explain the early phenomenal Islamic expansion critics have often suggested that Muslims used the sword. Medieval Christian writers would depict Muslim warriors with sword in one hand and the Quran in the other. This may well have been true in some cases and accounted for some conversions. For the vanquished there are obvious advantages in joining the victorious side. On the whole, however, this was a stereotype. We know that the sword is not an effective method of conversion, as history in our times shows us so dramatically.

No, we must look for other reasons. The first is the uncomplicated and direct nature of the Islamic message. Islam offered a religion of breathtaking simplicity. It has no complicated philosophy, no recognized hierarchy based on caste or wealth, no living spiritual head and no priesthood. In essence: one God, one Book and one Prophet. Each Muslim has access directly to God and to the Book and through it to the Prophet. Each convert – like every Muslim – feels Islam belongs to him or her. And conversion is simple: just the recitation of the declaration of faith. It is this simplicity which perhaps explains Islam's success, as indeed it does Islam's continuing appeal into the present day.

Another reason for Islam's popularity undoubtedly lay in its emphasis on the equality of people, irrespective of races and tribes. The only criterion of merit is goodness and piety – colour or birth or rank do not matter. To those living under the Persian, Byzantine and Roman empires the Islamic message came like a breath of fresh air. For the majority these empires were ridden with class hierarchy, sectarian prejudices and racial hatreds; corruption and oppression were the order of the day. Women in particular had few rights. Slavery was practised, and family, class and social connections determined privilege and promotion.

Islam also provided a healthy balance between affairs of the world (*dunya*) and those of religion (*din*). The choice between the world and religion was not *either* this *or* that, as in some religions, but *both* this *and* that.

Another section of society would also make loyal converts. The people of the desert and the mountains – the tribes – first introduced to Islam took to it instinctively like fish to water. These included the Berbers in North Africa, the Bedouin and the Kurds in the Middle East, and the Baluch and Pukhtuns in Afghanistan and Pakistan. These tribes would absorb Islam as part of their tribal consciousness. For them self-identity came to mean Islam; with Islam their tribalism was legitimized and completed. The Prophet's own tribal background enabled them to identify with him without reservation. Like him they knew what it was like to be a shepherd, to retreat into mountains and deserts, to expect loyalty – and enmity – based on tribal politics. It is tribalism that helps explain the actions of some of the early Muslims. When the Prophet announced his Islamic mission and was under attack by the powerful in Makkah who planned to do him harm, he was protected by his tribal kin. Many of his relatives did not accept Islam, but they were bound by tribal loyalty to shield him. And they did. Such is the code of the tribe.

The feeling of identity with Islam is important in understanding Muslim tribesmen. Even when they are berated by the orthodox from the cities for sometimes giving preference to distinctly un-Islamic tribal custom over Islamic practice, their response is of genuine amazement: we can be nothing but Muslims as our forefathers have been for over a thousand years; if we err then God is forgiving and merciful. It is the argument of the favourite: God knows we love and worship God even if we sometimes make mistakes.

The emphasis on courage, bravery and hospitality (*muruwwa*), which formed the ethos of traditional Arab tribal society, was mirrored in Islamic society. In Islam, therefore, the tribesmen found a sense of identity. It is a common saying among them that Islam is by definition part of their tribal identity; it is not a question of tribalism *versus* Islam but tribalism *and* Islam; the one is presupposed in the other (see Ahmed and Hart 1984).

Arab dynasties, Arab destinies

The first phase of Islamic history lasted for 600 to 700 years, producing first the great Arab dynasty of the Umayyads based in Damascus (661–750) and then the even greater one of the Abbasids in Baghdad (750–1258). Other significant dynasties like the Fatimids in Cairo and Umayyads in Cordoba are also worth noting.

In this phase of Muslim history, while mighty dynasties would rise and fall, renowned scholars produced great writing, famous artists made brilliant works of art, and rich patrons with an eye for symmetry and beauty assisted in the creation of splendid monuments. Through the rhythm of history, the ups and downs of dynasties, what emerges clearly is the creation of a distinct, rich and vibrant Muslim civilization that was truly universal. Indeed, during this period Islamic astronomy, geography and philosophy were influencing the West (through Muslim Spain). These are just some of the words imported into the English language from Islamic languages (Arabic and Persian): alchemy, alcohol, algebra, alkali, apricot, cipher, elixir, nadir, orange, pyjama, sherbet, sheriff, sherry, sugar, zenith and zero.

The influences of Muslim culture on Spain are numerous, sometimes overt, sometimes subtle. But it is remarkable that after 500 years a quarter of the words in the Spanish language are from Arabic. Even the name of the legendary national hero, El Cid (meaning the Noble Lord), is Arabic. The dances, the songs, the music, centuries after the Muslims ceased to live in the land of Andalusia, still echo their culture – from the *Olé!* as an exclamation in song and dance, which is a derivation of *wallah* ('oh God'), to the architecture and food.

Consider the unlikely example of Zorro, the masked and cloaked hero of the New World in America. The idea of an avenging swordsman dressed in black may well have come to Spain with the Muslims from North Africa. Certain tribes, like the Tuareg, cover their faces and wear loose, flying robes of a dark colour. The notion of an avenger wanting to establish justice and challenge tyranny is common in Muslim culture; there is even a name for him, *mujahid*. Both the Prophet, who in folklore is often referred to as the man in the black cloak, and Ali, who is depicted as a warrior dressed in black with sword in hand seeking to redress wrongs, provide models for the *mujahid*. From Spain this idea travelled to America.

The life of Ibn Khaldun, one of the earliest sociologists of history, who lived and worked in North Africa and Spain, but settled and died in Cairo, illustrates the universality and stability of Muslim culture. Albert Hourani describes these features of Arab history:

A world where a family from southern Arabia could move to Spain, and after six centuries return nearer to its place of origin and still find itself in familiar surroundings, had a unity which transcended divisions of time and space; the Arabic language could open the door to office and influence throughout that world; a body of knowledge, transmitted over the centuries by a known chain of teachers, preserved a moral community even when rulers changed; places of pilgrimage, Mecca and Jerusalem, were unchanging poles of the human world even if power shifted from one city to another; and belief in a God who created and sustained the world could give meaning to the blows of fate.
(Hourani 1991: 4)

Ibn Khaldun was not alone; some of the most famous Islamic writers, like Imam Ghazzali, Ibn Arabi, Ibn Battuta, led similar lives.

The sharp eye looks for convenient dates to mark beginnings and ends in history, but this is difficult for Muslim history. There were periods when it appeared nothing could stop Muslim advances, then there were times when it looked as though nothing could prevent total Muslim disintegration. At the turn of the eighth century it appeared that the Arabs were all over the known world, irresistible and triumphant: they landed on the southern coast of Spain, they conquered Sind on the river Indus and, further north, they captured the historic fort of Darbent, on the Caspian Sea, which was the key to the Caucasus mountains. They had also reached the river Oxus; the Central Asian tribes were poised to be converted.

But then let us move a few centuries ahead, to 1258. It was the year the Mongols, who had erupted from the Gobi desert under Chenghiz Khan, shattered Baghdad and destroyed the heart of the Abbasid empire. It appeared Islam was doomed, that nothing could stop its annihilation. But then, unexpectedly, the Mongols converted to Islam. In turn, they gave Islam a fresh wind. Soon the Mongols were carrying the message of Islam to the heart of Russia and back with them to China. Two centuries after the fall of Baghdad, Mehmet the Conqueror, in 1453, captured Constantinople, the ancient seat of Christianity and the heart of the Holy Roman Empire, and changed its name from Constantinople to Istanbul. Early in the next century Babar conquered Delhi and established the Mughal empire in India.

There are thus patterns, undulations and rhythms in Muslim history that defy easy analysis. When it appears about to collapse at one place, Islam takes root elsewhere. There can be no application of the simple rise-and-fall frame of history to Islam.

The Christian Crusades

Foreigners who are aggressive, ignorant, barbaric and unwelcome. Foreigners who are forever advocating their way of life and prepared to back it by brawling and fighting; foreigners with embarrassing and uncouth manners. Are we talking of Muslim immigrants as seen by Europeans in the late twentieth century? No. These are Europeans almost a thousand years ago in the Muslim lands of the Middle East. They came as individuals and as groups, as armies and as soldiers of fortune.

Muslims were not their only target; local Christians and Jews were also among their victims. In one instance their behaviour plumbed new depths. It was in the St Sophia church in Istanbul. They violated women, drank, and stripped the church bare. An eyewitness of the fourth Crusade was horrified: 'I Geoffrey de Ville Hardouin, Martial of the court of Champagne, am sure that since the creation of the universe, a plundering worse than this one has not been witnessed' (Efe 1987: 18). Compare this to Mehmet the Conqueror's entry when, with humility and awe, he fell to his knees, taking the dust from the floor and wiping it on his turban as an act of devotion (Efe 1987). Christians here have a saying: 'Better the turban of a Turk than the tiara of the Pope.'

As for the unfortunate Jews, they would be massacred by the Christians on their way to the Crusades and massacred by them on their way back from the Crusades. Not surprisingly Muslims thought that here was a civilization doomed to barbarism and backwardness for ever. It is noteworthy that local Christians in the Middle East supported Muslims in their fight against the Crusaders. This was an interesting crossing of religious lines and is reflected in the politics of the Middle East until our own times.

At the heart of the Crusades stood the city of Jerusalem, holy to Jews, Christians and Muslims. With Makkah and Madinah it is one of the three holiest places for Muslims, who call it, in Arabic, the Bait al-Maqdus, the Holy House, usually shortened to Al-Quds. The importance of Jerusalem is linked to the holy Prophet himself, to the night journey and ascension (Surah 17: verse 1). The Prophet ascended into heaven from the historic rock in Jerusalem over which the Dome of the Rock, the earliest Islamic monument, now stands. *Isra wal miraj* (the Night Journey) is remembered each year on the 27th of Rajab wherever Muslims live.

A mosque was built here by the caliph Umar in 638; the present dignified building was begun in 687 and completed in 691. The Dome of the Rock is more a shrine than a mosque, and another mosque was built nearby soon afterwards with much more space for Muslims to gather in. This is called the

1 The Quba mosque in Madinah (Medina), the holy city
where the Prophet is buried.

2 Frontispiece to part 7 of a Quran in seven volumes, copied by Muhammad ibn al–Washid,
illuminated by Muhammad ibn Mubadir and Aydughdi ibn Abd Allah
al-Badri in 704 AH (AD 1304) in Cairo, now in the British Museum.

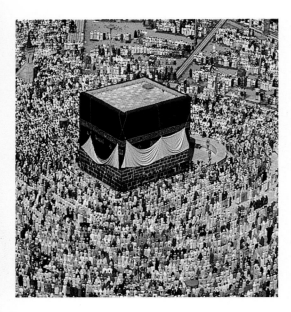

3 Pilgrims surging round the Kabah –
the central sanctuary – in the great
mosque at Makkah (Mecca).

Right 4 Aerial view of the great mosque
at Makkah during *haj*.

6 The Court of Lions, in the centre
of the Alhambra palace, Granada,
completed in the fourteenth century.

Left 5 A small Christian shrine inside the
original section of the mosque at
Cordoba.

———————————— ● ————————————

8 The exterior of St Sophia, Istanbul; built as a church by the Emperor
Justinian, it was converted into a mosque when the Turks
captured the city in 1453.

Left 7 Astronomers at work in an observatory, from an Ottoman
manuscript of the second half of the sixteenth century.

9 The Friday mosque in Isfahan, Iran, completed in the seventeenth century under the Safavids.

Right 10 The Gate of Victory at Fatehpur Sikri, built by the great Mughal emperor Akbar at the end of the sixteenth century. The architecture of Fatehpur Sikri is a synthesis of Hindu and Islamic styles.

11 Jahangir, who succeeded Akbar as Mughal emperor, contemplating a
picture of the Madonna.

Right 12 Aurangzeb, the sixth and last great Mughal emperor, at prayer.

13 The Taj Mahal at Agra, near Delhi, built by the Mughal emperor Shah Jahan as a mausoleum for his beloved wife Mumtaz Mahal in the seventeenth century.

14 The imposing mausoleum of Mr Jinnah in Karachi. The architecture of the tomb suggests that Pakistan has left its Indian legacy and is looking instead towards its Islamic past in the Middle East.

Below 15 The Faisal mosque in Islamabad, Pakistan. Named after King Faisal of Saudi Arabia, it was started in the 1960s and built in an international Islamic style.

Al-Aqsa mosque, meaning the 'furthest' mosque. Both the Dome of the Rock and the Al-Aqsa mosque are situated in the part of Jerusalem known as the Noble Sanctuary or Al-Haram Al-Sharif. It was towards this point that Muslims first faced when praying, before they were commanded to face the Kabah at Makkah.

The story is related that when Umar entered Jerusalem as a conqueror he refused to pray in the church which had been prepared for Muslim prayers after his followers had obtained permission from the Christian priests. Umar preferred an open space, because, he said, he feared his followers might make his attendance an excuse and convert the church to a mosque. Subsequent Muslim rulers of Jerusalem took their cue from Umar: Christians and their churches were unmolested, and Jews, long banned from Jerusalem by the Christian rulers, were allowed to return. After all, they too were 'people of the Book'.

Some centuries later, when in 1099 the Christians captured Jerusalem during the Crusades, the story was altogether different. They not only slaughtered its inhabitants – not even women and children were spared – but defiled the places of worship, including the Noble Sanctuary. The Dome of the Rock was converted into a church and the Al-Aqsa mosque, renamed the Temple of Solomon, became a residence for the king. Edward Gibbon described the Christian conquest of Jerusalem:

A bloody sacrifice was offered by his mistaken votaries to the God of the Christians; resistance might provoke, but neither age nor sex could mollify, their implacable rage; they indulged themselves three days in a promiscuous massacre; and the infection of the dead bodies produced an epidemical disease. After seventy thousand Moslems had been put to the sword, and the harmless Jews had been burnt in their synagogue, they could still reserve a multitude of captives, whom interest or lassitude persuaded them to spare.
(Edward Gibbon, in Watt 1991: 517)

One of my favourite Rider Haggard novels, *The Brethren*, describes the recapture of Jerusalem by Muslims in 1187:

Then Saladin showed his mercy, for he freed all the aged without charge, and from his own treasure paid the ransom of hundreds of ladies whose husbands and fathers had fallen in battle, or lay in prison in other cities. . . .

At length it was over, and Saladin took possession of the city . . . Thus did the Crescent triumph over the Cross in Jerusalem, not in a sea of blood, as ninety years before the Cross had triumphed over the Crescent within its walls, but with what in those days passed for gentleness, peace, and mercy. For it was left to the Saracens to teach something of their own doctrines to the followers of Christ.
(Haggard 1904: 337)

Saladin's conduct speaks of Muslim civilization at its best. The dramatic moment in the encounter between Christianity and Islam ensured that Saladin's name became synonymous with chivalry and culture in European mythology. Among Muslims, his courage, compassion, piety and respect for learning make him an ideal ruler.

Once again the Muslims reversed the Christian ban and allowed Jews to settle in Jerusalem. This characteristic Muslim magnanimity would resonate in history; in our own time the Jews would not only take Jerusalem from the Muslims but make it exclusively their own city.

The memory of the Crusades lingers in the Middle East and colours Muslim perceptions of Europe. It is the memory of an aggressive, backward and religiously fanatic Europe. This historical memory would be reinforced in the nineteenth and twentieth centuries as imperial Europeans once again arrived to subjugate and colonize territories in the Middle East. Unfortunately this legacy of bitterness is overlooked by most Europeans when thinking of the Crusades.

Not long after Saladin captured Jerusalem the power of the Arabs declined dramatically. After the Mongol destruction of Baghdad, after half a millennium of dominating most of the known world, the Arabs bowed out of history. By the sixteenth century there were three great Muslim empires and none of them was Arab. The Arab heartland (most of the Middle East) was ruled by two foreign powers: first the Ottomans and after them the Europeans. It is therefore not surprising that Arab writers even today blame their political problems on outsiders.

THE IDEAL MODEL OF EUROPEAN SOCIETY: MUSLIM SPAIN

Europe in the 1990s will be increasingly concerned to discover a model for its society. Numerous problems need to be addressed. How will fair play be ensured between races especially with regard to minorities? How will freedom of worship be guaranteed? Will intolerance – whether religious or ethnic – tear the fabric of society apart (as we see in the former Yugoslavia in 1992–3)? What will be the future of the immigrants who arrived in Europe from different parts of the world as a result of the colonial century? Can Europe's notions of humanism be sustained in the face of populations that are neither European nor white?

Some of these answers were successfully tackled by a European society which existed about a thousand years ago: Muslim Spain. If we define a civilized society as one which encourages religious and ethnic tolerance, free debate, libraries and colleges, public baths and parks, poetry and architecture, then Muslim Spain is a good example. Take the example of a library, always a useful index of civilization. The library of the ruler of Cordoba in the tenth century contained 400 000 volumes – more, it is said, than in all the libraries of Europe at the time.

We need to put Muslim Spain in the perspective of medieval Europe. At the time London and Paris were small towns. There was no notable art or literature or libraries or debate anywhere in Europe. Here, in contrast, was a sophisticated and powerful civilization with clear notions of harmony involving race and religion. Ideas of debate, libraries, love poetry, cleanliness and baths, were pervasive. Plato and Aristotle were discussed here.

The intermingling of race and religion in Muslim Spain produced a rich and dynamic culture. Intermarriage between Jews, Christians and Muslims produced many Muslim rulers with fair hair and blue eyes, according to the literature. There were alliances between Muslim and Christian rulers and a great deal of give and take on all levels. The near-legendary warrior El Cid fought against but also alongside Muslims; the Nasirids of Granada helped the Christians in their fight against the Muslims of Seville. This interchange is clear in the architecture too. The twelve lions at the Court of Lions in the Alhambra are heraldic, exhibiting Christian influences.

The American diplomat, Washington Irving, who encouraged the rediscovery of Muslim Spain through his writing in the last century, observes:

> As conquerors, their heroism was only equalled by their moderation, and in both, for a time, they excelled the nations with whom they contended. Severed from their native homes, they loved the land given them as they supposed by Allah and strove to embellish it with everything that could administer to the happiness of man. Laying the foundations of their power in a system of wise and equitable laws, diligently cultivating the arts and sciences, and promoting agriculture, manufactures and commerce, they gradually formed an empire unrivalled for its prosperity by any of the empires of Christendom. . . .
>
> The cities of Arabian Spain became the resort of Christian artisans, to instruct themselves in the useful art. The Universities of Toledo, Cordova, Seville, and Granada, were sought by the pale student from other lands to acquaint himself with the sciences of the Arabs and the treasure lore of antiquity.
>
> (Irving 1990: 52–3)

Although the picture of Muslim Spain may not always have been as ideal as this, there were certainly long periods when it was so. Europe would do well to look back to the past for inspiration in shaping the future.

Before we consider the achievements of Muslim Spain, let us recall the early arrivals of the Muslims from North Africa. The young Berber general Tariq had landed in 711 with 7000 troops. (Gibraltar is named after him: it derives from Jabal-al-Tariq or Rock of Tariq.) It was not a straightforward invasion but a response to a request from one faction of the warring Christian princes. Southern Spain was in turmoil under Visigothic rule; the Arabs called it Al-Andalus, from the name given to the Vandals, who had settled in the region.

During the next centuries Islam spread. When the Abbasids captured Damascus from the Umayyads in 750, Abdur Rahman, a member of the Umayyad family, fled to Spain and established a dynasty based at Cordoba. Under Abdur Rahman III (912–61) Cordoba became the most glittering city in Europe. Under Al-Mansor, prime minister of Hisham II (961–76), the entire Iberian Peninsula was finally conquered by the Muslims.

Muslim literature in Spain

The rich literature of Muslim Spain and its wider influences have been confirmed by scholars. 'Many people in North Africa today still regard Al-Andalus as the lost Garden of Eden,' observes Roger Boase.

> *This is hardly surprising because in Muslim Spain Arab civilization reached a level of artistic and intellectual refinement unattained elsewhere. This refinement was best expressed in poetry which since pre-Islamic times had been the art in which Arabs had always excelled. The style of this poetry could be described as Baroque and elliptical, at times even precious, because it relies on the use of striking similes, metaphors and conceits within a comparatively strict metrical system and a traditional framework of themes. The poet was a jeweller with words, seeking by means of verbal images to fix and thereby eternalize a fleeting experience of joy or sadness or aesthetic delight, seeking also to pay homage to a patron, to lampoon an enemy or to make a humorous observation.*
> (Boase 1989b: v)

The following examples of Muslim poetry in Spain will illustrate several points: the sophistication of the literature; the hedonistic lifestyle of the élite – alcohol and adultery, both forbidden by Islam, are celebrated in verse; the awareness of passing time, of imminent sorrow, especially poignant as Muslims began to lose power; and, finally, the Sufi themes of universalism and mysticism.

There is an interesting mirror image of Muslim poetry in India when Muslims began to lose power in the last century. Similar themes to those in Muslim Spain convey a similar message of hedonism as an anodyne drug to relieve the pain of uncertainty, of loss, and Sufism as an escape in a changing and hostile world. The famous names reflect these themes but in the context of their own part of the world (see, for instance, the verses of Mirza Ghalib).

The sophistication of Islamic poetry is contained in these lines which have the succinctness of a Japanese *haiku*: 'Look at the sun on the horizon; it is like a bird, casting its wing over the surface of the bay.'
Here is another perfect example:

> *The river is like a piece of parchment*
> *on which the breeze is writing its lines.*
> *And when the beauty of the river is revealed by these lines,*
> *the branches bend down to read it.*

Literary sensibility permeated society, and even kings expressed their love in poetry. Abdur Rahman V (1023–4), speaking of his marriage to his cousin Habibah, wrote: 'I have stipulated as a condition of marriage that I shall serve her as a slave and that I have conveyed my soul to her as my dowry' (Boase (unpublished): 15). The passion of a lover and the warrior's desire for honour on the battlefield – the essence of Arab chivalry – are intertwined in these lines: 'I remember Sulaymah when the heat of battle was like the heat of my body on the day that I left her; / I beheld her slender form among the lances and, as they inclined towards me, I embraced them.'

Andalusian poetry was set in a time of opulence and luxury; it reflected the hedonism of the élite. Ibn Zaydun's *Nuniyyah* speaks of glasses of bubbling wine mingled with water, but here wine is mentioned as a useless means of distraction. Ibn Zaydun, who shares with his beloved the cup of love, preferring the intoxication of love to that of wine, was improving upon a poem by Abu Firas (d. 967):

> *O night whose pleasures I shall never forget,*
> *When every delight was present;*
> *She was there, and I with her, and the wineskin made a third,*
> *And we spent the night until the morning giving each other to drink,*
> *As if the daughter of the grape*
> *Gave its choicest wine straight to her lips.*
> (Boase 1989b: ix)

The hedonism, with its obviously un-Islamic overtones, drew the commentary of Muslim writers. This type of love was codified by Ibn Dawud (d. 910) in his *Kitab al-Zahrah (The Book of the Flower or the Book of Venus)* and by Ibn Hazm (d. 1064) in his *Tawq al-Hamamah (The Ring of the Dove)*. It was discussed in more Neoplatonic terms by Ibn Sina (Avicenna, d. 1037) in his *Risalah fil-Ishq (Treatise on Passionate Love)* in a chapter 'On the love of those who are noble-minded and young for external beauty'. Ibn Sina wrote:

> If a man loves a beautiful form with an animal desire, he deserves reproof, even condemnation and the charge of sin, as, for instance, those who commit unnatural adultery [that is, outside legally allowed sex] and in general people who go astray. But whenever he loves a pleasing form with an intellectual consideration, in the manner we have explained, then this is to be considered an approximation to nobility and an increase in goodness.
>
> (Boase 1989b: x)

The sense of sorrow at the decline of Muslim Spain is found in Al-Rundi's elegy, written after the Christians captured Seville in 1248. The lines demonstrate how a universal literary theme, that of the lover lamenting over the departure of the beloved, could be applied to a political situation: 'The tap of the white ablution fount weeps in despair, like a passionate lover weeping at the departure of the beloved, / Over dwellings emptied of Islam that were first vacated and now inhabited by unbelief' (Boase 1989b: xiii).

The following lines from Muslim Spain's most famous Sufi mystic, Ibn Arabi (1165–1240), express a sentiment that is echoed in Sufic writings and sayings across the Muslim world, whether those of Rumi in the Middle East or Kabir, Ghalib and Iqbal in India:

> My heart has adopted every shape; it has become a pasture for gazelles and a convent for Christian monks,
> A temple for idols and a pilgrim's Kabah, the tables of a Torah and the pages of a Quran.
> I follow the religion of Love; wherever Love's camels turn, there Love is my religion and my faith.
>
> (Ibn Arabi, in Monroe 1974: 320)

The Andalus syndrome

In my book *Discovering Islam: Making Sense of Muslim History and Society* I described a feeling of strange melancholy that embraced me in Andalusia when I visited Spain as an undergraduate in the early 1960s. Here was a magnificent Muslim civilization which, after centuries, was abruptly killed off. Loss of political power for Muslims had meant physical expulsion, cultural annihilation. Yet the contours of Muslim civilization were visible in their buildings, such as the fortress palace of Alhambra and the mosque at Cordoba. I called this 'the Andalus syndrome' and suggested it has left a permanent scar in the Muslim psyche. Washington Irving, too, sensed the Andalus syndrome:

Never was the annihilation of a people more complete than that of the Morisco-Spaniards. Where are they? Ask the shores of Barbary and its desert places. The exiled remnant of their once powerful empire disappeared among the barbarians of Africa and ceased to be a nation. They have not even left a distinct name behind them, though for nearly eight centuries they were a distinct people. The home of their adoption and of their occupation for ages refuses to acknowledge them, except as invaders and usurpers. A few broken monuments are all that remain to bear witness to their power and dominion, as solitary rocks, left far in the interior, bear testimony to the extent of some vast inundation. Such is the Alhambra – a Moslem pile in the midst of a Christian land, an Oriental palace amidst the Gothic edifices of the West, an elegant memento of a brave, intelligent, and graceful people who conquered, ruled and passed away.
(Irving 1990: 54)

The mosque at Cordoba

When I revisited the Cordoba mosque in 1992 I felt profoundly saddened. The tangled architecture of the mosque was a metaphor for the Christian–Muslim struggle. Here was one of the most magnificent buildings in the world broken and disfigured. Abdur Rahman I had begun the mosque in 785 after buying the land at the site; in 1236 it was captured and converted to a church. Inside, rows of columns had to be demolished to accommodate the chapels and high altar. Arabic decorations and calligraphy were replaced and the main side of the mosque leading to the grand courtyard sealed off with a wall. In the early sixteenth century the cruciform church that now occupies the centre of the mosque was started with a transept and a lofty roof. Another sixty columns of the mosque had to be removed.

Shortly after, when Charles V, the King of Spain, visited Cordoba and saw what his priests had done, he was appalled. 'You have built here what you or anyone might have built anywhere else, but you have destroyed what was unique in the world,' he said with sorrow.

The church with its images of angels, death and crucifixion, the mosque with its calligraphy and flowers are like two different philosophies uneasily mixed together. As a metaphor for the Spanish *reconquista*, the reconquest, this was appropriate. But while the church did not quite kill the mosque, the mosque, in turn, did not allow full birth to the church either. The mosque at Cordoba is still known as La Mezquita, The Mosque; that is the great irony. If the courtyard is included, it is still today the largest home of worship in Europe save St Peter's in Rome.

'There is amongst the trees one which is as blessed as the Muslim – the palm' is a saying attributed to the Prophet. And the Umayyads from Damascus, who had still not quite shaken off their love of the desert in the gentle, green hills of Andalusia, set about re-creating a forest of palms in the Cordoba mosque. It was an exciting idea. The columns and arches inside would resemble palm trees and there would be rows and rows of them, one fading into another; and outside in the courtyard there would be a real forest of palm trees around the mosque. The effect was calculated to create a sense of an orchard of palms; a Muslim paradise. The delicate balance between light and shade, between illusion and reality, between the present and the hereafter, was achieved with dazzling effect.

Inside the mosque I pondered the fate of two of the greatest houses of God at the two opposite ends of Europe: the mosque at Cordoba in the west and the church at Constantinople in the east. The mosque was converted to a church by Christians, the church to a mosque by Muslims. Such forcible conversions sadden me, and I am reminded of the example of the wise and noble Umar at Jerusalem (see also chapter 5).

The fall of the Muslims

The story is told that when the Muslim ruler of Granada rode into the city after a victory he was hailed by his people as *El Ghalib*, the conqueror. He shook his head in humility, uttering: *Wallah ghaliba illallah*, 'God alone is conqueror'. This became the motto of the rulers of Granada. It is engraved, and repeated again and again in exquisite calligraphy, on the walls of the Alhambra. It is indeed an apt summary of Muslim history in Spain; of the passing of power, the transience of life.

Why was the Alhambra left intact and the mosque at Cordoba so cruelly destroyed? The Alhambra was a fort and could be used later; the mosque at Cordoba, the premier symbol of Muslim faith, had to be converted to a church in order to express the triumph of Christianity.

After the fall of Granada in 1492 Christian priests gave the Muslims and Jews a nightmare choice: either convert or leave the land. But even when they converted they were under suspicion and could eventually be burned at the stake as *conversos*. The Muslims who remained and converted to Christianity, the Moriscos, were finally expelled in 1609. Many were killed. It was not the first pogrom of its kind in Europe, but in its scale, scope and execution it was extraordinary.

Why did the Muslims collapse so totally in Spain? The first reason is that they were no longer united. This is the same story for the Crusades. When they united under Saladin they were invincible; when they fought each other they were easily defeated. Over the centuries they had been reduced to smaller and smaller fiefdoms and kingdoms, often fighting with each other.

Worse, their sources in North Africa were drying up; it was a period of tribal warfare, of decline.

Most important, there was a growing awareness in Spain of the need for a united front against the Moors; it was a call to destiny, to finish them off once and for all. A gigantic psychological, political and military momentum under Queen Isabella of Castile and King Ferdinand of Aragon had built up. The campaign to conquer Granada was personally led by the Queen. After Granada, that pent-up energy was then diverted to America. Gold and converts to Christianity awaited the conquistadors; loot and salvation went hand in hand.

The orthodox Muslim would say that Muslims collapsed because they were no longer God-fearing, they had lost their faith, there was too much pleasure, too much synthesis, too much corruption. But there were other causes too. When Granada fell in 1492 the world was at the threshold of a new era, one of those all-changing phases of history. New ideas, new technology and new political systems were beginning to herald the new age.

Perhaps the most important of the new ideas was that of the nation-state. This supplanted the idea of different, often warring, tribal lords and kings, sometimes united under an over-arching king or caliph. The *reconquista* ensured that the church played a central role in the concept of the nation-state.

Spain emerged early as the premier nation-state in Europe. Everything in it was to be subordinate to this idea. As a result it became the first major imperial power of Europe with extensive colonies especially in America.

1492 and all that

It is necessary to see 1492 in the context of fifteenth-century Europe. The fall of Muslim Spain had the same emotional and political impact on Christian Europe as did the fall of communism in 1991 on the West. For Europe, Islam had been the all-threatening alien force, both seductive and subversive.

The *reconquista* has to be seen through the eyes of Christians in Spain from the tenth century onwards. Every ambitious ruler, every courageous knight, every zealous priest dreamt of the day the Iberian Peninsula would be recaptured and freed of the infidel Moor. It was a cumulative dream, an objective that the entire population strove towards. The Portuguese and the Spaniards did not send people to the Crusades against the Muslims in the Middle East because they had their own Muslims on the Iberian Peninsula to fight. For the two to three centuries before the fall of Granada a determined and often systematic attempt, backed by the church right up to the Pope, had been made to defeat Islam on the Continent.

Whereas the whole business of Andalusia seemed peripheral and almost forgotten as far as the Muslim heartland was concerned, for Europe it was a central battle which was to determine the very future of its relations with Islam. Victory in 1492 unleashed all kinds of complicated processes. One was a dynamism that moved Europe towards the New World to create a fresh civilization there. More positively, the *reconquista* opened a door to the future in the form of the Renaissance. Arts, crafts, literature and new thinking suddenly became possibilities. Within two to three centuries Europe was poised to colonize the world not only politically but culturally and intellectually as well.

So the fall of Granada in 1492 was not just another military victory, a local triumph. In its impact it was the greatest event of its age. It is significant that Columbus himself linked the fall of Granada with his voyages:

> *On the second day of January I saw Your Highnesses' royal banners placed by force of arms on the towers of the Alhambra . . . and in the same month . . . Your Highnesses, as Catholic Christians and princes devoted to the holy Christian faith and the furtherance of its cause, and enemies of the sect of Mohammed and of all idolatry and heresy, resolved to send me, Christopher Columbus, to the . . . regions of India.*
> (Edwards 1992: 11)

A scholar of the period comments:

> *Thus the discoverer of America begins his diary of his first voyage by firmly placing the venture in the context of the conquest of Muslim Granada by his patrons, Ferdinand and Isabella. Modern historians, too, have recognised the connection between the whole New World enterprise and the Spanish Middle Ages.*
> (Edwards 1992: 11)

It is in this spirit that we must understand the arrival in America of the Spaniards from the Iberian Peninsula. Columbus, Pizarro, Cortez, Balboa – these men arrived like thunderbolts among the unsuspecting native population. They came with sword in one hand and Bible in the other, fresh from the triumphs over the Muslims. These Spanish conquerors would shatter the Aztecs, the Mayas and then the Incas, civilizations that stretched from Mexico down to the tip of South America. The Spanish robbed the Indians of their language, their culture and their dignity. They were raped and looted and burnt. They became third-class citizens in their own home. The poor Indians did not know what hit them. Smashing their temples, the Spanish placed the masonry at the base of the churches. This too was an architectural metaphor for the new reality.

The reawakening of Andulusia

Andalusia remained buried deep in the Spanish psyche. Until the time of Franco, Islam was officially banned. No one was allowed to forget or challenge the historical Spanish position on Islam. Memories of Muslim Spain littered the Spanish landscape: Santiago, a religious figure, given the title the Moor-killer, that is, the killer of Muslims; hotels called 'Reconquista', statues depicting Christian warriors in heroic poses, sometimes with their feet on the heads of fallen Muslims; and every year festivals called 'Christians and Moors' to commemorate the victory.

The celebrations in Alcoy, a small town with a population of less than 100 000, stretch over three to four days. The Alcoy festival purports to commemorate an actual historical event – the defeat of the Moors in 1257, with the assistance of St George. First the Moors win, then, finally, the Christians. It is good-natured fun, carnival kitsch. The Spanish playing the Moors paint their faces black; this is contemporary Europe's perception of Muslims. Functions as at Alcoy take place elsewhere in Europe also. These celebrations tie into modern European nationalism, a sense of soil, a link with the geography of an area. No such collective memory marks Muslim society. Muslim celebrations are religious festivals, the end of fasting, or commemorating Abraham's sacrifice to God or the birth of the Prophet.

Now, five centuries after the fall of Granada, the world media have helped to exorcise the ghost. There is an exuberant discovery of the past. Suddenly Andalusians are proud of the Moorish heritage. Indeed there are numerous converts among the Spanish to Islam. Suddenly the entire region is more at ease with itself. The exorcism is evident; Spain can now confront its past in order to move to the future.

Muslim Spain challenges some of our contemporary stereotypes. Here were Arabs as a vastly superior civilization, here were white Europeans still centuries to go before they could compete as a great civilization, and here was harmony in spite of the divisions of race and religion. It is a lesson we would do well to keep before us in a world of plural societies often at odds with one another.

THE OTTOMANS (1300–1922)

By the thirteenth century two of the greatest Arab civilizations had faded from history – one with its capital in Cordoba, the other in Baghdad. There were other great Muslim empires waiting to flourish, but they would not be

Arab. One such empire would be that of the Ottomans. In time it would rule much of the Arab world right up to the nineteenth and twentieth centuries.

The importance of the Ottomans must not be underestimated. Theirs was the pre-eminent Muslim empire. The fact that they ruled one of the largest and longest-lasting empires in history, the fact that they were the guardians of the holy places in Arabia, the fact that the caliph, the successor of the Prophet, was the Ottoman ruler himself and that they were Sunni Muslims and therefore self-consciously representative of mainstream Islam made them the rulers of the greatest of the Muslim empires.

If there is one central institution, one key symbol, one defining feature of the Ottomans, it is surely the Topkapi palace, the residence of the Ottoman rulers – called sultans – from the fifteenth to the end of the nineteenth century. Let us then enter the Ottoman period through the Topkapi.

The Topkapi palace

Situated in Istanbul, once the capital of the empire, the Topkapi was the head and heart of the Ottomans. Mehmet II (sultan from 1451 to 1481) chose a marvellous position for the building – Seraglio Point, where the Golden Horn meets the Bosphorus. Reflecting the might, diversity and span of the empire, the Topkapi palace – spread over thirty acres – overlooked three seas. Much of the Topkapi was constructed in the sixteenth and seventeenth centuries. At one stage the most renowned Ottoman architect of his time, Sinan, was in charge of it. Indeed one of Sinan's proudest titles was 'The Architect of the Abode of Felicity'.

The Topkapi, where the sultan and his family lived, was at the heart of the empire. In its splendour, scale and buildings it proclaimed the power and glory of the Ottomans. Its mystique was heightened by the stories and scandals of the harem.

There is no central plan in the Topkapi. Over the centuries sultans have added bits and pieces to it. One added the Baghdad pavilion after the conquest of Baghdad, another the Revan pavilion to commemorate the Revan campaign, and so on. Every part of it is to be considered a separate monument, a separate work of art. Similarly the presents, such as priceless daggers and vases, which were sent by foreign rulers over the centuries for rites of passage, accession or other special occasions, are now on display.

The Topkapi is an eclectic jumble of images, a cornucopia of the imperial imagination. Nowhere is it better displayed than in the room where the sultan sat to watch dancing (a discreet balcony allowed the princes to participate and still be out of sight). Pillars with Greek designs, grandfather clocks made in Europe, French paintings, Belgian mirrors and Islamic tiles: this could be a room in the Versailles Palace. Except for the Quranic verses we would not know that the owner was a Muslim. But the Quranic verses underline the fact that in spite of so many quotations from the Quran this was not Islam.

The sultan, his life ordered by the state rituals inherited from the Byzantines, was the living symbol of the empire. Protocol around the ruler was rigid. Only he could ride a horse through the main gate, and even ambassadors had to dismount. The sultan wore his silk robes once and then they were discarded. Many are preserved for us in the museum, which has one of the world's finest textile and kaftan collections.

Yet not only the power but also the weakness of the system can be traced to the Topkapi. It was in the harem that the all-powerful sultan spent most of his life. Every inhabitant of the 230 small, dark rooms was his to command. It is not difficult to imagine the unlimited sensual pleasures available to the sultan (the number of concubines often exceeded a thousand); and only to him: the permanent male staff consisted of eunuchs, their manhood destroyed before they even entered the palace.

Access to the sultan meant power. Little wonder, then, that the palace eunuchs and women wielded so much of it. Even so, no one was to be trusted. The sultan was shifted nightly to escape assassination. Favoured males were abruptly promoted to rule vast governorships – Syria perhaps, or Greece, both once part of the empire; out of favour ones were sent to the cage-like rooms in the palace from where there was seldom escape.

Women in the harem

The harem is a depressing place. Its silent, claustrophobic little rooms hint at dark tragedies and sufferings. Here hundreds of women lived out their lives in intrigue and boredom waiting for the ruler's notice. A slight mistake, a minor breach of etiquette, upset the established order of the harem and resulted in instant death. In the seventeenth century Sultan Ibrahim had 280 of his women sewn in weighted sacks and thrown into the Bosphorus. The view from the main court of the harem symbolized life for the inmates: the sea in the distance in front and the solid, heavily guarded buildings behind. The message was clear: here there was no escape.

The women in the harem came from all over the world – Chinese princesses, daughters of Moroccan chiefs, blue-eyed women from Europe and dark-haired beauties from Persia. Yet these princesses with their precious gems and jewels often had less freedom than a peasant girl.

The harem is extravagance, vulgarity, luxury – it is Orientalism, the stuff of European fantasy; it is not Islam. So much wealth, so much suffering, so much injustice are far from the ideas of marriage and married life in Islam. The verses from the Quran that are so prominent on the walls do not condone the spirit of the place.

Yet one can imagine the attraction in the harem for a family with a woman in here. It meant patronage, wealth and power. It meant access to the one man who mattered, the sultan. We picture the fear and suffocation a young girl felt when she was brought here. To her fear of being in a forbidding and strange place we must add the congratulations and triumph of her family. With our modern sensibilities we worry about the girl, but for her this was like a lottery she had won. Life would henceforth be one of comfort and influence. Perhaps she might even be the mother of the next sultan of the Ottoman empire, one of the most powerful men on earth.

Islam in the Topkapi

The self-conscious Islamic posture of the Ottoman dynasty is sometimes missed when seen through the secular idiom that has dominated modern Turkey. Inscriptions from the Quran are everywhere – from the main entrance, where the declaration of faith is inscribed in giant letters over the portal, to the rooms, to the lettering on the helmets of soldiers.

The Ottoman flag displayed the crescent and star of Islam (since adopted by many modern countries including Turkey); the sultan's bedchambers in the Topkapi had tiles with Quranic verses inscribed on them; the black eunuchs had their own mosque at the entrance of the harem with the Kabah painted on the wall; a gold 'Allah' sits on top of the Baghdad pavilion; and the Sheikh–ul–Islam in his person represented the authority of the *ulema* in the palace to remind the sultan – no doubt as tactfully as he could – of his Islamic duties.

Most prized of all the treasures of the Topkapi are those in the chamber of sacred relics. The centre-piece is the mantle of the Prophet which is made of black wool. In Muslim devotional poetry the Prophet is referred to as *kamli-wala*, the man who wears the black cloak. His standard and his footprint are also found here. These were brought from Egypt when Cairo fell to the Ottomans. They gave legitimacy to the Ottomans, whose sultan claimed to be the caliph of all Islam.

The Ottoman dynasty

The Ottoman empire derived its name from the eponymous ancestor Uthman (a namesake of the third caliph of Islam). 'Uthman' became 'Osmanli' and the name eventually became 'Ottoman'. Starting with Uthman, in the direct male line, thirty-six sultans ruled from 1300 to 1922. The empire is considered to have reached its zenith in the sixteenth century under Sulayman the Magnificent. In overall Islamic terms, new peaks of achievement in poetry, art and architecture were scaled during this period. This was also the time of the greatest expansion. The North African conquests date from then – all of North Africa except Morocco formed part of the empire, which stretched from Budapest to Yemen, from Baghdad to Algeria. In 1526 Sulayman came close to taking Vienna.

Yet the obsession with Christianity and Europe remained to challenge the Ottomans. When Constantinople was taken in 1453 by Mehmet the Conqueror it was renamed Istanbul, the 'city of Islam' (its earlier name Constantinople derived from Constantine the Roman emperor, who shifted his capital here from Rome). In these exchanges between Muslims and Christians, as fortunes changed, church was converted to mosque and mosque to church.

The most celebrated example of conversion is that of St Sophia. It is one of the best-known churches in Christendom, a marvel of architecture. The story goes that when its builder, Justinian, saw it on completion he thought of the Temple of Jerusalem and exclaimed, 'Ho, Solomon I have surpassed thee.' From the start it took its place among the wonders of the world. It was called the church of the holy wisdom, a wonder which had not been realized before. Not only the scale impresses but the massive, central cupola seems a miracle. God himself seems to hold it suspended in the air. And we must strive to remember that this is a sixth-century building. Muslims added the minarets to the building outside and some calligraphy inside; otherwise they changed little.

Sinan built the Sulaimaniye mosque deliberately to exceed St Sophia in height. The might and majesty of the Ottomans were proudly combined with the glory and greatness of Islam in the Sulaimaniye. But, however exalted the genius of Sinan, the impression of St Sophia is indelible on Turkish architecture. Most mosques until today echo it – a large imposing central dome with smaller domes at the base. The four minarets, lean and slender, seem almost an afterthought, even incongruous; remove them and it could be a Byzantine church.

Mehmet the Conqueror was twenty-one years old when he captured

Constantinople. It was not only the end of the Byzantine empire but one of the greatest victories in history, significantly shifting the balance of power between Islam and Christianity, Asia and Europe.

The consequences of the fall of Constantinople would be far-reaching. Muslims inherited the Byzantine rank structure, pomp, rituals and splendour, and inevitably they were affected. The eclecticism would characterize the Ottomans. Towards the end, by the last century, the palaces of the Ottomans could have been Parisian or Viennese. The chambers, dining rooms, windows, shutters, sofa sets, and their designs, colours and patterns were European.

Another consequence of the fall of Constantinople would affect Christianity itself. In the third century, Christianity had become more or less the official religion of the Byzantine empire, but it was still an Asian religion. But when the Muslims captured Constantinople in the fifteenth century the base of Christianity shifted to Rome. With this passage to Europe it became an increasingly Europeanized religion, further than ever before from the original. Here Jesus Christ in European art became a blue-eyed blond. Christianity was now Europe's response to Islam.

The Ottoman empire, so vast and varied, was noted for its eclecticism. It was widely influenced by those it incorporated. Thus Persian notions of absolute monarchy, the tradition of constant tribal warring from Central Asia, Byzantine ideas of government, and the Arabic script, sciences and religion became part of its character. The most significant influences came from Islam. In time the Ottomans would rule the Arab lands but their ideal would still remain an Islamic one. The Arabs would be to the Ottomans what the Greeks were to the Romans.

The ruling élite made their way up the social hierarchy through the state *madrassahs* or seminaries and the palace schools, up through a series of bureaucratic stages. They were always concerned with the needs of government and mindful of the restrictions of the *shariah*, the law of Islam. In its structure the ruling élite reflected a world of order and hierarchy in which promotion and status were rewarded on merit. Thus birth and genealogy, aristocracy or tribe became almost irrelevant to success in the system. Turk or Arab, Slav or Armenian, high or low – all were eligible to the highest posts in the land. Only one post, that of the sultan, was determined by birth.

The Janissaries (from *Yeni Ceri*, new soldiers) were almost all born Christian but raised as Muslim soldiers. Even some of the most famous Ottoman figures were not Muslim by birth. Both Sinan, the architect, and Barbarossa, the victorious admiral, were born Christians. Ali Bey, who became Sultan of Egypt and Syria in the late eighteenth century, was the son of a Caucasian Christian priest.

The Ottoman system, resting on scholarship and merit, encouraged art and literature. In particular poetry flourished. The work of two of the leading poets of the sixteenth century, Sulayman Fuzuli (1480–1556), who was influenced by Persia, and Abdul Baki (1526–1600), who developed, in contrast, a distinctive Turkish style, is well known. It was in the seventeenth century that Turkish began to supplant Persian influences. Scientific, historical and medical literature too were given a major boost by the opening of the schools adjoining the Sulaimaniye mosque. Geographical writing was stimulated by the expansion of the empire on both land and sea; historical writing stimulated by the need to record it. Historians like Mustafa Naima attempted sophisticated analysis based on their studies, relating historical causes to political events.

As always in Muslim society, the art of biography was highly developed. The renowned encyclopedist, Katib Chelebi (1609–57), related the contributions of various Muslim nations – Arabs, Turks, Persians – to Islamic civilization in his major work. In so vast an empire, one that set so high a standard on literacy, travel writing had to be popular. There were travel writers like Euliya Chelebi (1614–82), who spent forty years travelling in the Ottoman empire and in Europe, and then spent the last three years of his life writing it all up in the ten-volume *Book of Travels*.

After the second unsuccessful attempt to capture Vienna in 1683 the long process of Ottoman decline commenced. The later period of Ottoman history coincided with an increasingingly vigorous period of intellectual, industrial and economic growth in the major European nations. Soon Turkey would be known as 'the sick man of Europe'. At the same time European powers were expanding their borders. Covetous eyes were cast on the Ottoman empire. Slowly bits and pieces were bitten off or fell away. Some were claimed by local nationalism, others by European colonial avarice.

It is the sick phase of the Ottomans which created the popular caricature of Orientals in Europe. They were seen as debauched, untrustworthy, lazy and ignorant. The harem and the seraglio were fixed in European minds as symbolic of the Orient. The Topkapi became the secret treasure-house of the traveller dreaming of the wildest erotica. It is ironic that the un-Islamic sexual decadence and perversion associated with the harem provided the West with its images of Islam.

The resistance of the Greeks to the Turks also inspired European literary figures to fan the flames of anti-Islamic sentiment. The Greeks, inheritors of ancient Greek civilization, the fountain-head of Western culture, wished to shake off the yoke of the infidel Turk. This was a powerful message which few European writers could resist. Poets like Shelley and Byron jumped into the fray. The very word Turk became synonymous with treachery and cruelty; simply, as Carlyle put it, 'the unspeakable Turk'. Little wonder that Turks like Kemal Ataturk, who were born late in the nineteenth century, were repelled by their own past. Seeing little but decay and corruption, they wished to reject the past in order to establish a more respectable identity.

THE SAFAVIDS (1501–1722)

The Safavids, who created a Shia state, were strong enough in splendour and might to challenge the Ottomans in the west and the Mughals in the east. Perhaps the best way to understand the Safavids is through their paintings. These were designed primarily to illustrate manuscripts or to fill the albums of affluent connoisseurs. The Persian miniature offered a world of sparkling colour, exquisite delicacy and impeccable execution. The Islamic themes of fruits and gardens (natural to a desert religion) were combined with Persian sensuousness – in the miniatures of doe-eyed youths with waists tapering into nothingness, it was difficult to tell which was the girl, which the boy.

In time human emotions were explored with increasing boldness. Artists developed strands of blatant and even crude eroticism. Taboo subjects such as homosexuality were also depicted and lovers were shown in passionate embrace (for example, by Afzal al-Husaini at Isfahan, 1646).

The high point of Persian miniature painting was the illustration of Firdausi's classic epic poem, *Shah Nama* (Book of Kings), commissioned by Shah Ismail for his son Tahmasp in the sixteenth century. The scale of the project can be appreciated from the fact that it constituted 250 miniatures; until this work no manuscript had contained more than fourteen. The *Court of Gayumarth* (considered to be the legendary first Shah of Iran) is probably the masterpiece of the *Shah Nama*, indeed of all Iranian painting. The colours are riotous but controlled, the images of scintillating beauty, the rocks alive with hidden creatures, the figures fresh with animation.

For art to succeed on such a scale, patronage had to come from the top. The Safavids, like the princes of Renaissance Europe, were often artists themselves. Shah Ismail was a poet and Shah Tahmasp a painter. Such patronage, which included opening royal workshops for artists, created a favourable climate for the development of art. Above all, the Safavids personally encouraged and patronized art. The popular story has Shah Abbas holding a candle while his favourite calligrapher, Ali Riza, worked.

Not only miniature painting but metalwork, textiles and carpets reached new heights of perfection. The achievements of this era are most clearly visible even today by a perfunctory visit to the tombs and mosques in Iran: the tiles, the calligraphy, the colours of the painting and the symmetry of the buildings have stood the test of the centuries.

Isfahan: *Nisf-e-Jahan*

The artistic achievements and the prosperity of the Safavid period are best represented by Isfahan, the capital of Shah Abbas. Isfahan was the Paris or Washington of its day. Its parks, libraries, pavilions and mosques amazed Europeans, who had not seen anything like this at home. Iranians called it *Nisf-e-Jahan*, half the world – that is, to see it was to see half the world.

Built 1600 metres above sea level in the central Iranian plateau and surrounded by mountains, Isfahan became one of the most elegant cities of the world. In its heyday it was also one of the largest, with a population of one million; 162 mosques, 48 religious schools, 1801 caravanserais and 273 public baths were recorded in the city. The Chahar Bagh was a magnificent avenue four kilometres long, lined with gardens and stately homes. The city was 38 kilometres in circumference. Little wonder that Europeans visiting Isfahan were astonished by its magnificence.

The Naqsh-e-Jahan or 'map of the world', the central square of Isfahan – now called Imam Square after Imam Khomeini – is one of the wonders of the world. At its head is the jewel of Persian architecture, the Shah Mosque – now, of course, called the Imam Mosque. Opposite it is the market. On one side of the square is the pavilion called Ali Qapu, with the Bab-i-Ali, the Gate of Ali (named after the son-in-law of the Prophet). Opposite, across the square, stands the Shah Lutfullah mosque (for the exclusive use of the Shah). Behind the Ali Qapu pavilion, outside the square, there is an unusual if symbolically correct piece of Islamic architecture, mud-coloured and in the form of a tent, which provided a meeting place for Sufis.

Today the ghosts of the past and the rulers of the present meet here; splendid irony indeed. Hanging from the Ali Qapu pavilion, where the Safavid rulers viewed imperial troops and watched polo, are the gigantic paintings of the two main ayatollahs of Iran, both Ayatollah al-Uzma, Khomeini and Khamenei. They signify the end of kingship in Iran and the triumph of the Islamic revolution.

The Shia state

The state itself was founded by the Safavids, a Sufi order tracing back to Safi al-din (1252–1334). When the Safavids came to power in 1501, Shah Ismail was proclaimed ruler. The Shah's most important decision was to declare that the state religion would be twelve Imam Shiism, Ithna Ashari (it is a link that comes down to our own times in Imam Khomeini's declaration of loyalty to the Ithna Ashari). The state was to be a theocracy and the Shah was to personify the twelfth Imam (the hidden Imam) in the flesh. A vigorous campaign to convert what was then a predominantly Sunni population was launched. The Sunni *ulema* either left or were killed.

Shah Ismail's great-grandson, Shah Abbas (1588–1629), brought Safavid fortunes to their peak. By 1606 he had checked the Sunni advances of the Uzbeks on one border and the Ottomans on the other. Being hemmed in by the aggressive Sunni empires further reinforced the sense of Shia identity in Persia.

Peace allowed Shah Abbas to encourage art and industry. His rule saw the finest flowering of the Persian artistic genius, and it compares favourably with those of his contemporaries, Akbar of India and Elizabeth I of England.

By the eighteenth century, however, the Shahs were little more than drunken despots and the empire a house of cards waiting to be blown down. Their un-Islamic behaviour did not go unnoticed. It encouraged the *ulema* to challenge the royal notion that the Shah was the 'shadow of God on earth'. The *ulema* developed an alternative theory that only a *mujtahid*, one deeply learned in the *shariah* and one who has led a blameless life, can rule. In the reign of Shah Sultan Hussain (1694–1722) the religious leader Majlisi influenced government policy. He was able to impose his vision of orthodox Shiism on the state and made the Shah promise to abide by the laws of Islam. At his insistence tens of thousands of bottles of wine in royal cellars were publicly smashed. Yet such isolated acts of religious piety could not stop the empire from disintegrating, and for the next century or two it lay in a state of advanced decay. Bandit chiefs and feudal lords plundered at will, further weakening the empire, and people yearned for strong central rule and stability.

The rise of the Pahlavis (1925–79) this century thus saw the reaffirmation of strong central authority in Iran and the re-emergence of the dynastic principle. The discovery of oil early in the twentieth century and the interest in it of the British and then the Americans determined the style and role of the second Pahlavi Shah. The wealth from oil enabled him to head an opulent and corrupt court while the support of the West in exchange for oil concessions allowed him to play a pivotal role in the politics of the region. Imam Khomeini's movement changed all that in the 1970s.

Khomeini's religious challenge to the Shah's royal authority confirms the deep wells of tradition in society; we thus note the oscillation in Iran from one pole to another, from royal dynastic rule to religious authority; an oscillation fired by the need to purify, cleanse and redefine the self in the light of Shia Islam.

THE MUGHALS (1526–1857)

As we used the Topkapi to enter the Ottoman empire and Persian miniature paintings to approach the Safavids, we shall take Muslim architecture as a key to understanding the Muslims of South Asia. But while the Isfahan of the Safavids remained in present-day Iran and the Istanbul of the Ottomans is still in Turkey, Delhi, the capital of the Mughals, is no longer in a Muslim country. The Mughal buildings lie neglected and dilapidated. Even the Taj Mahal is threatened by industrial pollution. In Isfahan and Istanbul, by contrast, the buildings enjoy the full favour of government patronage.

The South Asian sub-continent is littered with noteworthy examples of different kinds of mosques, shrines, tombs and forts, some showing a degree of synthesis with Hindu architecture, others self-consciously retaining an Arab-Persian character. Before we discuss the Mughals, let us briefly introduce the Muslims in India.

The burden of history

The first introduction of Islam into India set the tone for the relationship between Hindus and Muslims. It came in the form of the Arab general Muhammad Bin Qasim, who invaded Sind in the eighth century, almost immediately after the advent of Islam. The image of the young, conquering Muslim warrior would be repeated for the next few centuries, but this time the invaders would come from the north. They were Turkish warriors, harder and fiercer about Islam, fired with the zeal of the convert. Their raids into India for loot and plunder would often be justified by the word *jihad* or holy war in the name of Islam. In fact they were establishing the image of the intolerant, fanatic Muslim, an image that is still current. Mahmud of Ghazni raided India seventeen times. After one expedition he took back with him the gates of the Hindu temple at Somnath. These were restored in the last century by the British when they brought them back from Afghanistan after a military expedition; Indian honour had been redeemed, said the British.

The Quran says Muslims must respect others so that they in turn will respect Muslims. Across the Muslim world there are still temples and churches standing centuries after Muslims ruled. Yet from the tenth century onwards there are examples of Muslims arriving in India with the idea that anything that distracted from the worship of the one God needed to be destroyed. They could not make sense of the Hindu idols and these often became a target. But these warriors were not the only Muslims coming to India; there were Sufi scholars and saints too (as we shall see below). Islam was spread by the patience and practice of the latter, not the force of the former.

No two cultures could be more different than Islam and Hinduism. Their notions of God, of life after death, of food, of marriage, of morality, of almost everything, are entirely different. Yet they have lived and survived together for a thousand years, often in genuine harmony.

Let me explain how this happened by painting a somewhat idealized picture. What evolved was a universe of separate communities living within smaller and smaller universes of their own, descending in smaller sizes, not unlike Chinese boxes. Yet they lived in harmony, aware of each other's differences, aware of the boundaries that separated them, but also aware that they needed to exist together. Whether ruler or ruled, their sense of self survived. The Muslims may have been the politically dominant force of South Asia but the Hindu sense of hierarchy placed Muslims at the bottom of the caste structure, as *mlechcha*, as ritually dirty and alien outsiders.

Complicated and intricate rituals further reinforced the sense of identity. Rules among Hindus dictated who one could eat with, sit with or indeed touch. It was a defined and organized world, and on the whole the Muslim rulers were not interested in either shattering or altering it. By and large there was tolerance and harmony, and in places even synthesis.

The synthesis between Islam and Hinduism in India is one of the most remarkable developments of South Asia. It added to the richness of both cultures, producing early on such attractive figures as Amir Khusro (1253–1325), the Indo–Persian poet. His mystical Sufistic verses with their universal appeal, his love of things Indian, of its flora and fauna, established a tradition of Muslims who felt at home in India. Another such figure is the fifteenth-century mystic poet Kabir, equally revered by Hindus and Muslims. The following lines by Kabir, translated by Rabindranath Tagore, state his philosophic position:

O Servant, where dost thou seek me,
Lo, I am beside thee.
I am neither in temple nor in mosque:
I am neither in Kabah nor in Kailash:
Neither am I in rites and ceremonies
Nor in Yoga and renunciation.
If thou art a true seeker,
Thou shalt at once see Me.

The content and style of the poem are reminiscent of Ibn Arabi, whose poetry was quoted earlier in this chapter. Kabir is reiterating the Sufi doctrine of *sulh-i-kul*, peace with all. It is a rich seam found wherever people of good will and good sense live, irrespective of their religion.

The Indian milieu allowed Muslims to debunk the empty hypocrisy of the religious functionary. Shah Jahan's son Dara Shikoh said paradise was to be found where there were no mullahs. The nineteenth-century poet Mirza Ghalib went further, pointing out the double standards of Muslim religious figures, as in the following well-known lines in which he accuses them of visiting places where alcohol was served: 'Where is the door of the inn and where is the religious figure? / Yet I know that when I was visiting it last night he was coming out of it.'

Eclecticism and synthesis are also to be found in the work of one of the most influential and important Muslim thinkers of the twentieth century, the poet Allama Iqbal. He throws a wide literary net, even beyond the confines of South Asia. By quoting Nietzsche and Lenin he is drawing in the Europeans. However, Iqbal begins to shift his position in his later work. The Islamic strand in his writing becomes more pronounced. Towards the end of his life he has moved from a position suggesting integration and synthesis with the Hindu majority to one demanding a separate identity for Muslims.

Something was pushing Muslims like Iqbal to change their earlier position of synthesis to one of separation. Perhaps it was the changing political climate and awareness that one day the British could leave India and Muslims would be at the mercy of the Hindus. Perhaps it was the resurgence of Hinduism in the Congress Party symbolized by the emergence of Mr Gandhi in the 1920s. Perhaps it was old age, the reversion of the elderly to tradition. What it did in Iqbal's case was to provide a clear vision of a Muslim homeland that would include North India, the traditional areas ruled by the Mughals; this would eventually become the movement for Pakistan.

The Mughal emperors

Many Muslim kingdoms were established in Delhi before the Mughals, but it was with the coming of the Mughals in the sixteenth century that Muslim power reached its height in India. Art, literature and architecture flourished. The royal family were patrons of art and books; many wrote excellent diaries. They revelled in nature, beauty and good company.

Six extraordinary emperors, in a direct line of descent from Babar, father to son, ruled between 1526 and 1707. The drama of their reign, their conquests, their loves, their personal tragedies survive through folk tales, novels and, now, the cinema. Blockbuster Indian films like *Mughal-e-Azam* (The Great Mughal) or *Taj Mahal* continue to romanticize and glorify the Mughals. These films are popular with both Hindu and Muslim audiences. The songs in the films – and no popular Indian film is without a number of good songs – carry a message of love, tolerance and humanism.

Babar, the founder of the Mughal dynasty

A mere boy, his father dead, his uncles gathering to divide his inheritance, Babar had little in remote Farghana but his dreams to cling to. His father's death was a turning-point; it would lead him to India and the founding of the Mughal dynasty. Some years ago I tried to capture the image of Babar at his father's funeral in this poem, 'Spring thoughts in Farghana':

> *The alfresco burial is done.*
> *The pipe and the kettle-drum*
> *have sung the warrior to his sleep;*
> *the mourners wail their way*
> *back to the village.*
>
> *High above,*
> *the mountains which stretch*
> *like a young man's ambition in springtime,*
> *an iced drizzle starts to speak*
> *of a last snowfall to come.*
> *Soon the passes will be clear.*
>
> *The boy, not yet twelve,*
> *gathers his father's breastplate*
> *sword and standard;*
> *his only legacy*
> *to work his fabled visions*
> *of empire and adventure.*

A bitter wind squeezes his face tight,
concurs a mood,
but in his clear eyes
are dreams of the golden kingdom of Samarkand.

Babar, the warrior, the poet, the romantic, has inspired biographers, historians and humanists (he was a favourite of E.M. Forster); now conquering an entire world, now throwing his life away while still in his prime to save his son in a mystical sacrifice that defies analysis. Honesty suffuses his autobiography, *The Babur-Namah*, and it would become a model for the later Mughals (Babar 1922). He records with equal candour the anguish caused by his infatuation with a boy and his vows to give up his beloved alcohol as a sacrificial offering if God gave him victory on the battlefield that would decide the fate of India. The tensions in Babar are evident. The two poles of Central Asian society (which we discuss in chapter 5) – the conqueror and the saint – are already causing contradictions in his Indian environment.

Babar's lineage was from a minor twig of the great tree that sprang in Central Asia and was associated with the house of Taimur (popularly known in the West as Tamerlane; see chapter 5). As a boy he would have been aware of the decline of the house of Taimur, of Central Asia reverting to chaos as war-lords battled each other. Adventurous and ambitious, he would reclaim Taimur's legacy and restore the lustre of Samarkand's name. On several occasions he tried unsuccessfully to take Samarkand and even Kabul. Then he crossed the Khyber Pass into India, a completely different world, yet his family would make it their own.

Babar arrived from Central Asia not as a barbarian bent on loot and plunder but with firm ideas about civilization, architecture and administration. He came with a rich cultural tradition, a knowledge of belonging to one of the most resplendent civilizations of the time.

There are interesting parallels between Abdur Rahman in Spain and Babar in India. Both came from far-off lands. Both were failures in their own world. Abdur Rahman's Umayyad kin had been slaughtered by the Abbasids in Damascus, which had, until the evening in 750 when he escaped with his life, been ruled by his family. He fled as far as possible from his ancestral home, across North Africa and to Spain. Babar failed repeatedly to take Samarkand and Kabul, the ambition of his life. Both would re-create as best they could images of the old world in the new. Both would give the name of their larger family to the dynasty: the Umayyads and the Mughals. Both would preside over dynasties that stood for tolerance, art and architectural and cultural attainment. There would be renowned names in their line but there would be no one quite like them. In their personality, courage, charm and curiosity they were in a class by themselves.

Mughal humanism

It is important to point out the spirit of humanism that pervaded Mughal rule. The synthesis with and respect for other religions was not a political ploy; it was deep and genuine. The reasons were partly sociological: many Mughal princes were sons of Hindu mothers, many powerful generals of the army and important figures in the inner court – the kitchen cabinet – were Hindu. But another reason was the confident, broadminded Islam that Babar had brought with him from Central Asia. Babar's first act after conquering Delhi was to forbid the killing of cows, because that was offensive to Hindus. The main inscription on the entrance to the Buland Darwaza, or Gate of Victory, in Fatehpur Sikri, Akbar's abandoned capital near Agra, cites Jesus:

> *Jesus Son of Mary (on whom be peace) said:*
> *The world is a bridge, pass over it,*
> *but build no houses on it. He who hopes for an hour*
> *may hope for eternity. The world endures but an hour.*
> *Spend it in prayer, for the rest is unseen.*

Sheikh Ahmad Sirhindi, one of the leading religious figures of the age, noted all this with disgust and criticized Akbar. 'The sun of guidance was hidden behind the veil of error,' the Sheikh observed. He was sent to prison for insisting too strongly on a more Islamic character to the empire. The emperor who imprisoned the Sheikh was Jahangir. His attitude to other religions is depicted in the portrait which shows him reverently contemplating a picture of the Madonna. Dara Shikoh patronized and translated the *Upanishads* and the *Bhagavad Gita*, classic Hindu texts, into the court language, Persian.

Some Indian historians depict Babar and the Mughals as foreigners. They are right: Babar was a foreigner; indeed, one of the most foreign of the Indian conquerors who came from the passes in the north. Most of the earlier ones were from Afghanistan. Many were Pukhtuns with tribal links on the Indian side of the Khyber Pass – the Lodhis, the Suris, the Khiljis. But here was another kind of conqueror, one who came from beyond the passes of the Hindu Kush; from beyond even the legendary Oxus, the river that demarcated Central Asia from Persia and Afghanistan. And he came not to destroy and plunder but to build and create. Little wonder that the genius of

Central Asia and the genius of South Asia fused and flourished under the Mughals.

Let us put the power and grandeur of the Mughals in a historical perspective. Take the field of architecture. Mulk Raj Anand, the Indian writer, compares Fatehpur Sikri, built by Akbar, to the London of the time:

> The total complex of private palaces, residences as well as the Imperial establishments, and the great mosque with the giant gateway, is one of the most considerable achievements in the history of world architecture. The Hampton Court of Henry VIII, near London, seems like a ramshackle barn as compared to Fatehpur Sikri.
>
> (Anand 1967:39)

Anand points out the scale of Akbar's achievement at Fatehpur Sikri:

> One has to remember that the city was built at the end of the 16th century, communications were difficult, materials inaccessible, and machine tools non-existent. And then one has to imagine the boldness of the conception, emerging from the social milieu of small moribund villages, where the construction of one grand mausoleum or mosque had been the only aspiration of the most powerful monarchs and Akbar must have seemed an eccentric even to his own nobles, to even those who were used to the heroic deeds of the Emperor when he ordained the building of a whole city.

England in the next century, the seventeenth, when Shah Jahan ruled India, and the Taj Mahal was built to symbolize the power, wealth and sophistication of the Mughals, was described by the British historian Christopher Hill thus:

> England in the early seventeenth century was a third-rate power. Governments of the old regime were both financially unable, and politically unwilling, to support the expansion of English trade, in the Far East, the Mediterranean, or in America. Charles I told merchants to keep out of the Mediterranean because he could not protect them against pirates there. (Nor indeed could he protect English vessels in the Channel or south-coast dwellers against pirates.) He could not even repulse an invading Scottish army. England, said the Venetian Ambassador, was 'useless to all the rest of the world', 'of no consideration'.
>
> (Hill 1991: 46)

Yet only two centuries later the descendants of these very Englishmen would terminate once and for all the rule of the descendants of Shah Jahan in 1857. The Mughal emperor, an old, frail and helpless prisoner of the British in Delhi, would be bundled off to Rangoon to die in exile. His male descendants would be herded together, lined up and shot. The man responsible, Hodson, was hailed as a hero. 'My dear Hodson,' wrote Robert Montgomery, Lieutenant-Governor of the Punjab (and another hero of that period), 'All honour to you (and to your "Horse") for catching the king and slaying his sons. I hope you will bag many more.'

Under the later Mughals the relationship with Hinduism was creating a major problem. Two distinct and opposed political models presented themselves to the Mughals. One was synthesis with Hinduism, some form of accommodation, at least on the cultural if not the religious plane; the other was outright rejection. Mughal princes like Akbar and Dara Shikoh represented the former position, Aurangzeb the latter. The choice would resonate in history and into our own times.

Muslim architecture in South Asia

Examples of Muslim architecture will help us understand both the Muslim past and the Muslim present. Our examples span time and space; they are also well known. Four of the seven examples are Mughal, but the others are also part of the story.

The thirteenth-century shrine of Khwaja Muin al-Din Chisti, the Sufi saint, at Ajmer in Rajasthan tells us of the coming of Islam to India. Muin al-Din arrived in India in the twelfth century, and the continuing validity of his message – 'peace with all', *sulh-i-kul* – is illustrated by the hundreds of pilgrims who daily visit his shrine. The majority are Hindus, and their presence is a testimony to the synthesis and harmony the Sufi saint effected. Unlikely connections confirm his message. For example, the compositions of Baba Farid, one of his disciples, form part of the holy book of the Sikhs – the *Guru Granth Sahib*.

Visitors come to the shrine to pray, seek spiritual solace, ask for favours and renew their religious zeal. The less privileged, in particular, revere the saint, and his popular title is 'the patron of the poor'. But the rich and the strong also come. At Ajmer the names of the Mughal emperors of the past jostle with the names of the powerful and famous of the present day – such as Benazir Bhutto and Begum Zia, two women Prime Ministers from South Asia.

Fatehpur Sikri was built by Akbar, the third Mughal emperor, as part of his attempt to absorb other religions into Islam. This was his new capital. Like Akbar's unique tomb at Sikandra, which is a tiered and domeless pyramid, Fatehpur Sikri is a synthesis of Hindu and Islamic architecture. Not long after its construction Akbar abandoned Fatehpur Sikri. Ever since, it has been a ghost town.

However, the real source of Mughal power lay in the capital at Delhi and in its heart, the Red Fort. As if to confirm this Shah Jahan had the celebrated lines inscribed here: 'If there is paradise on earth, it is here, it is here, it is here.' The Red Fort would attract foreign invaders and be sacked savagely over the last centuries. Now it is a symbol of modern India and is associated with major public events like the march past on Independence Day.

The Taj Mahal is ranked among the wonders of the world (see also below). It marks the high noon of empire, reflecting stability, power and confidence. The building is a mausoleum built by Shah Jahan to his wife Mumtaz Mahal and it has come to symbolize the love between two people. Here the Mughals appear sensitive, artistic, sensuous and extravagant – and all too human.

The Badshahi mosque in Lahore built by Aurangzeb, the sixth Mughal emperor, was said to be the largest in the Mughal empire, indeed in the world. It is the last great Mughal monument. The rise and fall of Muslim power affected the Badshahi mosque. When the Sikhs ruled Lahore, and later the British in the nineteenth century, it was sometimes used as an ammunition dump, sometimes as a barracks to accommodate soldiers and horses. Its minarets were damaged, its artwork destroyed. Vines and vegetation grew inside and all around it. Contemporary paintings depict a neglected structure in danger of being lost to the world.

In Pakistan today, the Badshahi is once again the jewel in the crown of Muslim architecture. The government lavishes its attention on it and worshippers flock to it. It is the symbol and pride of Pakistan. The mosque allows the newly formed nation to cultivate a sense of history, to maintain a direct link to the Mughals and thus legitimize the Pakistani claim to be the inheritors of the Mughal legacy. By the entrance of the Badshahi mosque is buried the poet who dreamt of Pakistan, Allama Iqbal, the architecture of the tomb corresponding to that of the mosque. A neat connection between the poet and the emperor is thus established. Together the two represent an essential part of the fabric of Muslim culture in South Asia.

The man who led the Muslims to Pakistan, Mr Jinnah, the Quaid-i-Azam, did not live long after the birth of his nation in 1947. A grateful nation built him the most costly and impressive mausoleum possible – situated on 60 acres – in Karachi. The mausoleum's Turkish design suggests a Muslim identity straining beyond the confines of India. It is significant that the most important monument made by Pakistan for the father of the nation was designed by a Turk. The mausoleum is a stolid, grey, imposing structure. The supporting minarets are dispensed with altogether. The architecture was also making a political point: Pakistan had left its Indian legacy behind and now needed to look to its Muslim past in the Middle East. But the past in this case hinted at Christian architecture (as we saw earlier in this chapter) that was inspired, however indirectly, by the St Sophia in Istanbul.

The Faisal mosque in Islamabad is one of the largest in Pakistan. It reflects the nation's attempt to identify itself with contemporary international Islam. Islamabad was itself built in the 1960s as the 'city of Islam'. The mosque is named after King Faisal of Saudi Arabia; its architects were mainly Turkish. The Turkish influence perhaps explains the thin, almost marginal, minarets so characteristic of Ottoman architecture. The architecture is not South Asian; there is no hint of the Mughals. The mosque shares the site with the international Islamic university; both hum with academic and diplomatic activity. Visitors to Islamabad are invariably taken to it as part of their itinerary.

During the time of General Zia ul-Haq and his drive towards Islamization the mosque became a hub of activity, a symbol of his era. The university was given a high profile by General Zia, who became its chancellor. He appointed the Education Minister, Dr Afzal, a relative, as rector (see also chapter 5). But its international tilt was clear from the composition of the other important posts: a Saudi was its pro-chancellor and an Egyptian its president. The Islam of the 1980s, assertive, confident and international, is reflected in the university.

From Ajmer to Islamabad, these architectural examples provide us with a commentary on the fortunes of the Muslims of South Asia. They inform us of the shrinking of Muslim power, a receding from the heartland of India, away from the Gangetic plain, back toward the north from where the Muslims originally came: the last three examples are situated in what is now Pakistan. One interpretation of these seven examples is to read them as the story of Pakistan.

Another lesson we can learn from our examples is how the people who are associated with the architecture are perceived in society. Those Muslims who stood for synthesis and tolerance, like Akbar and Dara Shikoh, are popular with Hindus but not always so with Muslims. Conversely, those who came to symbolize a strongly defined Muslim identity are most admired by Muslims. Among Hindus, Akbar is probably the most popular Muslim ruler and Aurangzeb the least liked; among Muslims the picture is reversed. For most Muslims, Aurangzeb is a hero and Akbar barely mentioned and then to be dismissed as a near heretic.

In our own times, Mr Jinnah is seen in a similar manner: for Pakistanis he is the greatest leader, for Indians the man who shattered the unity of India by creating Pakistan. The saint in Ajmer is an interesting case, an exception to the rule that divides Hindus and Muslims. He is universally popular, and his shrine remains a lively centre of worship, drawing large crowds from both communities. But it is the exception that proves the case for tolerance. Given the diversity of the races and religions of South Asia, perhaps this is the only viable approach to people's hearts and souls.

Taj Mahal: monument of love

If there is one romantic monument instantly recognized throughout the world that speaks to all peoples irrespective of colour or nationality or race it is the Taj Mahal. This was illustrated for me by Nasira, an Uzbek Intourist Hotel official in Bukhara in Central Asia. 'My only dream', she told me, 'was to see the Taj Mahal.' 'But why the Taj Mahal?' I asked, genuinely puzzled. We were not only hundreds of miles from India but in almost a different continent. 'I cry', she said, 'when I think of the Taj Mahal because it is a symbol of how much a man loved his wife in those days. Those men were different. They were not like the men today.' In the midst of the dreary Soviet repression, her culture, history and tradition had fused in the Taj Mahal. It was the symbol of love, of romance, of imperial luxury and extravagance; a symbol that was both Muslim and human, that spoke to her of her identity and, above all, that expressed human love, the love of a husband for a wife.

The death of his wife Arjumand Bano, given the title of Mumtaz Mahal, had shattered Shah Jahan. After emerging from a long period of depression he threw his energies into building a mausoleum in her memory. It is thought that 'Taj Mahal' – 'Crown of the Palace' – is an abbreviated version of Mumtaz Mahal's name (itself meaning 'Exalted One of the Palace'). Court histories from Shah Jahan's time simply called it the *rauza* (tomb) of Mumtaz Mahal.

Shah Jahan's selection of white marble with which to build the Taj was by no means an innovation. His genius rather is expressed in the overall concept and design of the mausoleum, in its power and execution. Both formally and symbolically he brought together fresh ideas in the creation of the Taj. Many of the skilled craftsmen involved in the construction were drawn from the empire – inlayers from Multan, masons from Multan and Delhi, garden designers from Kashmir. But many came from other parts of the Muslim world – calligraphers from Shiraz, finial makers from Samarkand, stone and flower cutters from Bukhara.

Calligraphy in the Muslim world is thought of as the highest level of artistic expression. It is notable that we see more inscriptions at the Taj

Mahal than on any other Mughal tomb, and almost all are from the Quran. The tone is set by passages of high moral purpose, like this one, to be read last before entering the garden:

> *O thou soul at peace,*
> *Return thou unto thy Lord, well-pleased*
> *And well-pleasing unto Him!*
> *Enter thou among My servants –*
> *And enter thou My Paradise!*
> (Pal *et al.* 1989: 58)

If Shah Jahan could not guarantee paradise in the next world for his wife he could ensure one in this world. Taking their cue from Shah Jahan, scholars have suggested that the Taj Mahal complex does indeed represent paradise. The Taj is flanked on one side by a mosque and on the other by a hospice for visiting pilgrims. During the day one can hear people chanting prayers. Clearly what is essentially an aesthetic sensation on the outside becomes on the inside a spiritual experience.

To see the Taj is to see the permanence of love, the eternal symbol of human affection, translated into artistic perfection. Every time I have seen it over the last forty years – the last time in 1992 – it has appeared different. It even changes with the changing light during the day. Yet it has always impressed me with its concept, its execution, its symmetry, its grandeur; it is simply the most exquisite building in the world.

★ ★ ★

In the end the three great empires faded away. Sooner or later every empire runs its course. These had become over-centralized, corrupt, their politics entangled in court intrigue, and they were not keeping up with the technological changes taking place in the world. Towards the end they were neither Islamic nor modern. Perhaps most important of all, by the nineteenth century the nations emerging in Europe had begun to compete with or to colonize most of the lands that had been part of the three Muslim empires, sounding a final death-knell. Democracy (inexorably moving to a full and free democratic order), industrialization, a belief in progress and in modern methods were to characterize the European powers.

FOUR

WHEN WORLDS COLLIDE: MUSLIM NATIONS AND WESTERN MODERNITY

●

Judged by Western criteria, most Muslim states fail the test of successful modern statehood. Dictatorships, poor literacy standards, maldistribution of wealth, nepotism and corruption appear to characterize them. Their record on human rights is unsatisfactory. This need not be so. Human rights, social and welfare programmes, universal education, democracy – the main criteria of modernity – are by no means incompatible with Islamic thinking. Indeed, Muslims claim these principles are embedded in Islam. In this chapter we shall explore the various aspects and nuances of Muslim nations grappling with modernity; it is an exercise that will take us far and wide.

In explaining the failings Muslims will say that Islam hardly features in the actions and ideas of most of their rulers; that only a more Islamic identity will solve their problems in the future; that many of their rulers are stooges of the West, conceding economic and political rights in exchange for arms and other support; that their societies still exist in the shadow of colonialism; that their cultural and political life is still influenced by the West. However, in spite of the obstacles, many countries, like Egypt, Turkey, Iran, Pakistan and Bangladesh, doggedly stay on the democratic path, attempting to create a civilized society, to encourage the arts and free debate.

In the first three sections of the chapter we shall look at three major Muslim nations – Turkey, Iran and Pakistan – which, each in its own way, are tackling the problems of modernity. The continuing impact of the colonial era is evident in their struggle. The examples of Turkey, Iran and Pakistan are made more relevant for us because they are the self-conscious inheritors of the great Muslim empires we discussed in the last chapter. In the last part of the chapter we shall broaden the argument and raise more general issues. We shall discuss the main Muslim dilemmas regarding modernity, including the role of democracy, family life, marriage and dress.

Of the three empires it was the inheritors of the Mughals who came closest to the Europeans in terms of the interaction between their own administrative structures and what eventually became the colonial ones. Modern education, transport and, above all, district administration structures were created by the British in the last century when they colonized India. But much was also borrowed from the Mughals (the district administrative structure, for instance). In contrast, the Ottomans continued with their own indigenous administration into the twentieth century. However, they responded to the West by imitation. The mimicry – in dress, life-style, training institutes and architecture – was most pronounced in the court and the élite. Kemal Ataturk merely continued down the same road, accelerating the pace of change. Perhaps the Safavids, fading away in the eighteenth century, and their successors, interacted the least with colonial Europe. In all three cases Islam tempered and guided dynastic ideas and practice.

The legacy of the past is visible in the actions of the founding fathers: Ataturk rejected the Ottoman structure and attempted to replace it with a modern Westernized one in Turkey; the Shah (like his son later) used the increasing oil revenues to build a centralized army and emphasized the Pahlavi and pre-Islamic identity of the Iranian state. In Pakistan the civil service and army, which directly reflected British influences, continued to be an important factor in social and political life. Mr Jinnah himself, the first Governor-General of Pakistan, was the very model of a British parliamentarian.

THE DILEMMAS OF MODERN TURKEY

Turkey is trying hard to sell itself to tourists as a modern nation. The nudist beaches, the shops with their stale global items, the postcards, the discos – all these are second-hand and even culturally debasing. Yet its own heritage, architecture and cuisine, its own past, are first-rate.

The rediscovery of the past
The challenge to the notion of Turkey as a European nation, the strong, unmistakable signs of Turks rediscovering their Islamic identity, are everywhere: the full mosques, the pride in the Ottoman past, the women with their *hijab*, even men wearing the fez. These are the first tentative steps. They are significant because they are reviving what Ataturk had buried in his

contempt for the past. For the Turks it is their legacy and they are set on reclaiming it; this quest will be the story of the Turks in the coming time. The push towards the Ottoman past is now too strong to stop. It has been fuelled by events in Central Asia whose only links with the Turks is through the Ottoman past.

Turks are a tough and proud people, with a developed perception of themselves as people of honour and worth. There is a story from the early 1950s about a Turkish brigade in the Korean war. Threatened by overwhelming communist forces, the Turkish commander refused to retreat. Defying the orders of his United Nations superiors, he sent a message back saying the word 'retreat' did not exist in the vocabulary of the Turks. The Turks were always in the front-line of Islam against Europe; but it was a sophisticated, cultured Islam embracing many societies. Here many systems thrived; here Jews and Christians lived in safety and comfort.

There is a central debate in Turkey now about how Islamic the Turkish past was at the time of the Ottomans. Although the debate may appear academic to an outsider, it relates directly to modern politics; it also reflects the central obsession in Turkish society, the relationship with Europe.

One school of thought maintains that the empire was simply an empire just like any other. Turkish Muslims who practise their faith say it was not particularly Islamic. They argue that the *shariah*, the law of Islam, was concerned with only family law. Foreign policy remained outside the *shariah*. The sultan did not follow the *shariah*; the Ottomans were dictators. In any case the Sheikh-ul-Islam, the most senior member of the clergy, was an official nominated by the sultan and thus under his power. Indeed, Kemal Ataturk's policies separating religion and state were, in a sense, a continuation of those of the Ottomans.

The other school argues that the Ottoman empire was self-consciously Islamic and based on the laws of Islam; that the *ulema* presided over courts which covered family law (this was most relevant to ordinary people); that, since by definition a Turk is a Muslim, the Turkish religion can be nothing but Islam. Turkish scholars like Professor Kemal Oke and Professor Nur Veergin maintain that during certain periods the Ottoman state was indeed Islamic. The debate has entered Turkish politics. The National Salvation Party, which preceded the Welfare Party, and like it saw itself as 'Islamic', contested the 1977 elections. It spoke of Turkey's 'national' heritage – meaning its Ottoman past – and of its 'national' moral values – meaning its Islamic traditions. It also advocated headscarves for women, and opposed usury and alcohol. For such Turks the Ottomans reflected the tolerance and compassion of Islam; they were generous to different peoples and faiths. These Turks point out that even today mosque, synagogue and church exist side by side in Istanbul.

Most important of all in the Ottoman empire, the *ulema*, the religious figures, could check and remonstrate with the sultan. In the figure of the Sheikh-ul-Islam the *ulema* had a voice in the palace. One sheikh was known to have warned a sultan that he was spending too much time hunting and in the harem. The spirit of Islamic justice was reflected in the 'Court of the People', where ordinary citizens could present petitions to the sultan, who had to appear in person. There were precedents, one dating from the rule of Mehmet II (1451–81), when a petition against the sultan led to his being tried by the *ulema*. Thus God's authority was established over the sultan's power.

Professor Oke, describing to me the Islamic legacy of the Ottomans and its relevance for modern Turkey, mentioned the insistence on justice as 'the governing spirit in administration and the foundation of all statecraft'. He also thought the Ottomans showed humanism 'with respect to upholding the rights of minorities or the people they conquered. I think Ottomans achieved a tremendous record there by putting all these people together and achieved a kind of peaceful coexistence.' It was rather like a 'united nations of the Ottoman Empire'. In addition he stressed the great advancement in science, art and culture, the sophistication of the Ottomans.

Kemal Ataturk

Kemal Ataturk (1881–1938) emerged at the time of the First World War to salvage the modern Turkish nation from the disintegrating Ottoman empire. Once he had formed a government in the 1920s, Turkey was set firmly on the path of Westernization. Ataturk was a military genius who commanded his nation like an army, issuing orders designed to create a modern Westernized state. Education, administration and culture were henceforth to be as closely European as possible. Islam and the Ottomans were at best a part of history that was dead and buried, at worst an impediment to modern progress, a cultural embarrassment. Ataturk depicted the Ottomans as drunk and whoring. The wheel has turned: Turks now depict Ataturk as alcoholic and homosexual.

In a series of dramatic moves Ataturk attempted to cut the roots of Islam in Turkish society. He could do so because of the immense prestige he enjoyed as the father of the Turkish nation (the meaning of the title conferred on him, Ataturk). In the 1920s not only did he reject the Ottomans culturally – mocking the red Turk fez, which he banned – but he abolished the caliphate, which had provided the Ottomans with the appearance of speaking on behalf of the Muslim world. The abolition of the caliphate reverberated throughout the Muslim world. So interconnected are Muslims, so developed the notion of the *ummah*, that for years there was agitation in India in support of the caliphate. Indian Muslims saw the abolition as a British-inspired plot to destroy Islam. They could not believe that the Turks themselves had abolished it.

As another measure to cut the Turks off from the Ottoman past, Ataturk shifted the capital from Istanbul and created a new one for himself at Ankara. St Sophia was converted from a mosque into a museum, Sufi orders were banned, and European legal codes replaced Islamic ones. So severe was the suppression of Islam that even today Turks speak of their affinity to Islam with caution. To be Islamic in Turkey invited the abuse *yobaz*, backward, fanatic. Ataturk's ubiquitous statues, in bow-tie or coat-tails, stare sternly to remind us of this extraordinary man. Such statues, prohibited in Islam, are also a reminder of how far the European obsession took the Turks. The drive towards Europe, as we noted above, had already begun in the eighteenth century, when army and navy training institutes were run by Europeans, and European literature was translated into Turkish. When Ataturk died in 1938 he was confident that Turkey had turned the corner and was on its way to its European destiny.

However, political life in Turkey has moved noticeably since the time of Ataturk. There is a new generation of political leaders. Many, like Turgut Ozal, the present head of government, are devout Muslims and at the same time comfortable in a non-Islamic government. Ozal was born in 1927, a few years after the death of the Ottoman empire, and can therefore look back to it objectively and without Ataturkian contempt. He has a two-pronged international strategy: to revive the position of Turkey in the Muslim world and to allow it to act as a bridge to the West: 'There is a large group of Islamic countries. Once they looked on the Ottoman empire as the leader of the Islamic world. We shall lead this group of countries and this will make us more important to the West. We are both a physical and a moral bridge from the West' (Ozal 1984: 3).

The debate between those who claim the Ottomans were genuinely Islamic and those who reject this view is thus about the nature of Turkish society, its identity and its future (including whether Turkey can find a place in the European Community). The question is: will Turkish society continue to imitate Europeans and eventually succeed in becoming European, or will it rediscover its own Islamic culture?

Islamic revivalism

The signs of Islamic revival are not difficult to read. At the 1991 election the Welfare Party, which represents Islamic revivalism, obtained 16 per cent of the seats in parliament. In November 1992 the party won nearly a third of the vote in the local elections in Istanbul. The party talks of closer ties with the Islamic world and a rejection of the West and its 'corruption'. According to recent surveys, some 70 per cent of Turkey's population of about 55 million claim they are 'devout Muslims' and about 20 per cent say they pray five times a day. About 20 per cent of the population proudly assert they are Muslims first and then Turk. But, significantly, only 3 per cent of the population wish to see the Islamic *shariah* law implemented in Turkey, replacing the secular state.

Apart from statistics and surveys, a casual visit to Turkey will confirm the trend towards Islam. There are over 3000 mosques in Istanbul and they are more and more frequented. After public clamour, prayers have been allowed for the first time since Ataturk banned them in the St Sophia in one of the side rooms by the entrance to the Topkapi. The call to prayer is in Arabic and no longer in Turkish (as once decreed by Ataturk). There are eight theological colleges with about 10 000 students. Women increasingly wear veils to emphasize their Islamic identity. The Directorate of Religious Affairs reports that there are now 57 000 mosques in Turkey. This number should dispel the notion of Turkish society as secular.

According to Professor Kemal Oke, although there is a revival of Islam in Turkey today, there is no large-scale political movement towards replacing the existing political institution with an Islamic theocracy like that in Iran. Most Turks simply want Islam to be part of their cultural identity. Fehmi Koru, chief columnist of the journal *Zaman* and an activist, would like to see a quicker pace of Islamization, a greater involvement in Muslim affairs abroad, both in the West and in Central Asia. He told me: 'The problem with today's Turkey is a kind of identity crisis. If we are Muslims we have to find our roots in Islam, but we haven't made our peace with Islam. If we are Turks, why are we staying aloof from the problems in Nagorna-Karabakh and Nishavand? If we are secular, why do we have a Directorate of Religious Affairs governing every aspect of religious life? So we have to find an identity for ourselves.'

Having established that there are definite signs that Islam is reviving, we may then ask why. There are several reasons of a cultural, political and sociological nature. First of all, Islam did not disappear under Ataturk (as was widely assumed) but simply went underground to wait for a better climate to emerge. In particular, rural society did not abandon it. Besides, the attempts at drastic Westernization did not solve Turkey's problems. Poverty and backwardness had not disappeared. Many Turks, although aware of Turkey's economic successes, were left wondering whether the sacrifices had been too much and the rewards too meagre.

Then there is the effect of the larger Islamic revivalism that swept the Muslim world in the 1970s and 1980s. Many Turks felt a pride in the Islamic assertion and turned their eyes to the Muslim world. It made ordinary Turks conscious of their 'Muslimness'.

There is another reason, which is linked to social developments in Europe. It is the growing awareness that however Westernized the Turks make themselves they will remain outsiders in Europe. Members of this proud race, once masters of the world, have become the despised immigrant underclass in Germany, the butt of the neo-Nazis. Horror stories of racist attacks in Europe triggered a reawakening of ethnic and religious identity among the Turks. Many feel that the price of becoming Europeanized is too high; many even challenged the official policy of trying to join the European Community.

Then there are the sociological factors. There is an element of class, the impact of urbanization and the demographic structure. The poorer classes, the recently migrated urban-dweller and the young seek solace in tradition and religion. For many of these Turks the ruling élite is alien, corrupt and far too Westernized.

There is also another – completely unexpected – development which will assume increasing importance in the future; it is provided by the Central Asian republics of the former USSR. Although to Europeans the Turk has always been the terrible Turk, the loathed hammer of Islam, the threatening invader, in Central Asia he possesses the opposite image, as a brave and honourable leader of nations. Some of the most renowned rulers of that region have been Turks and the major tribes proudly claim Turkish descent; indeed the entire area is called Turkistan – the land of the Turks. People look back to the past with great pride, as we shall see in the next chapter. Babar himself, reflecting the Central Asian tradition, was always proud of his Turkish ancestry.

For many in the Central Asian republics of the former Soviet Union emerging as independent countries, Turkey is a viable model (see chapter 5). Turkey is the inheritor state of the Ottomans with which they were linked; a motherland from which springs their historical identity. They already look to Turkey for cultural inspiration. More than ever Turkey will need to parade its past and emphasize its culture which is so closely linked to that past. It will not be simple. Many Turks and those in the former Soviet republics still owe allegiance to a secular ideology. Turkey's dilemmas will therefore assume an international dimension in the coming years.

IRAN'S ISLAMIC QUEST

To understand contemporary Iranian society and politics we need visit only two places in Tehran: the Shah's palace in the north of the city and the burial place of Ayatollah Khomeini in the south. Together they sum up an entire cultural, political and religious story.

Palace versus shrine

The Shah's palace is in the north, because that is where the élite lived, where the land slopes upwards towards the snow-covered mountains, giving it an air of a hill station, away from the hurly-burly and hoi polloi of the city. The Ayatollah is buried in the flat dusty plain on the road to the holy city of Qum. The Shah's palace is hidden in a forest where prying eyes would fail to see what went on behind the high walls. The Ayatollah's mosque is visible for miles around.

The architecture of the buildings and their contents inside are also completely dissimilar. The Shah's palace does not offer even a hint of Islamic culture and history. Inside is an Aladdin's cave of items from all over the world – massive dining tables, crockery, carpets, vases – but mostly from Europe. There is even a picture from Oxford: 'From Wadham College, Oxford, January 28th 1976, presented to H.R.H. Princess Ashraf Pahlavi on her honorary fellowship.' The date is significant; three years later the Shah was ousted.

The only concession to the Persian heritage is the set of four large paintings on a roof overlooking an inside hall. These are illustrations from Firdausi's *Shah Nama* depicting the exploits of the legendary warrior Rustam, which, however, emphasized Persian as against a broader Islamic culture coming from Arabia.

The buildings of the Shah's palace are large, square and characterless; they could be anywhere in the world – any large museum or office block. There is not a hint of Islamic tradition, no arches, no domes, no delicate Arabic calligraphy.

The Shah's palace is now called 'The People's Palace Museum'. I went round it with a group of Iranian peasants with their women in *chadors*. I heard their grunts and groans of disapproval. I saw the look of shocked disbelief on their faces as they saw the luxury, opulence and waste of the Shah's life. By one of the large dining tables, with all the expensive crockery laid out on it as if the Shah were expected at any moment, the administration had made a redundant political point by placing a photograph of some obviously impoverished peasants on a farm. The contrast was not lost on my group; more grunts and groans.

The Shah was a philistine in matters of art, taste and culture. Outside the palace there is a statue of a pair of gigantic riding boots which represent the legs of the Shah's father. The Shah's legs in Tehran, Saddam's hands in Baghdad – why do these despots imagine their limbs hold the slightest interest for any of us?

In sharp contrast, everything about the Ayatollah's burial place is consciously Islamic. The dome itself represents classic Persian Muslim architecture. It is more elongated, more bulbous, than the Ottoman domes and certainly more visually pleasing in its blazing golden surface. By selecting gold for the dome, Iranian clerics wished the shrine to echo the dome of the holiest shrine in Iran, that of Imam Raza in Shiraz. Inside, there is light and colour. The grave itself is simple. The only concession to poetic imagery is the depiction of a flower; rooted in Persian literature, it is a symbol of so many things – of martyrdom, of love, of purity. People come up and kiss the railings around the actual grave. The atmosphere is informal, as families – women and children – come to spend their time praying, chatting, seeing and being seen. On Thursday nights, which are traditionally considered holy, there may be up to 100 000 people here.

The grave has already become a religious shrine, part of the cultural tradition of Iran. Around the shrine a whole complex of hospitals, *madrassahs* (religious colleges) and student's quarters is being constructed. At night the complex glitters with green and gold lights and is visible from miles away.

The struggle for identity
Bearded clergy in flowing black robes, women covered in dark sheets, rituals centred around martyrs long dead, national hatred concentrated on the USA as the Great Satan – where does Iranian society relate to the USA? How do we make sense of the close relationship between the two up to the 1970s and then the almost obsessive mutual hatred in the 1980s? The answers are as complex as any pattern on an Iranian carpet; let us try to separate the strands.

In the 1980s two more different societies than the USA and Iran would have been difficult to imagine. It is well to remember that between the great events that inspire Iranian society and those that inspire the Americans there is a thousand years of history. The massacre at Karbala took place in the seventh century; the founding fathers landed in Plymouth a thousand years later. So one society was already old when the other was just beginning to be born.

The most important strand to identify is Shiism. Shia ideology in society encouraged people to respond in terms of good versus evil, of immense sacrifices, of martyrdom in the cause, and to accept the leadership of religious figures who reflected the authority of the Imams. The Safavid dynasty ensured the close working relationship between Shia ideology and the state.

The second strand reflects the oscillation in society between the dynastic principle of powerful kings and that of pious religious figures. The oscillation has been in evidence in the politics of Iran over the last few centuries. For example, we noted how Majlisi, one of the leaders of the clergy in the late seventeenth century, actually led a revolution, not unlike that of Khomeini's, to impose the will of the clergy on the Safavid ruler. The dilemma was difficult for the Iranians to resolve. According to one principle, power came from God, and humanity was to submit; according to the other, power came from the imperial dynasty, and genealogy decided authority. The problem was that the more the Persians emphasized their rich cultural heritage, the more they underlined the importance of royalty in their tradition, the further they moved away from the Islamic principle. So those who were against the Islamic principle would oppose it implicitly by talking of the glories of Persian culture, poetry and art. It was a subtext that announced their real political and religious positions.

Another strand relates to the geo-politics of the post-Second World War era which demanded that the newly emerged nations ally with one of the two superpowers. The Shah had placed Iran firmly in the American camp. Earlier Britain and then, increasingly, the USA took full advantage of their superior bargaining power in ensuring availability of Iranian oil at very cheap rates. The American connection was a logical outcome of an earlier British connection.

In Iran it is still widely believed that if anything goes wrong, if there is any conspiracy afoot, the British are behind it. There are numerous folk sayings and proverbs in circulation to confirm this. This is an exaggerated compliment, a memory from Britain's imperial past.

The British embassy in Tehran is seen as a central symbol of the country which has played such a vital role in Iranian politics. The British lions on the embassy gates in Tehran have seen much history. Inside we could be in a cantonment in Lahore or Peshawar or Delhi because of the North Indian nature of the architecture. The love-hate relationship between Britain and Iran is complex. On the one hand, the British love for Persian poetry, calligraphy and mysticism earned affection; on the other, British attempts to exploit and control Iran for the last hundred years earned hatred and anger.

In the 1950s, when the Shah was forced to flee Iran as a result of a popular movement, it was the CIA that engineered his return. This condemned him in the public mind for all time. The Shah was equated to the USA, and the USA to the exploitation of Iran and the corruption of its culture; such is the instant philosophy of the bazaar. What is less well known is that many Americans criticized the Shah and advocated genuine democracy. But in the public mind the Americans were seen as propping up the Shah and supporting his tyranny.

During the struggles against the Shah in the 1960s and 1970s thousands of men were mowed down by troops and Imam Khomeini's own son was killed. Khomeini himself was exiled from 1964 to February 1979. It was a land dominated by materialism, by the secret service, Savak, and by the corruption of the Shah and his family. But underneath it all the wellsprings of Islam remained, waiting to be tapped.

Modernity for planners and economists in Iran meant dams, roads and schools. But for people in the bazaars and the villages it also meant discos, jeans, strip-clubs, bars and cinemas – all of which antagonized ordinary people and infuriated the clergy. The moral and financial corruption of the Westernized élite, taking their inspiration from the Shah and his family, further added fuel to the fire.

The sociologist Dr Ali Shariati condemned the obsession with the West as *gharbzadegi* (being struck by the West). He remained popular, even somewhat of a cult figure; 100 000 copies of his lectures were published and thousands flocked to hear him speak. For them Shariati demonstrated the relevance of Shia Islam to contemporary life. A Sorbonne-educated intellectual, Shariati quoted Emile Durkheim, Max Weber, Frantz Fanon and Che Guevara. In his work he synthesized Shia Islam and Western thought. The challenge to the West was coming not only from the traditional clergy.

It was not hard to imagine the outraged feelings of ordinary Iranians about the Americans during the Shah's rule; and there were about 50 000 here – soldiers, advisers, technicians. Iran was an important bastion against the

Soviet Union, and this was the time of the Cold War. Bazaar rumours claimed that Americans had their strip-clubs, brothels and bars even in Isfahan. Iranians, passionately proud of their culture and history, were seething. Iran was a powder-keg and all that was needed was a match to blow everything sky high. It came in the form of Ayatollah Khomeini.

Imam Khomeini the scholar-activist

Imam Khomeini often backed his claims to speak for and represent the people on the basis of various *hadith* of the Prophet. 'The scholars are rulers over the people,' he would cite. His political writing and commentary – and he had a lifetime's scholarship behind him – thus had a powerful logic, since they were derived from early Islamic thought and history. His books and lectures on Islamic government became a major force during the revolution in the 1970s. Khomeini had already passed the greatest test of all, the respect of his fellow scholars in Qum, which was the final hurdle before a man was respected as an ayatollah. No formal title could confer this on a scholar. At the same time he had in no way compromised with the Shah's regime. Because of this unimpeachable position Khomeini occupied and held the high moral ground. The Shah did not have a chance once his army and secret police began to unravel.

No one understood better than Khomeini himself the importance of mobilizing the masses through traditional religious symbolism. He used the *tazyah* processions which commemorate Karbala, the seminal historical occasion when Hussain was martyred, to mobilize the people. In 1978 he sent messages from abroad to Iranians asking them to prepare for the massive marches of the month of Muharram. These would break the spirit of the military, who had no will to kill their own people. By converting the traditional mourning for Hussain during *Ashurah* into a challenge to the Shah, Khomeini again touched a deep chord in people. Hussain's martyrdom was in the cause of justice and his fight against tyranny. Modern Iranians understood the message. The Muharram of 1979 was used to pass the new constitution and further challenge the USA. In the next Muharram Khomeini directed people to return to their own neighbourhood, in an attempt to calm things down.

All this is not to suggest that Khomeini was manipulating people. He had deep convictions. Unlike many other Iranian clergy he always spoke of Islam – not the sect of Shiism. His greatest contribution to global Islam was his belief that there are no divisions between Shia and Sunni, that both are Muslims. For him Islam was a universal system, knowing no borders.

Indeed it took considerable argument to persuade him to speak only of Iran in order to mobilize the Iranian people. It required further discussion to convince him that the President of Iran must be an Iranian, not just a Muslim. It must be recalled that the first foreign dignitary he received after the revolution was Yasser Arafat. Though an Arab, Arafat symbolized an Islamic cause, that of liberating the holy places of Palestine.

None the less Islam for Khomeini meant Ithna Ashari or twelve Imam Shiism. While providing the Shias with an immense reservoir of religious passion, this inevitably acted as a barrier between the Shia and the Sunni areas and thereby created obstacles for Khomeini on the larger Muslim world stage.

Yet Khomeini did move Shia and Sunni towards each other by declaring they were one. Throughout the Muslim world, he had earned the respect of the people. His challenging the USA, his reputation for integrity and public espousal of the Islamic cause were widely supported. He had come to embody the mood of Islamic revivalism.

As the USA became the focus of both cultural and political opposition, and because it was the age of the Western media, Khomeini's image, in turn, became the symbol of all that was wrong with Iran in the USA. Khomeini was depicted as a humourless, cruel and medieval monk.

Yet Khomeini's writing represents a rich tradition in Persian literature. Apart from his serious work on religion and politics Khomeini tried his hand at poetry. Khomeini's poetry is seen as superficial love lyrics and dismissed by those unacquainted with the Persian tradition. What is not fully understood is that the imagery of such poetry is specific to Persian Islamic culture. The images and content represent a mystical tradition; wine is the metaphor of the intoxication that comes from divine wisdom and devotion; the pious believers who simply believe in outward ritual are seen as empty hypocrites, the drunkards who have human feelings are the real worshippers as they drink wine/wisdom, and so on. It is with this in mind that we need to approach Khomeini's poetry:

> *I've become possessed by the beauty spot above your lip, oh friend*
> *I saw your fevered eye, and fell ill*
> *Open the wine house door to me day and night*
> *For I am fed up with mosque and seminary.*
> *I sought help from the breath of the wine besotted drunkard*
> *Permit me to recall the temple of idols*
> *I was awakened by the hand of the idol of the wine house.*
> (Fischer and Abedi 1990: 452)

Islamic Iranian art

Iranians appear irrational, uncouth and uncivilized in the popular Western media. This is an entirely erroneous picture; their civilization and culture are highly sophisticated. I will illustrate this point by discussing contemporary Iranian paintings and posters. This art form allows the artist to comment on larger issues such as religion, history and politics.

Consider, for instance, the central emblem of the Islamic Republic of Iran. It is now the official logo and the source of inspiration for numerous derivative posters, stamps and media images. Although it is even on the Iranian flag, outsiders find it difficult to comprehend: 'It seems to me to drape itself like a mysterious veil over the whole country' (Danziger 1987: 51).

Let us attempt to remove the veil. The central calligraphy of the emblem represents *Allah-hu-Akbar*, God is great. It is composed of four crescents and a vertical bar with a short orthographic stroke above it. But in keeping with the sophistication of Iranian art and ideas the emblem suggests multiple readings (Fischer and Abedi 1990: 341–6). The emblem reads Allah, the name of God. The vertical bar can be visualized as a torch, a minaret or a sword and connects heaven and earth, representing the 'straight path of Islam'.

The central emblem also represents the figure 5, in turn representing the five holiest figures of Islam: the Prophet, his son-in-law Ali, his daughter Fatimah, and the sons of Ali and Fatimah, Hassan and Hussain. The figure 5 thus contains deep historical resonances for Shias. These five figures are the light of God and through their intercession God answers the prayers of the faithful. The orthographic stroke above the bar represents the angel Gabriel who joins the five holy figures, thus reaffirming the divine message.

The emblem can also be read as a *la*, a 'no'. Dr Ali Shariati had drawn attention to Islam as a religion of 'nos' – not so much a system of prohibitions but as a system of protest against false gods and false justice. He used the logo *la* on the cover of all of his books and published lectures. *La* thus combines graphically elements from Islam, modernity and Third World radicalism.

It can also be suggested that the pair of crescents on each side of the vertical bar have turned their backs towards the right and the left. They thus represent the modern slogan which Khomeini made his own: 'Neither East nor West, Islam is best.' In turn it reflects the Quran's *ummatan wasatan* or 'middle nation' (Surah 2: verse 143). Muslims in this depiction have turned away from the two contemporary superpowers.

Other common images in Iranian posters are the lamp, the rose and the tulip. The lamp is inspired by the Quran, which used the imagery of *nur* or light for God (Surah 24: verse 35). It is the light which guides people to the straight path of Islam. The flowers are celebrated in Persian poetry and associated with the blood of those who either die for the loved one or are martyred for their beliefs. The flowers have become a central icon of martyrdom for Iran. Two of the outer petals are often shown as falling, representing the price Muslims must pay to protect the 'light of God' and 'the straight path'. The two inner petals remain in the shape of *la* protecting the seeds of the flower and are illuminated by the inner light. It is significant that virtually the only pictorial representation above the tomb of Khomeini is these flowers. Paintings and portraits depicting a kindly Khomeini with a flower in the background are common. Indeed, the Hotel Intercontinental in Tehran is now called Laleh after the tulip.

As we can see there is much going on in the art of modern Iranian posters. Earlier, under the Shah, the official emblem of Iran was a male lion with a sword in its right paw. A rising sun in the background and an imperial crown completed the picture. Both sun and lion are familiar to royal iconography throughout the world. There was nothing Islamic in the Shah's emblem. The emblem of Iran today, by contrast, is rich with Islamic content.

The sophisticated and polemical nature of the poster artists is illustrated by the stamp issued in 1984 to honour Malcolm X, the Black Muslim leader. Malcolm X's picture is juxtaposed with that of Bilal, the first muezzin of Islam and a former slave in the time of the Prophet. His black colour made him a suitable if subtle choice for comparison with Malcolm X. The message was aimed at America's blacks: rise and shake off the shackles of your white oppressors.

Posters which depict Khomeini challenging the USA, Britain and Israel are also popular. The USA is equated to the Shah, who is usually draped in the stars and stripes. The Shah is also shown as a modern-day Yazid, the ruler who ordered the killing of Hussain at Karbala, the event above all others which inspires the Shia. It is clear, then, that we have in popular art a forceful and often sophisticated visual representation of religious themes combined with contemporary political discourse.

After the revolution

If Tehran represents the Shah, Qum represents Khomeini for most Iranians. Tehran itself is a modern city, grappling with modern problems: out-of-control inflation, disintegrating law and order, chaotic traffic and complaining citizens (everything is under scrutiny and one even hears criticism of the

'Mercs and perks' of some of the leading clergy). In contrast Qum, the traditional Iranian centre of religious learning, maintains its air of quiet dignity.

Qum is not unlike the university towns of Oxford and Cambridge in certain ways. Here, serious-looking religious scholars in flowing black robes are seen hurrying along with books in their hands. Sometimes they are on motorcycles or Japanese mopeds – a trend criticized by the more traditional who would prefer their scholars to be more dignified and walk.

Qum's importance derives from the shrine of the sister of the eighth Imam, Imam Raza. She is named after her ancestor Fatimah, the Prophet's daughter, but is known in the land as Masuma, the Innocent One. There are few shrines in the Muslim world as resplendent, as artistic, as full of worshippers as the shrine at Qum. Imam Raza himself is buried in Mashad. Of all the Imams he holds a special place in Iran: he is a 'local' Imam born and bred in the land.

Isfahan is different from both Tehran and Qum. It is the pre-eminent Persian city, the glory of the Safavids. Here I found people relaxed, including the women. Young couples were holding hands in some of the parks or sitting whispering together. When I expressed my surprise I was told they were in all likelihood married couples. But then, it was hastily added, before the revolution even unmarried couples would behave in this manner. The women did wear a scarf and modest dress, often a *chador*. Men wore trousers and shirts. Only some old peasants, from out of town, had on traditional dress or *shalwar-kameez* (baggy trousers and a long shirt).

The main avenues and main squares in the big cities were named after the Shah. All that has changed. They are now named after the heroes of the Islamic revolution. It was rumoured that some over-enthusiastic revolutionaries had lined up tractors to reduce Persepolis to a rubble but were stopped in time. But everything that is non-Islamic has not been swept away in Iran after the revolution. Firdausi's statue, which is distinctly un-Islamic, remains in one of the main parks in Tehran. So does the symbol of Iran Air, the mythical pre-Islamic bird, Huma. (Pre-Islamic mythical birds are used as symbols for other airlines owned by Muslim nations: the falcon representing the god Horus for the Egyptian airline, and the Garuda, half eagle, half man, ridden by the Hindu god Vishnu, for the Indonesian one.)

Imam Khomeini's photograph is everywhere, often alongside that of his successor as Ayatollah al-Uzma or the president, the one reinforcing the other – in airport lounges, in schools, in private homes. Khomeini's photos in Iran were almost unrecognizable compared to the ones we see abroad where he appears to glower and threaten. Here he is the soft-eyed, kindly uncle, the understanding scholar, with a gentle smile on his face. A flower in the frame lends a touch of elegance and poetic mystery.

What I did not see was anyone wearing a tie. It was regarded as a symbol of the West, of a Christian order, and that was positively discouraged. When we see Iranian ambassadors and cabinet ministers wearing smart Western suits we think that something is missing from their dress: it is the tie.

The Iranian government itself is led by sophisticated, intelligent people whose arguments and rationality would come as a surprise to those who imagine the stereotype of wild fanatics running Iran. Women have far more rights than is thought of abroad. There are ten women in parliament. Women have the right to work and some are prominent professionals.

With a population of about 60 million, with cultural influences rooted in history which extend to large parts of the region, with its vast natural resources and its perception of itself as providing revolutionary leadership to contemporary Islam, Iran has potentially a major role to play in the Muslim world, including some of the emerging Central Asian states. However, its revolutionary posture will continue to meet opposition in many Muslim states, especially Arab ones. Unless there is some kind of reconciliation the message of Islam will be lost in the rhetoric of revolution. Iran needs to strike a balance between spiritual commitment to Islam and finding a way of living in and with the world.

Khomeini's *fatwa* and Dante's *Divine Comedy*

A comparison between Dante's famous book and Khomeini's equally famous *fatwa* condemning Salman Rushdie to death offers an insight into the relationship between Iran and the West. It is now fairly well established by scholars that Dante's ideas of Islam profoundly influenced his work (Boase 1989a; Fischer and Abedi 1990; Menocal 1987). It is clear that the Islamic tradition known as the *miraj*, the Prophet's night journey to Jerusalem and ascent to heaven (described in chapter 2), provided the source of the plot and some of the particulars of Dante's *Divine Comedy*. Because Dante perceived Islam as a serious threat to Christianity his work was conceived, whether consciously or unconsciously, as a response, a counter-text, even an anti-*miraj*.

The lower part of Dante's hell is a city of mosques. It is here that those Christians influenced by Muslims are punished (like Cavalcanti, who was influenced by Averroës). Dante places the Prophet here also. He is torn to pieces by pigs; the irony will not be missed: the pig is an unclean animal for

Muslims. Scholars suggest that the reason why the Prophet is punished as a schismatic, that is one who creates divisions, rather than as a heretic was that he was associated with ideas which seemed to undermine Christianity. For Dante he symbolized 'the sowing of internal dissent in the Christian community' (Menocal 1987: 130). Professor Gabrieli, however, describes Dante's *Divine Comedy* as 'this grotesque fiction, the product of ignorance, fantasy and *odium theologicum*', and observes that 'the evil weed' that Dante sowed 'did not die with him but grew to become the *flagellum dei* both in the East and the West' (Gabrieli 1977: 14–15). Such is the power of literature.

Dante's fears of Islam as an irresistible force that could undermine Christianity were justified. After all, in his time Muslim Spain was a centre of 'high culture' for Europe (see chapter 3). Scholars found philosophy and science there, poets and artists found inspiration. Through Averroës (Ibn Rushd) and Avicenna (Ibn Sina) in the eleventh and twelfth centuries, Europeans learned of Greek philosophy and medicine respectively. Troubadour poetry was modelled on Arabic forms. Medieval Europe was enthralled by Muslim civilization. To Dante, Muslim civilization would have seemed like a great flood from which there appeared to be no escape; the lines around European culture and religion had to be drawn forcefully and firmly.

Interestingly, the same response for the same reasons seems to have accounted for the actions of Iran's ayatollahs in their vigorous attack on the West in the last decades. We are not analysing the merits of the foreign culture, whether it was better or more beneficial than the local one. We are pointing out that it was widely seen as monolithic, corrupting and inexorably advancing.

Fearful of America's irresistible cultural and political advance in their country, the ayatollahs decided that the best strategy lay in total rejection of the foreign. Because the USA had set out to Westernize Iran, it became the embodiment of evil: the USA was given the title the Great Satan. It was the reverse side of the Christian–Muslim encounter of Dante's time, with a new locality and in a different age.

Imam Khomeini's fateful *fatwa*, condemning Salman Rushdie for his novel *The Satanic Verses* (1988), needs to be set in this historical context. In Iran – as indeed in most parts of the Muslim wold – the novel was seen as a deliberate attempt to humiliate and ridicule the most revered figures in Islam. Any Iranian cleric would have done what Khomeini did. It is important to remember that Muslims in Islamic states are protected by laws of blasphemy. In Pakistan or Iran it is illegal under the constitution to mock the Quran or the Prophet. The point here is not that Muslims respect the Quran and the Prophet because of injunctions in their constitution, but rather that the constitution is now reflecting the wishes of Muslims by embodying this public demand in its legal enactments. In countries which are overwhelmingly Muslim no one would think of insulting the Prophet or the Quran.

It is in this context that we must understand the Muslim response to Salman Rushdie and *The Satanic Verses*. Certain passages were seen as particularly offensive. The Prophet, his most respected companions and – especially infuriating for Muslims with their sensitivities about women – his wives were depicted with irreverence, sometimes in scenes that involved sex. Fiction and fact were blurred as irony mixed with cynicism. For Muslims Salman Rushdie's sins were compounded by the fact that he was born into a Muslim household. If the author were ever to venture into a Muslim country his life would be in immediate danger. Since he has not made his peace with Muslims, the threat to his life still remains.

The implications that the Quran was written by the Prophet and the insults to the Prophet and those dear to him in *The Satanic Verses* would upset any Muslim. Most Muslims were disturbed by what they read in the novel, although not all supported the call for the author's death. But this exercise is not new; there are libraries full of similar material. What upset Muslims was something more complex and easily missed by the West. What really agitated them was the breach of *adab*. Islam is not just theology, Islam is also culture, civilization, behaviour and manners, as we have already noted. One thing good Muslims do not do is insult the revered figures or holy people of either their own or other religions: this is part of *adab*. Because Rushdie was Muslim – or at least from a Muslim background – he was expected to understand *adab*. By violating the rules of *adab* he appeared to be saying to Muslims: I understand your rules of behaviour and culture and I am violating them; let us see what you can do about it.

Muslims responded in anger to this. Had Rushdie not been a South Asian there would have been no problem. Muslims would have known that his book was yet another in the long series of attacks on Islam. His violation of the manners of South Asia was another matter and not to be forgiven. It was really South Asians who took the lead against Rushdie; the book was burnt by them in Bradford and they were killed demonstrating against it in Islamabad and Bombay. The Iranians were quick to follow.

When Ayatollah Khomeini issued the *fatwa* the matter took another twist. It became a question of national honour; every Iranian was now bound to support the *fatwa* and the younger generation of radicals now rallied to it. The response was no longer purely cultural or religious but also political.

In South Asia groups like the Barelvis, mainstream Sunni Muslims who derive their name from their leader Ahmad Riza Khan of Bareilly, India, see the Prophet as almost semi-divine, present everywhere and not made of flesh. Ahmad Khan stressed the Sufi concept of the 'light' of the Prophet (*Nur-i-Muhammadi*) which came from God's own light and existed from the beginning of creation. Similarly, among the Shias with their great emphasis on the genealogy of the Imams (the leaders of the age, directly traced to the Prophet), the position of the Prophet is supreme. Neither of these philosophies prevails in quite the same fashion in the Arab world. So although there was a reaction against what was said in the book it was not as intense, emotional or personal as the reactions among South Asians and Iranians.

Arab writers Muslim themselves detect a subtle difference in the response to the novel between South Asian Muslims and Arab Muslims:

> *The influence of the 'Asian' branch of Islam was illustrated during the row over Salman Rushdie's novel* The Satanic Verses. *The Muslim minority in Britain is mainly of Asian origin, and it was they who initiated questions which were put to Ayatollah Khomeini at a prayer meeting early in 1989. Khomeini originally spoke in general terms in response to a question which did not specify Rushdie by name. He was asked whether an apostate should be killed, and confirmed that this was so. Later he was reported as having spoken in more explicit terms which were interpreted, mainly by Muslims outside the Arab world, as an order to kill Rushdie. The 'fatwa' was not taken up or repeated by Islamic authorities in the Arab world, although Rushdie's book was condemned in the Arab press. Huge demonstrations against* The Satanic Verses *and its author were held in Islamabad, Karachi, Tehran and Dhaka, but much less interest was shown in Cairo, Damascus and Riyadh.*
> (Heikal 1992: 62–3)

Late in 1992 the Rushdie affair flared up again. The foundation in Iran which had offered 'bounty money' to anyone who would implement the death sentence increased the sum. Although the foundation is not an official government body, this caused an international hue and cry against Iran.

For people in the West, the main scandal was the fact that the *fatwa* appeared to be an actual death sentence imposed on Rushdie by the government of a nation of which Rushdie was not a citizen. In other words, Islamic law was being applied to someone not living in an Islamic state, the *fatwa* was equivalent to a death sentence on Rushdie wherever he lived or travelled, and Muslims were more or less being commanded to kill him. Salman Rushdie has wide public support in the West, not just from people who are prejudiced against Muslims, but from those who are generally tolerant towards Muslims but who do not accept that the Islamic law of a Muslim theocracy should be applied outside that country. Thus the possibility that Rushdie might never again be able to visit a Muslim nation is not the main objection; the fact that he lives under the threat of death in a Western country – whether the UK, the USA or Germany – is generally opposed on the grounds that only the law of the land should be applicable there.

Both Muslims and non–Muslims continued to misunderstand the opposite point of view. Muslims never appreciated how deeply the death threat to the author and the burning of his book offended the West, that these revived memories of Nazi Germany. After all, the core of Western civilization rested on notions of free speech and freedom; for many in the West, Muslims appeared to threaten all this. The secular West, on the other hand, did not appreciate the respect religious societies accord to their revered figures.

INDIA AND THE CREATION OF PAKISTAN AND BANGLADESH

The story of the Muslims of South Asia is the attempt to maintain, or define, Muslim identity in the face of an established majority culture, namely Hinduism. Accommodation and confrontation – rarely indifference – mark the historical relationship between Islam and Hinduism. This has been the central obsession of South Asia up to the present day, and it reflects the confrontation between India and Pakistan. It can be said to throw light on a number of contemporary issues including the nuclear programmes of India and Pakistan, the present uprising in Kashmir, the Hindu campaign to demolish Babar's mosque in Ayodhya in order to build a temple to Lord Ram on the site, and the eternal, bloody communal killing in India.

We need to go back a few centuries to trace the origins of the movement for Muslim separatism which grew into the demand for Pakistan. The eighteenth century saw the disintegration of the Mughal empire; old clients (like Hyderabad in the south) declared independence, while new powers (like the Marathas in the west) emerged. More important was the arrival of the Europeans. Slowly and steadily the British gained ground over the other Europeans. Establishing forts and annexing territory, by the early nineteenth century they were poised to declare their supremacy. With the final collapse of the Mughal dynasty in the mid-nineteenth century Muslims woke to a new and shattering reality.

Mughal authority and influence had been irreversibly declining over the course of the eighteenth century as the other power groups emerged. By the nineteenth century the emperor was a mere shadow of his illustrious ancestors, his authority confined to Delhi itself. None the less the person of the Mughal emperor and his capital, Delhi, with its court and rituals, provided important symbols of Muslim rule; they meant continuity, a legitimate reminder of imperial greatness. Politically impotent, the court channelled its energies into fostering one of the most glittering periods of Urdu literature. Ghalib, Momin and Zauq recited their poems for the last Mughal emperor, Zafar, who himself was a noted Urdu poet. But these props were an illusion and the awakening would be a bitter one.

After the abortive uprisings of 1857–8 (or what is known as the Indian Mutiny in British history books) the Muslims were transformed from the ruling élite of India to a subordinate group deprived of power. They were viewed with suspicion by the British for their leading role in the revolt. This was the nadir of their fortunes. In 1857 at one stroke Muslims lost a capital, an empire and an emperor.

1857 and the birth of Aligarh

For the Muslims of India, 1857–8 was a major turning point in history. Delhi was almost razed to the ground. The Red Fort and the Juma mosque, the two central symbols of Muslim rule, were almost blown up. To be Muslim was to be an enemy of the victors, the British. Sir Sayyed Ahmad Khan reacted as the Japanese did after the Second World War: he would admire the conquerors racially and culturally and be as much like them as possible. Critics would accuse him of cultural sycophancy.

But his ideas produced the college at Aligarh. Its very name suggested the synthesis Sir Sayyed had in mind – the Mohammadan Anglo-Oriental College (later upgraded to a university). Its Anglo-Muslim architecture reflected his position. The main buildings, the clock tower, the cricket fields were nineteenth-century ideas of English architecture and their alliance with a Muslim one. But Aligarh started something important.

Aligarh would be the Muslim answer to modernity; a universal Muslim response to the changing times (although not all its students were Muslims). It gave Muslims a sense of direction and confidence. To say that you had been to Aligarh was to declare your credentials. It also provided a focus for Muslims all over the sub-continent. From Quetta at one end of India to Dacca at the other, Muslims came to study here; this forged a sense of brotherhood, of nationhood. It produced those Muslims who would eventually lead the community to Pakistan. Indeed it was, in the end, like a Who's Who of South Asia, having produced at least half a dozen presidents and prime ministers.

The emblem of Aligarh expressed its Islamic stance. In the centre stood a date palm (recall the Prophet's saying about the tree, in chapter 3), on the right the book of learning – no doubt the Quran – and on the left a crescent, symbol of Islam. Now it seems oddly out of tune with the Indian times, in the heart of Hinduism, which is undergoing a massive cultural and religious revival with a focus of hatred on the Muslims. Murderous riots recently in Aligarh saw Muslim women and children being burnt alive.

Sir Sayyed was not alone, nor the first, in arguing that Hindus and Muslims formed separate and distinct nations in India on the basis of different cultures and religions. But he had shifted from an earlier position of accommodation with Hindus.

The struggle for Muslim self-identity and expression was slow in starting. Muslims appeared dazed, and lost in the last century; too much was happening too fast; the world was changing and they were out of step. From the total collapse of the Mughals in the mid-nineteenth century to the creation of Pakistan in the mid-twentieth century lies a period of Muslim struggle for identity. It would eventually take the shape of the demand for the creation of a separate Muslim homeland, a land of the pure or *pak*, a Pakistan.

From the beginning the Congress Party had failed to broaden its appeal to Muslim opinion. Muslims comprised about a quarter of the population of India but only 10 per cent of Congress delegates in 1899 were Muslim. This further shrank, as Muslims suspected that the aim of the Congress was simply to replace the British Raj with a Hindu Raj. Early this century a group of prominent Muslims created the All-India Muslim League. This formally ended Congress hopes of representing both Hindus and Muslims. But it was not until a few decades later that, under the leadership of Mr Jinnah, the trickle of Muslim separatism became a flood.

Mr Jinnah: the Quaid-i-Azam of Pakistan

For the Muslims of Pakistan Mr Jinnah is the Quaid-i-Azam or great leader. A successful Westernized lawyer, wearing Savile Row suits and a monocle, Mr Jinnah first supported synthesis with other communities. Indeed, he was called the ambassador of Hindu–Muslim unity. But then, disillusioned with the Congress, he became the champion of the Muslim cause. Taking on both the Indian Congress and the British, he led them successfully to the creation of Pakistan in 1947. Pakistan was created in two halves, East and West Pakistan, separated by a thousand miles of a not always friendly India. Like many Muslims he was not happy with the Pakistan he got; 'moth-eaten' and 'truncated', he called it. But he knew it was better than none at all.

However Westernized and liberal Mr Jinnah may have been, when he led the Muslim League, his emotions and thinking reflected broad Muslim sentiment. Again and again Mr Jinnah's sentiments would echo the need to champion the Muslim cause: 'I will never allow Muslims to become slaves of Hindus.' He was emerging as a modern Saladin, but a Saladin speaking the King's English.

Championing the Muslims did not mean he was a religious bigot. The opposite was true. For example, his staff always had Hindus on it. After becoming the first Governor-General of Pakistan he rushed to the site of a Hindu–Muslim clash in Karachi and announced to the press: 'I am going to constitute myself the Protector-General of the Hindu minority in Pakistan' (Gandhi 1986: 178).

What has always impressed me about the Quaid is his acknowledged integrity. It is a quality not always found in politicians. There is a story about Mr Jinnah that sums up this integrity.

The Quaid's main lieutenant had managed to secure copies of a batch of personal letters that had passed between Lady Mountbatten, the viceroy's wife, and Nehru, the leader of the Indian Congress. In a private meeting the letters were handed to the Quaid. The lieutenant was jubilant, declaring that the next morning they would print the letters on the front pages of the party newspapers. Other lieutenants joined in, saying it would finish Nehru and expose him as a playboy mixing politics and passion, and that the letters would expose both their adversaries, the British and the Congress.

But the Quaid took the letters, put them in a drawer and locked it. This was not his kind of politics, he said; they would fight on principles, not with underhand tactics.

Leading a Muslim movement
Mr Jinnah, rigid, even inflexible in his demand for Pakistan, would be prepared even to change his lifestyle if it pleased his followers. He gave up his English suits, a habit of a lifetime, and adopted the *sherwani*, *shalwar* and *karakul* cap. Although the dress was an amalgam of various cultural streams, in part reflecting one ethnic group, in part another, it became the national dress of Pakistan. Cynics may dismiss these gestures by Mr Jinnah and say this conversion came too late in life to be sincere, but we must place it in

context. So great was his influence over his followers, so powerful his charisma that he need not have made these gestures. That he did so reflects his desire to create a more authentic identity, one that would drive Muslims towards discovering their roots, one that would be more indigenous and more true.

It is also significant that, however Westernized he was, when his only daughter wished to marry a non-Muslim all hell broke loose. He never forgave her for that act. In the recesses of this seemingly Westernized lawyer there were deep wells of traditional feelings, which towards the end of his life began to express themselves more and more openly, challenging all that he had stood for as a younger man.

The desire for synthesis and integration that he once believed in was refuted at the end of his life. He had come to the conclusion that the only way ahead was the path of separation for Muslims. He may not have wished for a theocratic or religious state but he certainly wished for a separate homeland for Muslims where they would be able to preserve their culture and identity.

Mr Jinnah led the Muslim League to the creation of Pakistan; and he led it skilfully and successfully. But he was representing a movement that had begun almost a century ago and was evident in the writings of Sir Sayyed Ahmad Khan. Sir Sayyed's discussion of two distinct communities in India, both needing to live in harmony but as separate entities, had already laid down the map for a separate polity. This argument was substantiated and fed by subsequent ones. And it culminated in the poetic vision of Iqbal of a distinct geographical area for the Muslims of North India. Chaudhri Rahmat Ali in Cambridge gave the name Pakistan to the area (each letter of the alphabet represents a distinct Muslim area – thus P for Punjab and so on; as we know, it also means the land of the 'pure' from *pak*). Mr Jinnah, then, was voicing the sentiment of Muslims, not creating it. To see him as the Pied Piper who mesmerized his followers and led them to Pakistan is incorrect.

The Partition of India in 1947

Even Iqbal the visionary poet or Jinnah the humanist could not have envisaged the extent of disruption at the Partition of India. The massacre, uprooting and migration were unprecedented. It has been estimated that about one million people were killed and ten million migrated from their homes, Muslims fleeing to Pakistan, Hindus to India. But not all Muslims in India could or indeed wished to migrate to Pakistan; these remained in India (and will be discussed in chapter 5).

A communal madness seems to have gripped the land in 1947. It appeared that centuries of fear and hatred that had been suppressed and buried by the British presence now exploded into savagery. No one was spared – young or old, male or female, high or low (for graphic accounts of the violence, see Chaudhuri 1990; Singh 1988).

The events of Partition still haunt South Asia: for India the nightmare of disintegration; for Pakistan the terror of the violence inflicted by the majority. This mutual hatred still feeds into the complex political configuration of contemporary India and Pakistan. India's nuclear programme, and Pakistan's desire to develop one, the struggle for independence among the Muslims of Kashmir, the maintenance of large armies by both countries and the geo-politics of the region all reflect the perceived threat that is rooted in history. The crisis of identity among South Asian Muslims still awaits resolution.

Nuclear weapons on the one hand and starving peasants on the other: this is the reality of South Asia today. At the cost of keeping one-fifth of humanity firmly in poverty (incomes per capita range between $200 and $400 in these countries), the region continues to maintain huge armies. South Asia has produced world scientists and writers – indeed even Nobel Prize winners – and yet cannot better its pathetic record on poverty and peace because of the expenditures on defence. The neurosis, suspicion and short-sightedness of dealing with the 'enemy' are thus explained.

So overriding is the horror of Partition that Indian intellectuals refuse to use the word 'religion' and instead use the word 'communal' as a code for Hindu–Muslim clashes. When we read in the press that communal violence takes ten or twenty lives it is difficult to tell whether they are Hindu or Muslim. Another code word is 'secular'. On one level, it means simply belief in the dominant Congress Party as representing a way of life. On another level, it means modernity and distance from religion and tradition. In the subtext in India, 'secular' means Congress; 'religious' or 'communal' means the BJP (Bharatiya Janata Party).

The problem of identity

Although the creation of Pakistan had solved one problem, that of establishing a separate homeland for Muslims, it did not solve the problem of identity. The debate about identity within Pakistan ensured stormy and unsettled politics; periods of martial law were almost inevitable. Corruption and nepotism were also widespread. Bengalis in East Pakistan complained of being treated like colonial subjects by West Pakistanis and in 1971, helped by

Pakistan's war with India, broke away creating the nation of Bangladesh (as we see below). After 1971 what remained of Pakistan was plunged more directly than ever before in attempts to resolve the dilemma of identity. Mr Bhutto (and later his daughter Benazir) wished for a democratic, Westernized Pakistan, General Zia ul-Haq for an Islamic one.

There have been gains. The number of universities and medical colleges has increased enormously. Agriculture and the textile industry have shown remarkable development. Income per capita has risen to twice that of India. The Soviet invasion of Afghanistan allowed Pakistan in the 1980s to play a major role in the region. Pakistan's self-conscious Islamic posture allowed it an important voice in the Muslim club of nations.

Yet Pakistan's population of almost 110 million people has begun the 1990s with uncertainty. Ethnic tensions, breakdown of law and order and an unpredictable international climate after the collapse of the Soviet Union create problems for Pakistan. In this bleak situation national unity is being encouraged from an unexpected quarter. India is perceived as threatening and aggressive. India and Pakistan have so far fought three wars. The rise of the communal BJP in India and its campaigns such as the one to destroy Babar's mosque at Ayodhya confirm in Pakistani minds their worst fears of Hindu domination; in retrospect the orthodox Aurangzeb, not the tolerant Akbar, is vindicated. The BJP recognize this, almost as in a mirror, and have a contemptuous title for the Muslims of India: *Aurangzeb ki aulad*, 'the children of Aurangzeb'.

Despite all its problems, however, Pakistan has tenaciously kept to the democratic path. In 1988, when General Zia ul-Haq was killed, many people thought martial law would be declared. It was not. In the elections later in the year General Zia's rival, Benazir Bhutto, came to power.

Pakistan is more than a country; it is also an idea, a cultural expression of identity. It is architecture, language, dress and food. It is a link in the chain that takes Muslims back to the past. When the critics of Pakistan cried jubilantly in 1971, 'Pakistan is dead', they were wrong. It is very much alive both on the ground and in the minds of Muslims.

A school in Pakistan today
When I recently visited my old school, Burn Hall, in Abbottabad, Pakistan, little had changed on the surface. The grounds, the buildings, even some of the staff were the same. The boys were wearing the old school uniform, ties and blazers and appeared sure of themselves. But I discovered an unhappiness and uncertainty among them. They complained about their courses,

their books and the shortage of facilities. In particular they complained about low standards. Some of this is the usual moaning of schoolboys to a sympathetic ear, some requires attention.

Faced with this rather gloomy picture we may ask: why has the Muslim world failed to produce great scholarship and great literature recently? The fact is that books and authors exist in a particular social, intellectual and cultural milieu. They are not isolated from their environment. Libraries, intellectual circles, trade journals, publishing houses and critical reviews nourish them. This structure is largely missing in the Muslim world – although parts of it may be found in some cities like Cairo and Karachi. Today bureaucratic interference, political pressure, the materialist milieu and local jealousies ensure that the author remains stunted or frustrated. The wonder is not why great works of literature have not been written in recent years but that even the second-rate stuff continues to be produced.

In my schooldays the more academic students took the Senior Cambridge exam which was marked in England, while the less academic ones were asked to do the Matriculation, which is a Pakistani exam. Today the two are equated for purposes of promotion, and boys often prefer to do the Matriculation and save a few years. Besides it is much easier to pass.

Two intellectual traditions appear to be developing in Muslim societies: one working in English with an international network and standards in mind; the other local, temporary and with an immediate social and political aim. Both traditions appear to exist separately from one another, rarely feeding or interacting with each other. The former is limited, often on the defensive and in danger of dying. The latter thrives and flourishes. Indeed, its very life-blood is the younger generation of restive, enquiring, intensely patriotic Muslims. Their sense of identity is further reinforced by what they read in the vernacular journals. Indeed there is a perverse pride in rejecting English as a language of the West and a falling back on the local language as an assertion of identity. The rupture does not bode well for those who seek harmony and dialogue.

Pakistan and the birth of Bangladesh
Pakistan does not represent South Asian Muslims alone: there are more Muslims in India and there is also a third great concentration of Muslims in Bangladesh. There are somewhere around 100 to 110 million Muslims in each of these countries and together they constitute about one third of the world's Muslim population. But such statistics are intelligent estimates, little more.

Pakistan and Bangladesh were one until 1971 when the Bengalis of East Pakistan split away to form Bangladesh. Earlier this century the Bengali leadership had enthusiastically embraced the idea of a separate land for the Muslims. But once Pakistan was created Bengalis felt, rightly, that although they had the majority population they were bullied and pushed aside by the more dominant West Pakistanis. Most importantly, the West Pakistanis controlled the two key instruments of government, the civil service and the army. The political and cultural feelings of alienation developed into an irresistible ethnic movement for independence which was given its final shape in 1971 when the mainly West Pakistani army posted in East Pakistan attempted to control that province by force. Atrocities were committed, as West Pakistani soldiers attempted to suppress the Bengali uprising, and as Bengalis sought revenge on West Pakistanis where they could find them or their allies the Biharis (mainly non-Bengali-speaking refugees from India). An adverse international public opinion against Pakistan was thus created. India was actively involved in the developments, and the war it fought with Pakistan towards the end of the year ensured that East Pakistan was quickly recognized as a separate and independent country.

Although Bengalis shared Islam with West Pakistan they looked to Calcutta for their poetry and literature. Their ideas were laced with the intellectual arguments emanating from the coffee-shops and salons of Calcutta. They were a quick-witted and gifted people, eager to embrace democracy. They were also far more aware politically than the people of West Pakistan, who until then were largely led by feudal lords in the Sind and Punjab and tribal chiefs in the Frontier province and Baluchistan. West Pakistan would begin to shake off this feudal and tribal way of thinking only a generation later.

However, the relationship between India and Bangladesh soon soured and it now veers between being formally correct and overtly hostile. Matters are made complicated for Bangladesh because its population of about 110 million has a Hindu population of about 10 to 12 per cent. Riots against Muslims in India inevitably create anger in Bangladesh against Hindus. The cultural and political arguments that had led to the creation of Pakistan have not entirely disappeared. Indeed there is increasing talk of closer ties with Pakistan. But the creation of Bangladesh ensured that the Muslims of South Asia would now be divided into three distinct bodies increasingly isolated from one another. Yet each one is aware of the mutual predicament of living in South Asia with and in the presence of a far larger majority, that of the Hindus concentrated in India.

ISSUES IN MODERNITY: DEMOCRACY, FAMILY AND IDENTITY

What constantly struck me as I travelled in the Muslim world and heard the debate and saw the dilemmas was how eternal and recognizable were the themes that engaged the earlier Muslim thinkers like Abduh and Iqbal. The issues they raised, the conflicts they identified, the boundaries they wished to draw around Muslim identity found an echo in my own time. Despite changes in the political and cultural context the call for Islam's reawakening, the threat from the West, the dangers of materialism still marked the parameters of the debate. We have heard some of it in Turkey, Iran and Pakistan; let us hear it in the Muslim heartland, the land of the Arabs.

The Arab predicament

In the world media Arabs are often depicted as xenophobic, quarrelsome and out of step with the times. Their leaders are shown as either tyrannical dictators or pleasure-loving princes. Here is a mass of people – about 200 million – possessing some twenty countries stretching from Morocco, across North Africa, the Middle East and the Arabian peninsula and up to the borders of Iran. The area contains vast natural resources; the people for the most part speak one language and follow one religion. Yet there is little unity among them and the range of political leadership is bewildering: from benign kings to ruthless Stalinist dictators. Although from the outside the Arab world may seem a monolith, in fact there are notable differences among them in behaviour, organization and values; indeed, even the notion of all Arabs being Muslims is incorrect, since there are large non-Muslim communities, like the Christians.

To understand the Arab predicament we need to appreciate the factors that explain their complex history and society. The most important explanation is provided by Arab history itself. For Arabs their history means Arab culture, tradition, language and, above all, religion. It is one of the richest cultural traditions of the world and the Arabs are justly proud of it. It allows them a sense of self, of worth, of pride. But the splendour of the past contrasts with the reality of today. The memory of past greatness thus both acts as a haunting dream to inspire Arabs and creates a haunting crisis in society, provoking demands for change and true identity.

Another explanation of the Arab predicament comes from the effects of colonization, first by the Ottomans and then by the Europeans. After the First World War, Britain, France and Italy divided the Arab lands. Then, after the Second World War, the Europeans left behind artificial states and boundaries, often cutting tribes and nations in two. Arabs therefore dream of a united Arab nation stretching from Morocco to Iraq: one language, one culture, one religion.

Many Arabs complain today that although they are ostensibly free their societies are still in bondage to Western imperialism – whether political or cultural. Their rulers, they say, depend on the West for support and, in return, give away rights to natural resources or military bases. From this historical background emerges a major factor causing anguish and anger among Arabs: the creation of Israel after the Second World War. This episode of history is painful to Arabs, for it reflects their impotence and injures their pride.

The creation of Israel

The Arabs argue that Israel was created and is sustained by the West to keep them weak and divided. Israelis' perception of Arabs as impoverished, powerless and backward acts as a cultural challenge. The loss of territory and the routine humiliation of the Palestinians (which over the last few years has won them some international sympathy) was bad enough but the loss of Jerusalem, or Al-Quds, one of Islam's three holiest places, was shocking not only for Arabs but all Muslims everywhere.

Al-Quds is one of the most powerful and recognizable symbols throughout the Muslim world. I saw a replica of its central symbol, the Dome of the Rock, in the office of the Sheikh of Al-Azhar in Cairo; I saw it in the large paintings on office blocks in Tehran with Imam Khomeini exhorting people to support its liberation, and it appears on the 1000-rial Iranian note (a main square in Tehran is also named Al-Quds); I saw it as a poster in the basement room of the cook in the residence of the Pakistani ambassador in Moscow with the Quranic verse promising that victory is at hand: *Nasrun-minallah Fateh-un-Karib*. There are regular rallies protesting against the loss of Al-Quds throughout the Muslim world, from Nigeria to Pakistan.

The holy sites of Al-Quds are effectively out of bounds for the Muslims of the world. In October 1992, as I stood on the small ramshackle Bailey bridge, alongside the destroyed Allenby bridge, over the river Jordan, the main land entry to Israel, I thought of Al-Quds less than an hour away; but I could not visit it. I felt the same sense of injustice and frustration that millions of Muslims feel.

With Israel came cultural, intellectual and political ideas that were alien to the Arabs. So Israel represented more than a military threat. It is this complex hatred among the Arabs that explains their rallying behind any Arab leader who is prepared to stand up to Israel and the West, and the two are seen as interchangeable. A generation ago Nasser symbolized the Arab challenge; in the 1990s it was Saddam Hussein.

With regard to the contemporary relationship between Muslims and Jews as a consequence of the creation of Israel, Muslims are often accused of being inherently anti-Judaism, anti-Semitic and anti-Zionist. This is incorrect.

The roots of prejudice against the Jewish people are complex and originate from different sources: prejudice can be religious, that is anti-Judaism; it can be racist, that is anti-Semitism; and it can be political, that is anti-Zionism. Prejudice may combine all three types, but prejudice of one type does not automatically subsume the other two; for instance, those who oppose the political philosophy of Zionism do not necessarily have to be either anti-Judaism or anti-Semitic.

By definition Muslims cannot be anti-Judaism. Whatever internal differences with Judaism, it is part and parcel of the Islamic cultural and ideological tradition. Jews are very much 'people of the Book'. Culturally the affiliation is evident in the Judaic names which are common among Muslims such as Musa (Moses) or Ishaq (Isaac), the name of the current President of Pakistan.

Similarly Muslims cannot be anti-Semitic because the original Muslims, the Arabs, were themselves Semites. Anti-Zionism is a different matter. Zionism, politically organized in modern Europe, was basically alien, a foreign import, to the Middle East. The differences in the two, European Zionists and Middle Eastern Arabs, are brought out in this illuminating analysis by a Jewish writer:

> The European Jews who built Israel came out of a culture of sharp edges and right angles. They were cold, hard men who always understood the difference between success and failure, and between words and deeds. Because the Jews were always a nation apart, they developed their own autonomous institutions and had to rely on their own deep tribal sense of solidarity. This gave them a certain single-mindedness of purpose. (Friedman 1990: 126)

He contrasts the Arabs:

> The rhythm of life in the Arab world was always different. Men in Arab societies always tended to bend more; life there always moved in ambiguous semicircles, never right angles . . . In Arab society there was always some way to cushion failure with rhetoric and enable the worst of enemies to sit down and have coffee together, maybe even send each other bouquets.

16 Reading the Quran in a mosque in Lahore in Pakistan.

17 The Youth Memorial on the seafront at Marmaris in south-western
Turkey. Kemal Ataturk leads two young people who are dressed
Western-style in short skirt and shorts.

Right 18 Painting of Mr Jinnah, the Quaid-i-Azam or great leader of the
people of Pakistan, which hangs in the National Assembly, Islamabad.

19 Uncle Sam – a street mural in Tehran, Iran.

Right 20 Anti-American demonstration in Tehran on the anniversary of the occupation of the US Embassy in 1979.

22 Feeding the poor during
Ramadan in Cairo.

Left 23 Jordanian students at
Amman University wearing
traditional head-dress.

Opposite 21 A Muslim praying
in Sakkara, Egypt.

24 The Dome of the Rock (left), the earliest Islamic monument, and the Al–Aqsa mosque (right), built soon after, in Jerusalem, both among the holiest places of Islam. In the foreground is the Wailing Wall.

26 Muslims in Bradford in the north of England.

Left 25 Women arriving at the Regent's Park mosque in London for *eid* prayers.

27 Studying the Quran in a Quranic school in Uzbekistan. Throughout the
new Central Asian republics Islam is being rediscovered.

Right 28 The Sher Dar *madrassah*, built in the first half of the seventeenth
century, in Registan Square, Samarkand.

29 A young Palestinian in Ramallah in the West Bank, during the *intifada*, the Palestinian uprising which began in 1987 in protest at the Israeli occupation.

Right 30 *Mujahidin* guarding positions in Kabul, Afghanistan, after their victory in the war.

31 Demonstrators in Amman after the Gulf War cease-fire.

It was natural, therefore, that 'The Arabs, for the Zionists, fell into two subsets of goyim – agents and enemies. Agents you ordered and enemies you killed' (Friedman 1990: 127).

The success of Zionism in creating Israel complicates matters for Muslims. The loss of land for the Palestinians and the loss of the holy places in Jerusalem are viewed with a sense of injustice and anger among Muslims. In the rhetoric of confrontation, many themselves blur the distinctions between anti-Judaism, anti-Semitism and anti-Zionism. Such Muslims thus make the mistake they accuse others of making about them – seeing all Jews as homogeneous, monolithic and threatening.

The people of the Middle East – Muslims, Jews, Christians and others – need to find a way of living peacefully together; the violence and hatred must end if the next century is to be one of peace in the region.

Tensions in Arab society

The wide disparity in income and lifestyle between the ruling élite and the rest of the population is another factor that causes tension in Arab society. The view from the balcony of the Rameses Hilton out over the Nile is a reflection not only of Egyptian society but of many Muslim cities today. The pleasure boats, the tourists, the island of Gezira with its club and racecourse, the high-rise hotels and Nasser's tower, built opposite the American embassy, are impressive signs of modernity. Far in the distance, but visible on a clear day when the smog and pollution allow, are the pyramids. What is missing is the Islamic skyline; no domes or minarets. In the other direction one can just see the shanty towns, the squatters, the favelas. These live cheek by jowl with the rich, the opulent and the corrupt.

A few decades ago, Nasser talked of three concentric circles that provide the Egyptian identity: Arabian, African and Islamic. Today the West has penetrated and scrambled the circles. Egyptians may say they hate the West because of its imperialism, in particular Britain and France, but they are also fascinated by it. Education at the American University in Cairo is seen as a right step in the marriage market. Young men wear jeans and American consumerism is the rage among the middle class. Nasser's circles today would be replaced by two opposed positions: Islam and the West.

From the 1970s onwards a combination of factors have fed into an Islamic revivalism: the success of Sadat's October war against the Israelis in 1973; the use of oil as a weapon by King Faisal of Saudi Arabia; the general resurgence of Islam – the triumph of Imam Khomeini in Iran and General Zia's Islamization programme in Pakistan. Henceforth Islam was to become increasingly a force in Arab politics. Islam meant cultural identity and pride; it also meant social and moral purity in a world seen as corrupted by the West. Furthermore, it was a local native response to organizing and living in the world, not something imported from Moscow or Washington. But Islam would not have an easy run; Muslim activists would be killed and jailed and tortured in their thousands. Their legitimate participation in elections would be frustrated and their aims deliberately distorted in order to misinform people. The struggle is far from over (see below, for instance the Algerian experience).

Problems of democracy

There is a debate raging in Muslim society which attracts adverse publicity in the West because it touches on one of the most cherished Western notions, the idea and practice of democracy. When a Muslim leader like General Zia ul-Haq of Pakistan says that Islam does not believe in democracy he conveys the idea to the world that Islam is a religion of dictatorship and military rulers.

Yet the egalitarianism in Islam is more pronounced than in any other religion in the world. There are no caste systems, no priests, no differences between rich and poor in Islam. This is best seen at prayer-time when Muslims stand shoulder to shoulder in the mosque. In their anonymity they are one. In numerous ways the Prophet emphasized that all human beings – men and women, rich and poor, black and white, Arab and non-Arab – are equal before God.

None the less General Zia was right in one sense when he said Islam has serious reservations about democracy in the manner it is practised. The experiments with democracy in Muslim lands have not been a success. Dynasties, corruption and nepotism often accompanied the so-called democratic leader. Democracy is far from perfect even in the West. It grants concentrated powers to one man in America who then, however good or indifferent, has the capacity to obliterate life on earth. In its European variety it can allow a minority once elected into government to rule a majority for decades (the example that springs to mind is that of the Tory Party in the UK which has only 40 per cent of the electorate supporting it). None the less there is no better way of conducting affairs in our times. So, while the old structures in the West, whether feudal or monarchic, have now been replaced by a democracy in which individuals have – or at least appear to have – control over their votes, this is not so in Muslim countries.

While Muslim countries are generally if erratically moving towards the acceptance of the notion of democracy, or some form of controlled democracy, the old structures – feudal or tribal or monarchic – continue to remain in place. True democracy cannot function with such structures constantly interfering and subverting it. On the surface there may be democracy but in practice it is another form of tribalism in one place, feudalism in another. Democracy in a country like Pakistan means that the tribal chief or his son will win the elections in Baluchistan and the feudal lord will invariably do so in the interior of Sind. Little has changed except the terminology of democracy as a figleaf; it ensures a greater tyranny of the traditional structures over the less privileged. It is a halfway house, neither quite traditional nor quite modern.

Traditional structure, although it had many faults, none the less provided two or three crucial elements which helped give stability to society. It provided an equilibrium and a source of patronage. Strong chiefs often acted with a sense of responsibility towards the people. This was paternalism, but it did not lack compassion; honour and reputation were involved. It also represented the continuity of custom and history. It helped to keep in check many of the elements that would plague modern Muslim societies, such as dacoity (gang robbery with violence), rape and ethnic conflict. Finally, it gave the individual a sense of identity. Even those who did not belong to the dominant classes knew what their universe was, who they were, where they came from. People felt secure in a kind of static, unchanging manner. Doors were closed but life was not unbearably uncomfortable.

In the present situation Muslim societies find themselves in a quandary. They cannot fully convert to the democratic process without jettisoning traditional structures. Too much democracy would mean a straight plunge into anarchy for some states which are still evolving and whose borders are still flexible. Internal groups demand autonomy and sometimes secession; external enemies cast covetous eyes on chunks of territory. Powerful factions would not think twice before changing their masks and creating fresh disturbances to further their own ends.

An example of this comes from Pakistan. The first free election in the history of Pakistan in 1970 resulted directly in the break-up of the country. Bengalis had formed a majority, about 55 per cent of the population, but they lacked power in the civil service and army, which were dominated by West Pakistanis. In 1970 the Bengalis voted for Sheikh Mujeeb-ur-Rahman's Awami Party which was flirting with ideas of autonomy bordering on secession. Once it was clear that he would have the majority in parliament, the road was open for a declaration of independence, and the separate state of

Bangladesh was formed. It is little wonder that rulers in developing countries would prefer to keep the lid on democratic activity rather than risk political changes which may be catastrophic for the nation.

Another example is taken from India, which has, by and large, a comparatively satisfactory record of conducting democratic elections. However, elections in Kashmir have been constantly postponed. The United Nations resolutions that Kashmiris be allowed to vote in a plebiscite for their future, as promised after the clashes in 1947–8, have been flouted by the Indian government. The reasons are the same. Political analysts suggest that if allowed a free vote Kashmiris would clearly voice their disenchantment with India and might opt for either Pakistan or even complete independence. This could result in communal violence and jeopardize the safety of Muslims in the rest of India. In addition, Kashmir has a strong economy and internationally recognized geographical and political significance. Other groups, like the Sikhs, also test India's democratic will. So rulers in developing societies remain uncertain about how to cope with democracy.

However, tyranny and injustice cannot be imposed on one people on the grounds that democratic change may affect another people elsewhere. The answer is to find solutions for the people of Kashmir and those elsewhere in India without which democracy is an incomplete system. In the absence of any solution, unimaginative bureaucrats impose harsh, authoritarian rule over Kashmir. Greater hatred is created and feeds into the cycle of violence.

Democracy and double standards: the case of Algeria

Recent events in Algeria have highlighted further problems for Muslim societies moving towards democracy. With a population of 25 million Algeria is no marginal country, no newly emerged Muslim state. Algeria is one of the leaders of the Third World, one of the earliest to win independence. It emerged trailing clouds of glory for its heroic struggle against France's colonial rule in which countless Algerians suffered. Algeria led by the FLN (National Liberation Front) was set on the path to democracy and modern statehood. It then slowly sank into a morass of corruption and stagnation. The world forgot Algeria.

Then, suddenly, because of the stories of Islamic resurgence, Algeria was in the news again. The Western media were alarmed: here was another potential Iran; they looked for another Ayatollah Khomeini. Once again, not understanding the sectarian or social structures that make such comparisons so invalid, Western commentators waited for the Islamic revolution. It came in the form of the victory for the FIS (Islamic Salvation Front) in the elections.

Now the West was put to the test. What would its attitude be? Would it wait and give the FIS a chance to run things in the way it wished? Or would it be pleased if the FIS was frustrated and power denied? For better or worse the FIS was poised to win the election and take power. At this juncture the elections were postponed and the military moved its tanks into the streets. It was an old ploy.

In the event, when the army prevented the FIS from taking power and the tanks rolled into the streets, the West was jubilant. The beatings and killings, even in the mosques, the arrests and harassment did not appear to dim Western joy. The main news was that another Islamic movement had been stopped. There were no tears for the death of democracy.

Muslims were appalled at the double standards of the West. Had there been a similar military action, say in Pakistan, the Western media would have become hysterical with stories of the tyranny of martial law. They would have paraded the old arguments about the death of democracy in Muslim society, the inherent predilection of Muslims for authoritarian rule. But here was a situation where the West was gloating over the denial of power to the duly elected FIS. The double standards cause Muslims to ask, 'Why is the West constantly hostile to us?' They point to Algeria. If Algeria is not so far inclined to an extreme Islamic position – for all kinds of social and sectarian reasons – this manner of negative Western response will provoke a virulently anti-West position.

Certain facts need to be considered in the Algerian situation. Algeria is not Iran. The FIS has not swept to power in revolutionary blood and neither is its rhetoric fired by anti-Western sentiment. Indeed its leaders talk in conciliatory terms of encouraging Western investments and maintaining close contacts with the European Community. Overwhelmingly, FIS supporters are young people angered by the corruption of the fossilized FLN and its failure to tackle the rising unemployment, poor economic growth and acute housing shortage.

The victory of the FIS must also be seen in the context of North Africa. The victory has repercussions in neighbouring Morocco and Tunisia. It has decisively ended the dominance of post-colonial politics. It has declared the Islamic message to North Africa and served notice to its rulers.

The hostility of the European countries does not help the situation. For instance, France, which has so many Algerians in its southern towns, was particularly alarmed at the emergence of the FIS. Immediately questions were thrown up about the future of Algeria: What will happen to the bars? Will alcohol be banned? What about the discos? Many Frenchmen played the immigration card, and raised the alarm about the possibility of being swamped by 'fundamentalists' in the future and argued vigorously for the closing of borders. But there was little sympathy for and little understanding of what was actually happening on the ground. It was once again clear that the gaps between Islam and the West remained wide.

The centralized state

One of the main causes of the failure of democracy in the Muslim world is the recently formed state which in most African and Asian countries is insecure and tends towards centralization. It uses the weapons of the police and the army to suppress any dissidence. Lacking in imagination, vision, humour and warmth, it rapidly alienates itself from the people. We note the paradox: the conversion of a generally contented though impoverished populace at the time of independence to disillusioned mobs breaking the law and resorting to violence. Worst of all, the centralized state robs the individual of the dignity of tradition, custom and ethnic pride. Stripped of dignity, the individual drifts to the urban areas, reduced to the level of a desperado looking for some means of material advancement.

In these states there is no kind of social security system. An individual depends on the family for a safety net. Unemployment or sickness can make the whole family destitute. It is this that keeps the individual clinging to a job or patronage. The challenge for Muslim societies would be to create infrastructures allowing individuals some security. This in turn would encourage healthier thinking, healthier politics and healthier societies among Muslims.

The reversion to primordial identity, the falling back to the old ways, is one way of regaining lost dignity. A woman wearing a *hijab* or a man cultivating a beard are both attempting to relocate a sense of pride. They are making a point: by asserting themselves and their sense of identity they aim to recapture some of the dignity that is so deeply required by all human beings.

Islamic punishment

Ideas of law and order and of punishment are another crucial area of the debate on modernity. The image of Islamic punishment in the West is a harsh one. The Western press picks on the chopping off of hands for theft as a symbol of a barbaric punishment and indeed society. Islamic law is seen as incompatible with democracy and modernity. A comment is therefore important.

Islamic punishment rests on two assumptions: first, rules are laid down for the maximum limits of the punishment for a particular crime which is designed to discourage its repetition. For instance, the punishment of cutting a thief's hand freezes crime. Because this is practised in Saudi Arabia it is still possible to see shopkeepers leaving their shops unattended during prayer-time without any fear of theft. It would be a foolish person indeed who would try to steal from them. This state of affairs can be compared to other societies with highly developed and sophisticated police forces where theft, burglary and rape are common because there is no fear of the law or indeed of the punishment it provides.

It may be added that although the cutting off of hands is an Islamic punishment it is very rarely practised in Muslim countries; it is not known in the Muslim countries of South Asia. Even during General Zia's decade of Islamization this punishment was never implemented.

The second assumption is that, once the maximum ceiling of punishment has been determined, the spirit of Islam dictates its usage. Compassion and kindness are underlined; the spirit of mercy and balance runs as a theme throughout the Quran. For example, if a man commits a murder and there are strong extenuating circumstances or if the murdered person's nearest relatives are prepared to forgive the murderer, then Islamic law will take this into account. In the West the law must prevail at all costs; very often two deaths result instead of one. For Muslims the electric chair is as barbaric as some Muslim punishments are for the West.

The role of witnesses is crucial, and the moral character not only of the witness but also of the judge is an important factor in the case. The idea in trying cases is not to humiliate or demean people but to create a just, pious and safe society for all citizens.

It is well to recall that the symbol of the great empires, like the Mughals, was the scales of justice (it is found in the Diwan-i-Khass in the Red Fort, in Delhi, where the emperor attended court). Most pious rulers prided themselves on their sense of justice. The best of them – like the caliph Umar – were known to have wandered in the streets after their official work to ensure that ordinary citizens had justice. Indeed many a powerful ruler, from the Ottoman sultan to the Mughal emperor, accused of falling short of the Islamic notion of justice has had to face legal proceedings in his own court.

In the West the emphasis is on law and the text, on the need to implement it and uphold it. The accused and society are secondary to this process. In many rape cases the victim suffers the ordeal again and again as an unsympathetic police force and judicial system drag the case on for months, sometimes with blatant scepticism towards the victim's story. In contrast, under Islamic law a decision is made immediately after witnesses have given their evidence. There is no hanging about, no postponements. Justice is accessible, swift and visible.

It is for these reasons that a person like Waseem Sajjad, the Chairman of the Senate of Pakistan, in spite of a law degree from Oxford, supports the *Shariat* (from *shariah*) Bill, that is, the introduction of Islamic law in Pakistan. He explained that in the ordinary course of law judges do not have any special expertise in religious matters. They would not, for example, be able to understand fully the meaning of the Quran or the *sunnah* of the Prophet. Besides, Pakistani civil and criminal codes still derive from colonial British laws. Therefore the *shariat* court was established, with judges who have special expertise in religious affairs and issues. However, Pakistan still has a long way to go before Islamic law prevails in the land. Once it does, Waseem Sajjad is confident that the Quranic concepts of *adl*, equilibrium, and *ihsan,* compassion, will guide society. But more orthodox Muslims, like Qazi Hussein Ahmed, head of the Jamaat-i-Islami party, complain that not enough is being done in Pakistan to implement the *Shariat* Bill.

Class, corruption and communism
Regardless of the injunctions to care for the poor in Islam, the differences between the rich and the poor appear to be huge and are, if anything, increasing. Visiting the suburbs of a large city like Cairo or Karachi, the Western visitor can be forgiven for feeling that there are people who live exactly like rich people do at home, with all the latest comforts. In addition servants and guards isolate the rich in luxurious surroundings. But stepping into the bazaar or a favela in the city the visitor is immediately struck by the poverty. Social services seem to have come to a halt or broken down. Electricity and water supplies and telephone communications are erratic.

Why is there this discrepancy? Do the different sectors in society have any contact with each other? How long will this state of inequality exist? These are valid questions and need to be answered by those who are ruling Muslim societies. The inequality cannot last because Islam emphasizes the equality of all people. It emphasizes the need to care for the hungry and the less privileged (the Prophet said that if a neighbour has the means he must care for the neighbour who is in need). So the inequality that we see is not

Islamic; it is the asymmetry typical of post-colonialism. It is the greed of rampant capitalism. It is the selfish and myopic acquisitiveness of the élite. It is doomed.

If capitalism has failed, what of communism? Was communism a viable answer to the problems of Muslim society? Muslims largely looked on it with undisguised revulsion (see also chapter 5). It clashed directly with Islam's notions of God. Apart from the theological aspect, communism's centralized state and police structure revolted Muslims. Islam's ideas of compassion and humanity were not to be even glimpsed in the way in which communists conducted their governments. In their purges, in their forced resettlements, in their destruction of traditional rural life, in their secret police, in their torture cells, communists were seen as a curse.

This is not to say that many Muslims have not flirted with communist ideas. Indeed, some eminent Muslim thinkers felt that this was the only alternative to capitalist America and openly declared their allegiance to communism. One of the best-known modern poets of Pakistan, Faiz Ahmad Faiz, was known to be sympathetic to communism; indeed, he was awarded the Lenin Peace Prize in Moscow. His poetry reflects a mixture of traditional Urdu romantic poetry and communist ideology. Warm-hearted and generous Faiz remains loved in Pakistan and among admirers of Urdu.

None the less communism translated badly into Muslim societies. In Iraq and Syria it meant hero-worship of the leader and ubiquitous statues to him; it meant a secret police and torture; it meant a suppression of Islamic identity and pride. It meant the butchery at Halabja in Iraq and Hama in Syria for opposing the dictator.

If Muslims rejected communism, however, this does not mean they have embraced the Islamic parties. Because of the inflated attention that Islamic parties receive in the Western media, it is not fully appreciated that the Jamaat-i-Islami party in Pakistan and the Muslim Brothers in Egypt win no more than 5–10 per cent of seats in parliament. Even in Iran there are ominous rumblings against the 'Mercs and perks' of the ayatollahs, as we have noted. In none of these countries is there any danger of the Islamic parties having a free run in parliament.

Tribal or ethnic loyalty – which translates as nepotism and corruption – also draws justifiable criticism from the West. Such loyalties affect politics, society and indeed the economics of Muslim society. It is a fact of life that the leaders of many Muslim countries, whether kings or socialist dictators, function as tribal chiefs, appointing their near and dear in key positions. Similarly, most of the business houses are run like family concerns.

Modernity has done little to break up the family structures which simply transfer from one field to another.

While providing continuity and a sense of cohesion, this tends to ignore the notion of individual merit or talent. Tribal politics also means trouble if your tribe is out of favour or power. So if Saudi Arabia pampers tribal and nomadic groups – there was even an allowance for tribal camel owners, and one frequently sees camels, looking dolefully embarrassed in pick-up vans, being hurtled across the length and breadth of the land – in other states there are savage attempts to suppress them. Iraq's treatment of the Kurds is an example.

Rulers then and now

Why were Muslim rulers centuries ago more tolerant, more sympathetic, more compassionate, more learned than those today? What has gone wrong? The answers should help us understand not only Muslims but also how they view modernity in our world. The early Muslim rulers were first and foremost Muslims situated in a specific cultural context: they responded to life around them as Muslims living in a dominant, meaningful Islamic milieu. The *shariah*, the *hadith*, the sayings of wise men, meant something to them. They were not the final arbiters of authority, simply custodians on behalf of God who was watching. So even wayward sultans would be conscious of doing wrong and indeed would be criticized by the learned for doing it.

In contrast, Muslim rulers today have mostly come to power through the modern political or administrative structure. Many of them are in power simply because they happen to be at the head of the army at a certain stage in their country's history; they declared martial law and took over as the president. Although many of them are pious and inclined to Islam in their private lives, in public they act and behave like any other politician anywhere in the world. Others, though elected through a democratic process and using the rhetoric of democracy, are in fact dictators prepared to use their powers to stay in office illegally.

This is not to say that rulers in earlier times did not attempt to suppress opposition. Many highly respected Imams were imprisoned, publicly lashed and humiliated by the rulers of the day. But they were able to bring immense moral pressures on the rulers, challenging their hereditary status and even their right to rule.

In that sense the criticism of the establishment is not new. What is new is that in the old days the opposition would focus on the moral imperative of the ruler to rule. The arguments would be different today. They would focus on the lack of elections or democracy or viable economic planning. Few opposition leaders – except those leading the Islamic parties – would launch a programme against a Muslim ruler based only on the argument that his rule was insufficiently Islamic. The idiom, therefore, has changed, and so has the content of the argument. It allows the ruler to respond as any other political ruler by using the almost inexhaustible means of the state and its resources.

Intellectual opposition or creativity are the first victims. In the repressive cultural and intellectual milieu that prevails in the modern Muslim state it is wise for a writer not to write, for a thinker not to think; it is prudent to be a coward. Otherwise, to oppose is to challenge not only the injustices of the time but the modern state itself with all its sophisticated and brutal instruments of repression. It is no wonder that most original writers are either abroad or broken or silenced. They are bought off either by comfortable jobs or by other means if they choose to stay at home. Or they become intellectual and cultural nomads, moving from one country to another. Paradoxically a home is provided for them in the West, usually in the USA and the UK which attract the highest number of intellectual writers and artists from the Muslim world.

The Muslim family

The central institution of Muslim society is the family. In the West, the Muslim family structure is often seen as oppressive and backward, an obstacle to modernity. For their part, many Muslims are concerned about the frequent breakdown of marriages in the West, and worry that their own societies may be heading along a similar route. Muslim families today have to cope with the problems of rapid urbanization, and the pressures of living in cities and in cramped accommodation. Although there has been an alarming increase in the divorce rate among Muslims, none the less Muslim marriages tend to be far more stable than Western ones, because they are based on an entirely different set of assumptions.

These assumptions are founded in the Muslim notion of the cosmos. As there is order and balance in the universe, there is a similar natural pattern in society which is reflected in the Muslim household. In a conceptual sense, one mirrors the other. Thus each individual member plays an equally significant role in his or her own capacity which is related to the other members of the family. Each person is special and yet different. It is the difference that ensures the balance and harmony.

The proper behaviour of all the members of the family is constantly emphasized in the Quran and *hadith*. Ideal behaviour encourages dignity and modesty in the family. The father, the mother, the children and the elders all have a positive and defined role to play. In each case the model of ideal behaviour comes from early Islam. The Prophet was both the ideal son and later the ideal husband and father. The women of his household – like Khadijah and Fatimah – provide the ideal for Muslim women.

For Muslims, then, the family is *the* central institution; it is at the centre both of theology and sociology: 'The family is a divinely-inspired institution that came into existence with the creation of man. The human race is a product of this institution and not the other way round' (Ahmad 1974: 13). Not surprisingly, the most intricate rules and regulations guide family life. About a third of the legal injunctions in the Quran deal with family matters. These aim to produce the attitudes and behaviour patterns that Islam wants to foster in society. And they cover different generations: a Muslim family is an extended family, normally with three or four generations within its circle.

Islam is the religion of equality. This principle is never more explicit than in the Quranic instructions to men and women on how to become good Muslims. 'If any do deeds of righteousness – be they male or female – and have faith, they will enter Heaven' (Surah 4: verse 124). In Surah 33, verse 35, the equality of men and women, the need for both to believe, to speak the truth, to be humble, to give alms, to fast and to be modest, is emphasized by constant repetition of the words 'men . . . and women . . .'

Even in the controversial area of divorce it is necessary to point out that both men and women have the right to divorce. The first divorce initiated by a woman was granted by the Prophet himself on grounds of incompatibility. This gives women tremendous leverage in society.

At the same time, men have duties towards the women of the family. A wife must be maintained by her husband, even if she has means of her own. This practice is used to explain the inequality of inheritance – a man receives a larger share of a family legacy than does a woman.

Muslims are known to be extremely affectionate towards their offspring. Little girls and boys are constantly spoilt, sometimes to the point where it is harmful to them. In particular grandparents dote on grandchildren. As the young are loved, the aged are revered. With age people gain in status and influence. It is the duty of every child to care for parents: 'Show kindness to parents . . . Lower to them the wing of humility out of tenderness' (Surah 17: verses 23–4).

Mothers in particular evoke a very strong emotional response of affection among Muslims. Heaven, the Prophet had said, lies beneath the feet of the mother. The following lines were dedicated by me as a young man to my mother:

When I walk at night alone,
in the deep wadis of her sobs
or when I know that each time I drive fast
or delay reply to her letter
when I know that at midnight
she sits up praying to her God
to keep me warm and whole,
when I know that she will still bless me
though I give her eyes cause to tears
when I know that all my warts and ways
will turn to gold at her simple touch
then I see through her the God she sits rotating her
* beads to*
and then I know that her God
will always be there for me to reach out and touch.

Polygamy in Islam

There is another idea about family life that is difficult to lay to rest in the West. It is of Islam as a man's paradise with every man possessing at least four wives. This is, of course, a stereotype and not a real image. In my anthropological fieldwork in Pakistan which cast a wide net over an entire section of a major tribal group (the Frontier Pukhtuns) I discovered that only 0.02 per cent of men were polygamous (Ahmed 1980). Personally, too, apart from one or two people in the older generation, I know of no friend or acquaintance who has more than one wife. The vast majority of men are monogamous.

In Islam it is always important to look for the spirit behind the word or law – whether it is in criminal punishment or polygamy. The fact that a man is allowed in extraordinary circumstances to marry up to four wives must be seen in this context. It is quite clear that the ideal is one wife, and the Quran emphasizes and indeed advocates it. However, there are situations in times of war or famine or social upheaval when it is better that a woman is safely and honourably married than has to fend for herself as a destitute or even prostitute her body. It is therefore the spirit that must be understood, not the letter of the law.

The Quran has clearly given permission for men to marry more than once, and in certain circumstances this is a social necessity: 'If you are afraid that you will not treat orphans justly, then marry such women that may seem good to you, two, three or four' (Surah 4: verse 3). But in the next line the Quran lays down a clause: 'If you think you will not act justly, then one.' This is a stringent condition making it difficult for a person to marry more than once. Indeed the Quran itself says that polygamy is not possible: 'You will never manage to deal equitably with women no matter how hard you try' (Surah 4: verse 129). The true spirit of the Quran thus appears to be monogamy, because marriage to more than one wife is contingent on absolute equality and impartiality between wives.

None the less Muslims are not apologetic or defensive about polygamy. A liberated, female Indian Muslim writer makes the following point while supporting polygamy in Islam:

> Islam accommodates human weaknesses and needs. It aims to create a society based on natural instincts. It sanctions re-marriage and divorce but discourages flagrant immorality and sex outside marriage. Polygamy is a provision and not a compulsion.
>
> The Western pattern and definition of women's liberation is not the only one. If a woman is content with being a second wife why should anyone tell her she should feel otherwise? Polygamy provides a hedge for increased female population due to disasters like wars. The clause legitimizing multiple wives is in the interest of 'the other woman' as it gives her moral, social and legal rights. One man one woman relationship is merely an Anglo-Saxon concept of purity.
>
> The oppression of Muslim women in the sub-continent is a result of feudal-social attitudes and has nothing to do with Islam. Some of the laws in these countries are detrimental to women and need to be reviewed in the Muslim framework. Islamic jurisprudence provides the liberal and progressive basis for a moral and a just society in recorded history.
>
> (Dehlvi 1992)

Marriage in Islam is not a temporary union and is meant to last for life. Dissolution of marriage is, however, permitted if it has irretrievably broken down. However, before actual divorce Muslim law demands an attempt at reconciliation. The natural prevalence of monogamy as normal is more and more the practice in Muslim countries. Nevertheless, a limited polygamy is seen as a realistic need in certain circumstances, and indeed as preferable to the concealed polygamy without responsibility, in some ways tolerated in Western society. 'Islam is a practical religion and is meant for the guidance of human beings made of flesh and bones' (Ahmad 1974: 21–2).

Arranged marriages

As most young Western couples select their own marriage partners, the arranged marriage appears odd and outdated to them. Although most Muslim marriages are arranged even today this does not mean that marriages are forced upon young people. What it does mean is that parents and senior relatives often discuss various possibilities, yet all the while consulting the person involved. This allows them, over a period of time, to assess the weaknesses and strengths of the future partner. In Islam both partners must clearly and before witnesses agree to be married; no one can be coerced into marriage. Usually marriages take place within the extended family or even the same ethnic or tribal group. It is difficult in such marriages for husbands to be mean or cruel to their wives because husband and wife are related and such behaviour would cause adverse comment in the family. After all the uncles and aunts of the wife would also be the uncles and aunts of the husband. Arranged marriages are perhaps one of the reasons why Muslim marriages are so stable. There are few comparative statistics but many young Muslims even in the West enthusiastically support the notion of arranged marriages, particularly in the light of the high statistics of divorce in the West.

Are arranged marriages still viable among Muslims living in Western societies or highly Westernized families in Muslim cities? We already hear of more divorce cases in this generation than in the previous one. Is this a trend? If so, will the trend spread to the more traditional rural areas also? Does it indicate a breakdown of the arranged marriage system? These are questions that need to be addressed by all Muslims today.

Muslim women

Women in Islam have the right to inherit property, to divorce, to demand a say in the house and in public life, to conduct business, and to have access to information and knowledge. Take the matter of inheritance. In Arab countries prior to Islam, inheritance was passed down in the male line, that is the patrilineal. Women in Arabia as in many other cultures were excluded from inheritance. However, the Quran emphasizes the right of individual members, including women, to inherit. These rights were superimposed on earlier practices. It is often pointed out by Muslims that these measures of equality were only won in Western society in the last century, whereas they have existed in Muslim law since the time of the Prophet.

The women in the Prophet's household provide ideal models for Muslim women. They are caring, committed and, most important, involved in life around them. Above all, they have immense dignity. These are not the shy, retiring, ineffectual creatures of the Orientalist stereotypes. They participate in the lives of their family, contributing to and enriching it. Not surprisingly Khadijah and Fatimah are very popular names among Muslim girls. Fatimah has a central role as the Prophet's only surviving child, the wife of Ali, the mother of Hassan and Hussain. The Prophet himself has underlined her status in Islam: 'Fatimah is a part of my body; whoever hurts her, has hurt me, and whoever hurts me has hurt God'. Like her sons who were martyred, she embodies a life of dedication, suffering, sharing and compassion.

Muslim women are confident when Islam is secure; they are unsure and insecure when it is on the defensive (see Ahmed 1988: 184). Where Muslim civilization is dominant, women play their rightful role in society, fully and unhindered. Where it is threatened or damaged, a curtain descends over Muslim homes, and women are hidden away from prying, alien eyes. When Mughal rule was at its height in India, the Muslim women matched their men in every field of human activity, often surpassing them in some. As writers, saints, rulers and artists, they were central figures in the Mughal empire for two centuries. Bringing angry male relatives together, consoling those who were down on their luck, helping those in need, distributing favours to the poor – these were the Mughal women. In spite of their high profile they did not draw the criticism of the orthodox for un-Islamic behaviour; that is, they played a full part in life and yet played it within the bounds prescribed by Islam. These Mughal women were illustrating balance between *din* and *dunya*.

Women in the modern world

A simple formula assumed by critics of Islam is that women are treated badly in traditional homes and marginally better in more modernized ones. This is not so. Many paradoxes and surprises emerge if we look closely at Muslim family life. Modern marriages in Cairo or Karachi can often be unsatisfactory. Husbands and wives are sometimes involved in extramarital affairs; the pressures of city life, of competing and attempting to live up to a higher standard of living, can become unbearable.

The more traditional homes, on the other hand, provide greater security to the family, particularly women. Women have control over affairs of the family and have a defined role and place in society. Perhaps through their traditional faith, perhaps through their disinclination to wander into new areas of controversy or challenge the established order and tradition, they appear more content than their sisters who have opted for a more Westernized lifestyle. 'Modernity has very little effect on how women live, or indeed on how they want to live,' Dr Helen Watson, a Cambridge anthropologist, noted after a visit to Cairo:

Familiar western concepts of sexual equality and the liberation of women are irrelevant and unnecessary from local women's point of view. At the core of this conviction is the perception that gender roles and male and female responsibilities are fully complementary. There is a male sphere of influence and activity and a female one; both are separate and distinct, but in combination they form the basis of a stable society.
(Watson 1992: 6)

The Western assumption that Muslim wives are helpless prisoners in the home needs to be corrected. There may be some husbands who are tyrants but the actual picture is usually of strong wives with authority and much to say in the running of the household. Traditional women emerge as powerful mothers who control the lives of the members of the family with skill and confidence. As the husband grows older and more involved with matters outside the home the wife's authority increases.

Indeed I have rarely come across a situation where a husband can mistreat his wife over any period of time and get away with it. Not only would she not tolerate it but her relatives and the immediate family prevent this from happening. This is not to say that men sometimes do not behave in a brutal manner. Stories that reach us are sometimes horrifying. But these are men drunk with either tribal or feudal power. Their response is Pavlovian. They are asserting their physical superiority or their feudal or social position. They do not respect Islamic behaviour.

As most homes remain what are known as joint family homes – that is, more than one family lives in the home – the slightest hint of incorrect behaviour would come to light. This would create a scandal and start tongues wagging. Such fears, combined with Islamic practice and tradition, add up to check the man who may wish to do injustice at home.

To critics in the West it appears that Muslim men impose a rigid seclusion on their women through the use of force. The reality is often surprising, as Dr Helen Watson explains:

Despite how it might appear to an outsider, this is not a system which is imposed on women in any obvious sense of the word. The segregation of the sexes and observance of a strict code of conduct is valued and actively maintained by women themselves. An ideal female way of life is popularly expressed in terms of the cloistered seclusion women enjoyed in the past. Secluded quarters and confinement are no longer possible, although women know of a few rural élites who can afford to keep their female kin in seclusion and do without their labour in the fields. This is discussed with a candid and clear envy, since the women's own families relied heavily on their agricultural work before migration. The equivalent urban image of a secluded lifestyle is that of a rich businessman's wife who never leaves her luxurious home and spends all day watching television after ordering groceries by telephone. Conscious that the lifestyle they desire is

denied to them by poverty, local women's positive view of seclusion is dominated by the idea of liberation from financial problems and hard unfulfilling work.
(Watson 1992: 5–6)

To support the claim that Muslim men treat their wives as subordinate, as inferior, Western critics argue that they make their wives walk a few paces behind them. This is an obvious misunderstanding of how and why this happens. It has little to do with theology and more to do with sociology. Men are extremely conscious of the honour and respect to be given to women. They walk ahead symbolically to confront or block any possible danger or situation so that their women remain as safe and as comfortable as possible. It underlines the high status and respect of their women. It is the equivalent of the English gentleman of an earlier period giving his left arm to the lady he was escorting in order that his right arm may be free to protect her.

Another criticism of this kind is that Muslim women do not eat with the men but eat afterwards. The implication is that they are not considered good enough to sit with the men at mealtimes or that they are given the leftovers. This again is incorrect and has no basis in reality. Those commentators who may have observed this practice may have been correct. But the women eating later may have had more to do with the observation of *pardah* (veiling, modesty) from a stranger or male guest than with inferiority. Very often if the male visitor is entertained at a traditional Muslim home the wife may well eat separately in order not to violate the injunction to be modest. It has nothing to do with inferiority.

It is also argued in the West that Muslim women are not allowed to visit cemeteries, go to funerals or indeed even to mosques. This too is incorrect. The reason that they tend not to visit these places is as much social as religious. At any rite of passage or public gathering there is a great deal of hustle and bustle and even rowdiness. Women are thus given the privilege of choice. If they wish they can say their prayers in the mosque where there is always a separate place for them (as at the Cambridge mosques where women do come for prayers). However, if they prefer they can offer their prayers at home. If men had been given this privilege many of them would have availed themselves of it, for it is an additional hardship on them. For instance, men and women are expected to go to the Friday prayer at the local mosque. This is often difficult for many in the West as they must obtain special permission from their non-Muslim employers.

One effective argument used by critics of modern Islam is that if Muslims came to power (for instance in Algeria) women would be threatened, that they would be forced to stay at home and not work. This is false propaganda. Even in Iran women work and are prominent in parliament. Pakistan was led by Benazir Bhutto and Bangladesh is led by Begum Zia, both democratically elected. In their ability and intelligence these women are obviously in no way inferior to their male colleagues. Their impact has been revolutionary, and they have provided authentic role models for Muslim women.

However, it is generally true that in Muslim society women often face discrimination in public life. They may find it difficult to use public transport, they may find it equally difficult to adjust to the atmosphere in an all-male office. The social climate does not encourage easy movement.

In certain tribal areas of Afghanistan or Pakistan, women who violate custom can be easily accused of promiscuity and punished according to the tribal laws of *tor*, black. The colour black signifies evil and death. In some cases, when a woman is accused of commiting *tor* she can be taken out of her home and shot because she is said to have disgraced her family. This is not Islam.

Neither is the mutilation women suffer in certain parts of Africa Islamic. There is persistent misinformation and misunderstanding about clitoridectomy. The mutilation of the clitoris of a woman is incorrectly associated with Islam. But this is a practice of some African tribes, and clitoridectomy is most common in Somalia, where all girls are infibulated between the ages of five and fifteen. Circumcision, excision, infibulation, female genital mutilation – none of this is Islamic. These are various pre-Islamic or non-Islamic African customs absorbed into Muslim tribes and retained as custom. They find no sanction in the Quran. Indeed they are against the spirit of the Quran, which emphasizes compassion and kindness. But for the last century these practices have been regarded as Islamic by many Western writers.

The spirit in which women are regarded in a Muslim society is summed up by Qazi Hussein Ahmed: 'In our society, women are very much respected and they are treated as a special sacred type of people. They are provided special protection. The husband, or the son, or father, or brother, they are responsible for all the needs of women.'

Muslim dress and the *hijab*

Islamic clothing affects Islamic thinking and vice versa. As the Quran teaches modesty for both men and women (Surah 24: verses 30–1) clothes are meant to emphasize modesty and dignity both in men and in women. Thus clothes that either suggest the contours of the body or expose it are avoided except, perhaps, among some members of the fashionable, the young or those who live in the cities.

Modesty is also behaviour, speech and conduct. It is in this context that respectable men and women wear clothes that appear formal and dignified. They need to cover all parts of their body. Flowing robes are probably the best method to do so. To see a sheikh or an ayatollah in his robes is to see a person of dignity, learning, authority and grace in his own society.

Loose clothes are worn because they allow people to say prayers which include prostration, bending and sitting. It is not easy to do these things in tight-fitting clothes. Loose clothes are also worn because of the dietary pattern. Most Muslims, because they are often up early at dawn for prayers, tend to rest in the afternoon; for most the afternoon meal is usually heavy, and the midday sun makes work difficult. There is also the force of tradition. People often tend to wear what the previous generation has worn before them. It does not mean that there is no change. Even in the rural areas of Pakistan men and women once wore pyjamas or *shalwars* which ran literally into yards and yards of cloth. Now the *shalwar* is much tighter and neater, although to outsiders it looks very baggy.

Muslim women appear to be divided on the subject of the veil. The covering of the face by a veil has never been universal in the Muslim world. Country women go to the fields without a veil, women in some parts of the Muslim world have not adopted it, others during the last decades have discarded it, yet others rediscovered it. But the Quranic injunction to modesty, however it is applied, cannot be set aside. Its interpretation has varied, and does vary, but its importance is basic. One interpretation of what constitutes modesty is the long skirt and headscarf worn by many young women – a stricter interpretation than that of some of their mothers.

The *hijab* or veil presents us with some useful sociological insights into Muslim society. Its source as an Islamic dress is debated. 'The true veil is in the eyes of the men' is a saying of the Prophet. Tribal society, as Arabia was in the seventh century when Islam came to it, would have two or three distinct features regarding women which we can reflect on with a degree of accuracy. Women would have been far more free than we can imagine. This is a tribal characteristic. People are related on the genealogical charter and everyone knows everyone else. Molesting a woman or raping her would mean committing virtual incest.

Although the notions of female honour and sexual conduct are highly developed in the Muslim tribal areas, there is no concept of the veil, which begins to appear once you come nearer the towns. Indeed a woman in the tribal areas will come up and shake hands and say, 'How are you, brother, would you like a cup of tea?' She has the kind of confidence which would be difficult to find in her better-educated sister in the city.

Although the *hijab*, *chador* or even the *pardah* are not in early Islam according to some scholars, in time they became associated with Islam. These customs were assimilated from the conquered Persian and Byzantine societies and were considered to reflect the Quranic spirit. It may well be that seclusion and veiling reflected the upper-class, urban women who would protect themselves from the gaze of those in the bazaars and in the fields. Over the centuries, however, this spread to other parts of society. In certain groups it had unfortunate consequences. Women in towns and cities were often confined to small houses with limited social contacts and therefore barred from community life.

Professor Nur Veergin, Professor of Sociology in Istanbul, although intensely supportive of Islam, is scathing about the long black *chador* or veil, even blaming it on Christianity. She explained her argument to me:

> *I must say that these categories have been influenced by Christianity. For instance the veil. It's claimed that horrible black* chador *that one sees now more and more in Istanbul streets is something to do with Islam, that has nothing to do with Turkish Islam anyway. It comes from Byzant [Christianity], it comes from Iran, but it certainly doesn't derive, doesn't stem from the Turkish national culture or the Islamic culture of Turkey.*

The *hijab* in the 1980s and 1990s has become a fashionable and recognizable symbol of Muslim identity among young girls. It must be emphasized that it is not worn out of fear or pressure from the home. Many girls wear this in spite of opposition at home. It is a neat way of saying: this is where I stand and I am proud of it.

★   ★   ★

Let us end this chapter by emphasizing a crucial point that must be borne in mind when considering Muslim responses to modernity. Western commentators commonly make the assumption that once Muslims are set on the path to democracy (and modernity) they will become more like 'us' and, as in most of the West, eventually separate the religious from the secular in their lives. Yet Muslims are either Muslims or they are not; there is no halfway house. They cannot just take bits and pieces of Islam and still remain Muslims. If they do, they become something completely different. Evidence of this is most explicit where Muslims live as a minority in non-Muslim states, and we shall discuss this in the next chapter.

FIVE

MUSLIMS AS MINORITIES

———————•———————

In the last chapter we focused on countries where Islam is the dominant religion. In Turkey, Iran and Pakistan – and in the Arab countries – about 90 to 95 per cent of the people claim to be Muslims. Many of these countries use the word 'Islamic' in their self-description; thus the Islamic Republic of Iran and the Islamic Republic of Pakistan, where the *shariah* is the law of the land. We will now look at Muslims in countries where the majority population is not Muslim. The important point to keep before us is the wide range of the Muslim experience as minorities. In one place they are comfortable and adjusted, in another resentful and deprived; Stornoway in the Outer Hebrides is an example of the former, Samarkand, under the Soviets, of the latter. We shall look at both in this chapter.

In discussing the problem of Muslim minorities in my book, *Postmodernism and Islam: Predicament and Promise* (1992), I mentioned Kashmir, Palestine and the Central Asian republics of the Soviet Union. But events now make the third example redundant. Over the last few years we have seen the Soviet Union disintegrate and the former Soviet republics in Central Asia emerge as independent states. We can no longer talk of the Muslim republics as a minority within a non-Muslim majority. But because their problems derive from their former situations as a minority we shall discuss them below.

THE 'PROBLEM' OF MUSLIM MINORITIES

It is not difficult to see why Muslims who live as a minority in non-Muslim countries like India or Israel are seen by them as a problem. The reasons are relatively simple. Wherever Muslims live as minorities they increasingly face problems of discrimination. These are partly due to historical and political factors, partly due to the media, which have confirmed for many that

Muslims are violent, unreliable and prone to anarchy. There is another reason. Most non–Muslim countries in which Muslims live have an image of themselves as plural, tolerant, secular and modern societies. Muslims somehow challenge this image. They provoke the worst aspects of the state. In the main, instead of solving the problems of the Muslims in a manner that would be mutually beneficial, the state tends to ignore or minimize them.

In the former state of Yugoslavia the Serbs went one step further with their Muslim minority. They systematically killed them and drove them from their homes in Bosnia. The world called it 'ethnic cleansing' and did nothing. Bosnia was added to the list of recent Muslim losses.

What offends Muslims living in a country as the minority community? What is the Muslim 'problem'? There are two or three things that Muslims are most sensitive about. The most important is religion. Muslims would like to be able to visit their mosques and say their prayers peacefully without interruption, without being beaten up, without being picked up for interrogation. They would also like privacy in their homes where they can lead their lives as Muslims. They would like dignity and honour for their families – in particular, for the elderly, the women and the children. They do not like police or paramilitary forces to burst into their homes and humiliate their families. They would like some control over their lives, some perpetuation of their own customs and values, the construction and maintenance of mosques which are the focus of social and cultural life, the capacity to read the Quran and the chance to live as Muslims and by Muslim traditions. These include family laws, inheritance, religious holidays and religious festivals. When these are threatened, Muslims are threatened; confusion and anger ensue.

It is not difficult for non-Muslim rulers to concede these facilities to Muslims; when they have been conceded, Muslims have lived harmoniously. History confirms this. It is the modern state that creates the problem. Because the modern state is so centralized and because it often lacks imagination in dealing with its minorities, Muslims are constantly under pressure. Merely wishing for the minimum, Muslims are seen as people who demand separation and indeed secession.

There is a cultural problem also for Muslims living as a minority. Non-Muslim tourists visiting Muslim holy places cause offence by eating there and loitering, playing loud music on their radios. Islamic culture, *adab*, is directly challenged. In some cases there is a direct physical threat to these holy places, such as the demolition of Babar's mosque in Ayodhya, India. The inevitable religious clashes cost lives. There is also the more sinister danger of actual history being changed and Muslim culture being depicted in official textbooks as barbaric and worthless (as has happened in Spain).

A discussion of Muslims as a minority is important for several reasons. First, the populations we are discussing are large. Indeed, Muslims who live as a minority constitute about a quarter of the total number of Muslims. The problem is serious because it is ongoing and does not involve only one or two countries; it is global. A list of countries in which Muslims live as a minority includes the USA, India, Russia, the UK, France, Germany, Israel and Singapore. In India alone there are said to be anywhere around 110 million Muslims. No religion in the world has so many people trapped in an alien environment as the Muslims. Neither Christians nor Jews, nor Hindus, none of the major world religions have such large numbers in so many countries dominated by people of other religions.

The second reason is that the sharpest and most brutal political confrontation is taking place in these societies. We learn of the most compelling stories of injustice and brutality as Muslims struggle for self-dignity and identity. The images that are shown on television and the reports in the press confirm for us the plight of the Muslims.

Thirdly, because of the notion of the *ummah*, because of the manner of the suppression of these groups, Muslims in neighbouring countries are deeply concerned. The struggle of the Kashmiris in South Asia and the Palestinians in the Middle East draws in large Muslim populations outside the national borders. The geo-political situation remains tense; indeed it can escalate to war at any time. It is well to recall that the major powers in both areas have gone to war three or four times because of these Muslim minorities.

Finally, some Islamic ideas place Muslims and the non-Muslim majority on a confrontation course. The Islamic ideas are notions of the *ummah*, which transcends national borders, and the idea of *jihad*, struggle, the need to fight for a just and correct order. On the other hand these non-Muslim nations need to respond to security requirements and geo-political strategy. The Muslim minority is often caught in the crossfire.

There are agonizing dilemmas facing Muslims living as a minority in certain areas. In a different time, in a previous age, Muslims persecuted by the majority could do one of two things: they could pack up and leave, that is exercise the right to adopt *hijra*, or they could fight for their rights, that is *jihad*. Today, because of the power, the highly centralized security and administrative structures and the strongly manned borders of the state, neither option is really feasible. Besides, it would be difficult to exercise the option of *hijra*. As recent history shows us, migrant communities do not settle down easily and merge; they take a long time to do so. Any influx of large numbers of refugees causes all kinds of social and political problems to the host community, however welcoming they may have been at first (see also below).

This leaves the option of *jihad*. That too is difficult in our age. A small deprived minority cannot easily take on the power of the state, but it can try. The attempt to assert independence, to fight for one's dignity and culture, explains what is going on in Kashmir and Palestine. Communication between the government and these groups appears to have broken down. For Muslims the state is represented by the brute force of the soldier and the policeman. The women in the area live in dread of their honour and dignity being violated; young males in the constant fear of being picked up for interrogation and torture at any time on any flimsy pretext. For the elders there appears to be no real alternative but to give free rein to the youth in their attempt to break loose and create their own response to the world, whatever the costs. It is a dreadful choice, full of pain and disruption. But when dialogue breaks down it appears to be the only one open for the time being.

An important aspect of these movements is their direct involvement with the geo-politics of the region. The Kashmir movement is seen in India as entirely a creation of Pakistan. This perception is simplistic and disregards numerous factors: the notion of the *ummah* which generates sympathy for Muslims wherever they are in trouble (although the Kashmiri cause has great sympathy in Pakistan, so does the Palestinian one); the strong feelings of injustice in Pakistan regarding the legality of the state of Kashmir and the manner it was incorporated into India; the many Kashmiris who have settled in Pakistan (the present Prime Minister, Nawaz Sharif, is of Kashmiri origin – as was the poet Allama Iqbal); the failure of the central government over the last decades to integrate these areas into the larger body of the nation. All these factors militate against integration.

There are also certain Muslims who out of enthusiasm or ignorance or even mischief would make demands which not only clash with the state but suggest its disintegration. These create problems for everyone concerned. For instance Dr Kalim Siddiqui's call for a Muslim parliament created all kinds of doubts in Britain in the early 1990s. Did Muslims want to create their own country in Britain? Did they want independence? Were their threats of forcing an Islamic order on to Britain to be taken seriously? Such questions obviously cause resentment and anger in the majority. This reaction, when fed into the existing stereotypes about the minority, creates a

153

sense of contempt and revulsion against it. Muslims appear to be largely unaware of this aspect of their relationship with the majority.

The inexplicable fear of Muslim minorities

I find it surprising, even intriguing, that there is such a pronounced fear of Muslim minorities, whether in India or in Israel. In India it is even reflected in its attitude towards Pakistan. India, a country far larger in size, its armies and air force always maintaining a ratio of four or five to one, and now with a sophisticated nuclear programme, lives in strange psychological fear of Pakistan, the smaller, poorer, lesser-armed country.

Similarly, the Israeli notion of the Arab threat is exaggerated. Here is a modernized nation possessing one of the most sophisticated defence services of the world, including a wide range of nuclear weapons. It is supported by the USA, which, when there is war against the Arabs, enters the fray with an almost unlimited supply of the most up-to-date weapons. Israel faces poorly equipped armies often manned by demoralized soldiers. Arab leaders are usually politically divided whatever their rhetoric of wiping Israel off the face of the earth. Yet Israeli leaders sound like David facing Goliath.

It must be, I imagine, the atavistic fear of Muslim warriors in the past. Nothing else could explain the neurosis of such powerful countries contemplating their weaker Muslim neighbours. These are deep and complex psychological fears, but they need to be confronted if they are to be laid to rest.

Muslim governments have rarely exhibited this tension with regard to minorities. Minorities have always been part of many Muslim countries and on the whole they have been left alone, indeed often participating in the state by holding the highest positions. The problem is therefore not only of the minority but of the majority. If the majority is a little bit more tolerant and imaginative it will be able to deal with the minorities more fairly and more kindly, and Muslims in return would respond more positively. Power is both corrupting and dangerous when it is unchallenged and concentrated in the hands of the majority as it is in Israel and India. The non-Muslim voices of tolerance and compassion are easily drowned.

In the selection of officers for defence and the civil services and in the distribution of economic permits and sanctions, the state tends to encourage the oppression of the minorities. It also does so by suggesting a certain kind of Muslim as a 'good' Muslim in the media. The definition is centred on someone who is prepared to abandon Muslim customs and indeed faith. He or she thus becomes a good or moderate Muslim. In contrast anyone wishing to assert their culture and identity is seen as a fanatic or a fundamentalist – in the terms of the state, a troublemaker, a separatist, a communal creature.

The resources of the state are infinite, the energy of the security forces and their strength is inexhaustible. In comparison the protesting individual has limited resources and lives at the centre of a web spun by the state. The fact that Muslim groups have fought so long for their rights simply underlines the desperation of their position. Imagination and wisdom demand that the state responds to them with understanding and tolerance. Using more force, more torture and more suppression implies not only the failure of the state but a serious misreading of the situation.

The burden of the immigrant

But the position is more complex than a straightforward clash between majority and minority. What is not so well known in this context is that Muslim groups fleeing to neighbouring Muslim countries have also had a difficult time. The Muslims of India who migrated to Pakistan found a great deal of succour and support in the early days. In recent years, however, a confrontation has developed between them and the local majority based on ethnic and economic factors. Refugees from India were seen as monopolizing better jobs. Notions of cultural superiority, language differences and ideological arguments about identity all widened the gap between the minority and the majority.

The result was that in the last decades we have seen these very minorities in direct conflict with the majority population – although both are Muslim. So while Sindhis battled it out with refugees from India in the Sind province of Pakistan the Jordanian government fought it out with the Palestinians using tanks and heavy weapons to dislodge them. It was a cruel, paradoxical and even unexpected development. But it showed how deeply interconnected countries and problems were, how impossible it was to view the problem of the minorities in isolation.

By the time of the Gulf War in 1991 we saw how the role of the Palestinians affected and divided Arab opinion. Because of their support for Saddam – which seemed to have developed only because of his vocal support for them – they were victimized and hounded out of countries that had once allowed them employment. The ideological and emotional support for their cause was clearly subordinated to the antipathy they were arousing by their political position.

The Afghan refugees arriving in Pakistan provide another example.

Although they were welcomed when they arrived in the late 1970s, most Pakistanis soon began to view them with unease and then open resentment. Stories of kidnapping, drug-smuggling and robbery were publicly linked to them, and Pakistanis began asking their guests when they would return.

Similarly, the Muslim minorities appeared to be out of step with the majority in Britain. During the Gulf War the Muslim conference in Bradford which claimed to speak for all Muslims in the country *unanimously* supported Saddam against Britain. British Muslims were concerned about the bloodshed and damage that would be inflicted on the Iraqi people. They were right to be concerned. But it also convinced many in Britain that here was a potential fifth column, a minority which in the middle of a war situation was prepared to side with the enemy. The leaders of the Muslim minority were out of tune with the times. The racial harassment that followed was only to be expected. It would have been far worse if the war had continued and large numbers of British soldiers had died. Coffins coming home would have triggered racial violence on an unprecedented level. Fortunately for the British Muslims, the war ended quickly. As there was no hand-to-hand fighting or set-piece military engagements, British casualties were at a minimum. But the British majority had been made aware that the Muslim community had voted against them. Henceforth a question mark would hang over the loyalty of the British Muslims.

MUSLIMS IN THE WEST

For the last thousand years the West treated Islam as the 'other', as 'over there'. In the main this is still true: the bulk of the Muslim population lives in Africa and Asia. But today this simple world-view has been complicated by the presence in the West of over ten million Muslims. About five or six million Muslims live in Europe and about four or five million in America; the exact numbers tend to be somewhat unreliable, since immigrants and converts sometimes do not wish to declare their identity or register and are therefore difficult to enumerate.

Muslims living in the West are theologically in harmony with the Quranic position. Again and again the Quran has emphasized that God's domain is not restricted by East or West: it is everywhere. 'To Allah belongeth the East and the West. Whithersoever ye turn there is Allah's countenance' (Surah 2: verse 115). So Muslims can practise their religion whether in Cairo or California, in London or Lahore.

We need therefore a new frame of reference. It can no longer be seen as Islam *versus* the West; it is Islam *and* the West or Islam *in* the West. The growth of this Muslim community has been impressive to judge by the mosques: both Germany and France have about a thousand, Britain about 500 (although many may only be a room or two). The central mosques in London and in Washington symbolize this growth: the mosques are full of worshippers, they are beautifully constructed and are the hub of Muslim social and religious activity.

But if there are no theological obstacles for Muslims in the West there are certainly sociological and political ones. The Muslim presence in the West has added fuel to anti-Islamic sentiments. Young girls wearing the *hijab* in France have become the subject of hostile national news; Muslims wanting separate schools in England are at the centre of a heated national debate; the Salman Rushdie controversy continues to involve the Muslims and the majority in a virulent confrontation.

This charged atmosphere encouraged the growth of European racism dramatically in the 1980s. It was symbolized by Le Pen in France. So rapidly did his popularity escalate that few politicians could ignore his message. Soon, even the distinguished offices of the French Prime Minister were talking of 'smelly and dirty immigrants'. It had become fashionable to speak of immigrants with open contempt. Politicians called for rigid immigration controls, even for deportation. This kind of public position was quite unthinkable only a generation ago when the figleaf of European humanism would have covered such racist expressions.

Apart from an increasingly hostile environment in some Western countries several other factors have sharpened the Muslim sense of identity. It is for this reason that so much alarm is being caused. It explains the platform for politicians like Le Pen. The international political climate which changed dramatically in the 1970s struck a chord among Muslims in the West. This was the period when King Faisal of Saudi Arabia used oil as an Islamic weapon and Imam Khomeini in Iran and General Zia in Pakistan talked of Islamic revolution and Islamization. This kind of political leadership triggered Islamic revivalism throughout the Muslim community, wherever they lived in the world.

The younger generation

A younger generation of Muslim immigrants has come of age in the West; about half are now born in the West as distinct from their parents, who migrated here in the 1950s and 1960s. The young people rejected the integration and assimilation that their parents often desired. They were no longer the meek, invisible immigrants grateful to be allowed in at all; they wished to assert themselves. In this situation issues of race and religion often fused, as growing racism forced them into a greater sense of religious identity.

In the mid–1960s when I was in Cambridge there was no place for Friday prayers. Now, in the 1990s, there are three and they are invariably overflowing with worshippers on Friday. At various sessions of *Seerat-un-Nabi* conferences (in honour of the Prophet) organized by the Pakistan Cambridgeshire Association, which I chaired, around 200–250 Muslims, entire families, turned up. This type of phenomenon appeared to be happening all over the world. In 1989 on my way to Hawaii for a conference I was invited to speak at the recently constructed mosque in Seattle after the evening prayer. There were about 200 Muslims present; many were women – again a sign of our times. The questions were sharply focused on the role of Muslims living as a minority.

There is also an economic factor. The younger generation are better educated than their parents, who in the UK, for example, had arrived largely to take up menial jobs as bus conductors or factory workers. Young Muslims now compete for places at university with ambitions of becoming doctors and engineers. They wish to share the good life of the West, to own smart homes and cars.

Not all analysts are convinced that the signs of Muslim activity are evidence of Islamic health. Some of the trends among the younger genera-tion of Muslims cause pessimism in certain Muslim quarters. Older Muslims living in the West are worried that their culture will be weakened over time. For example, Dr Muzammil H. Siddiqi refers to a recent study of immigrant Muslim communities in the West which showed that with each succeeding generation there was a decline in strict adherence to specifically Islamic values:

> *Thus it is observed that few Muslims care for five daily prayers. Some do not feel bad about drinking, dating and dancing. Some Muslim girls feel there is nothing wrong in marrying non-Muslims as long as they love and care for each other. Seventy to eighty percent of all Muslims do not belong to any Islamic centre or mosque, and do not care about them. Many think that Muslim countries (especially the oil-rich countries) should build mosques for them, and they do not even contribute one percent of their income to the Islamic centres and organisations.*
> (Siddiqi 1991: 12–13)

The American versus the European experience

There are some interesting differences between the USA and Europe which help us to understand better the phenomenon of Muslims living in the West, and which also highlight the broader historical differences between the USA and Europe. The main difference is the social and economic composition of the Muslim community. In the USA it is largely middle class – doctors, engineers, academics. This gives the community a greater social confidence and a positive sense of belonging. In Europe by and large the community remains stuck in the working class or even the underclass. Its failure on the political scene is spectacular: although Britain has almost two million Muslims they have not been able to win a single seat in Parliament. Worse, their leaders tend to be divided, particularly over where to draw the line between integration and traditional Muslim identity; they seem more interested in attacking each other than representing the community.

Another difference is that in the USA there is a greater geographical spread; Muslims are not concentrated in one state or city. In Europe there is a tendency to concentrate; Bradford in England is an example. The concentration allows the leaders of that particular city to emerge as spokesmen. During the Rushdie crisis the leaders of Bradford were constantly consulted by the media and, it was assumed, spoke for the entire community. It allowed the media to simplify questions of leadership, values, strategy and organization among Muslims. Only subsequently did people realize that although the Bradford spokesmen broadly reflected the general opinion of by no means elected or unanimously accepted leaders of

UK.

in specific communities has another import and perpetuate its sectarian and . The traditional sectarian tensions in Deobandis were lifted *en bloc* to the UK. between these sects are confusing and lain by an example. For the Barelvis (who vince of Punjab) the holy Prophet is a e is all around us at all times; he is *hazir*, or flesh, but *nur*, light. The Deobandis, gue he was the *insan-i-kamil*, the perfect rtal. This explains why Kalim Siddiqui in tation of the *fatwa* against Salman Rushdie his most sympathetic audience among the of mosques that they have organized.

Europe itself has changed dramatically in relation to its immigrants and their culture. For example, from the early 1950s to the early 1990s a number of developments took place in Britain on all levels of society: from seven curry restaurants to seven thousand, from a few mosques to 500, from no African or Asian television presenters and journalists to dozens, from only a few African or Asian authors writing in English to a number of Booker Prize winners. All this was to the good; British culture was that much richer. But it is easy to understand the British fear that perhaps too much may have been happening too fast. After all, Britain is a deeply conservative and insular society, and no such foreign influences – and from such far lands – had made themselves felt before. The fear fed easily into feelings of racial animosity.

Muslims in the USA are conscious that they are there by choice. They have opted to be American. America is, after all, the land of the melting pot, where everyone is ideally equal. This contrasts with Muslims in Europe. Many feel that they are in Europe simply because their parents migrated or were forced to migrate for economic reasons. This makes for disenchanted and alienated citizens.

Muslims in Europe have a direct relationship to the colonial period. The UK ruled South Asia (British India), and therefore most of its Muslim immigrants tend to be from Pakistan, India and Bangladesh (of about two million the biggest single national group is Pakistani). Moroccans and Algerians drifted to France (about half a million of the former and one million of the latter of France's three million Muslims). Because Germany and Turkey had a relationship going back to the First World War, Turks went to Germany (most of Germany's one and a half million Muslims are Turks). The Netherlands has about half a million Muslims who are mostly from Surinam. In Portugal most Muslims are from the former colonies in India or southern France; in Spain they are from Morocco or Algeria. In Italy, where there are estimated to be about 200 000 Muslims, they are mostly from Libya.

In both the USA and Europe, ideas of local ethnicity also affect Muslim self-awareness. The rise of black power in the USA helped to create a mood of assertiveness, of identity, of exaggerated self-importance in the Muslim community. Black Muslims like Malcolm X and Muhammad Ali in the 1960s became symbols of Muslim pride. This did not happen in Europe. There were no superstars to rally behind. The vast majority of the Muslims were marginalized in low-paid jobs and there were few intellectual or media figures speaking on their behalf.

There is also the geo-political factor. The USA is, by and large, neutral in its dealings with Muslims. So, while it is seen as anti-Libya, anti-Iran or, more recently and more famously, anti-Iraq, it is also seen as an ally of Egypt, Saudi Arabia and Pakistan. Its relationships, therefore, depend on its geo-political strategy. Racial or imperial prejudices which often colour the view of the European powers are less visible.

Muslim integration in Western nations

It is a common assumption that the Muslim presence in Europe began after the Second World War; it is fed by media stereotypes and racist polemics of Muslims invading and flooding Europe. But the roots of Muslim immigration go back much further (Nielsen 1992). The origins of the Muslim community in Germany lie in the close relationship between Germany and the Ottoman empire through periods of war and peace. Even earlier, Muslims had settled in the southern German states after the second siege of Vienna in 1683. After that period Prussian kings often employed Muslim soldiers. It is the same link that allowed the Ottoman sultan to patronize the mosque built in a Muslim cemetery in Berlin in 1866. The economic and diplomatic relationship between Turkey and Germany thus has deep roots.

The picture is the same for France and Britain, where many immigrants arrived during the last century. Seamen from Africa and Asia settled in London and other ports. We know of the early Yemeni settlements (Halliday 1992). The first mosques were opened for these seamen, and mosques were then opened in Woking in 1889 and Liverpool in 1891. The Liverpool mosque did not survive the outbreak of the First World War. In 1935 the mosque in Woking declared its adherence to Sunni Islam (earlier it had been associated with the Ahmedis). Marmaduke Pickthall and Abdullah Yusuf Ali, whose translations of the Quran into English continue to be read all over the world, were both associated with this mosque. In 1944 King George VI inaugurated the Islamic Cultural Centre on a site near Regent's Park in London, in exchange for a site in Cairo for a new Anglican cathedral. In due course Britain's main mosque would be built there.

France shows an even more pronounced pattern of immigration than Britain before 1945. Mohammad Ali of Egypt in the last century had encouraged Egyptian students, scholars and business people to go to France. Before the First World War immigrants from Algeria, mostly from the Kabyle tribes, were drifting to the Marseille region for jobs in the olive oil refining and related industries. During the First World War Moroccans, Algerians and Tunisians joined the civil and defence industries. It was in recognition of this that the French allowed the opening of a mosque in Paris

161

in 1926. During the Second World War the Vichy government in 1942 imported North African labour to help Germans in their war effort. By the time of the 1954 census there were 200 000 Algerians in France.

Immigration was caused largely by the European governments them-selves, who actively encouraged people from their former colonies to emigrate to the 'mother country' because of the need for labour in the post-war reconstruction. For example, in Britain, at a time of full employ-ment in the 1950s it was difficult to recruit people to work in the most menial and arduous jobs; the governments therefore sought to attract Asians and West Indians to Britain and offered them the worst jobs, those that they could not fill with native British. This occurred throughout Europe. It is often forgotten by native inhabitants that Muslims were actually invited by the governments.

Most of these immigrants had no intention of staying permanently in Europe. But most did. At first their problems were not so severe. However, changes were taking place in Europe. The colonies had disappeared. The economy was stagnant and the oil prices began to rise sharply. The question of race was now in the air. European countries reacted by stricter immi-gration laws, Britain being the first with its Commonwealth Immigration Act in 1962. This did not prevent immigration from continuing and indeed increasing. But there was a difference: wives and children were now arriving.

As the governments had only wanted immigrants for their labour, they tried to restrict immigration when Muslim men started to bring their families over. By this time the governments had achieved their objectives and did not assume responsibility for the break-up of Muslim families as a result of migration.

When discussing Muslims in the West we often overlook the 'local' convert. Many Europeans and Americans are attracted to Islam, especially its Sufic strand. Small communities, such as that at Norwich in the UK, became famous for attracting British middle-class converts. In the 1970s they drew attention because many of their members were academics and intellectuals and some from influential families. Interestingly, these groups have now been marginalized by the more noisy, aggressive, turbulent and ethnic Muslim politics of the 1980s and 1990s.

What can Muslims do to improve their chances in the West? Some answers are provided by a sympathetic Christian scholar in the USA (Poston 1991). He believes that five main actions are crucial for the future wellbeing and expansion of Islam in America: (1) The need to develop an indigenous

American leadership: American converts should be trained quickly and thoroughly for positions of leadership in order to avoid the categorization of Islam as a foreign 'cult'. (2) The stereotypical negative image of Islam must be transformed through proper use of the media. (3) Provocative anti-Christian polemics should be avoided lest they provoke a strong reaction among Christians (whether practising or non-practising). (4) Muslims should attempt to reach more achievable goals by promoting co-operation among themselves instead of focusing their concern on homogenizing diverse Muslim ethnic groups. (5) Muslim individuals should become involved in *dawah* (social welfare and missionary) activities in order to overcome the powerful assimilative influence of the American mainstream.

These are practical and sensible suggestions, and most Muslims will find little to argue in them. Many Muslims may have reached these conclusions themselves but as communities they are still some way from implementing them. Unless they do so, strife will result from their minority position. Muslim leaders and writers need to do more serious thinking.

In the midst of accounts of prejudice, alienation and anguish there is a success story of integration and harmony. It is located in the unlikely setting of the Outer Hebrides, off the Scottish coast.

STORNOWAY: MUSLIMS OF THE OUTER HEBRIDES

Stories have long circulated of a small Muslim community in the Outer Hebrides. Idyllic tales describe how integrated they are, how their members speak Gaelic and how they have fused into society. It was in search of this community that I visited Stornoway in the summer of 1992.

Stornoway (or, to give it its Gaelic name, Steornabhagh) is the main town of the island of Harris and Lewis in the far north of Scotland. This is the land of the Macleods who once dominated the Hebrides and the Mackenzies who ousted them; this is the Gaelic heartland. It is bare and windswept, and sparsely populated. The Muslim community, of Pakistani origin, is itself small, about fifty in number, and indeed very well integrated. There are no overt signs of racism and the loyalty of the community to the soil is total; they live here and they wish to die here: 'We are real Scots but also Muslims.'

Selling furniture, hardware and crockery in his general store, the elder of the community is grateful. He contrasted the peace and tranquillity of his life here with the social and political turmoil in Pakistan. There is no doubt in his mind of where he would want to be buried.

On Sunday there is no ferry, no plane, nothing; this is strong Presbyterian country, and Sunday is exclusively given to the Lord. No washing is hung out, the parks are closed, the children's swings chained and padlocked. Even the public toilets are shut. No one in Stornoway would violate the cultural code that demands that people stay indoors, least of all the Muslim minority.

The island's economy is based on sheep farming, fishing and tourism. No one starves, but there is a high rate of unemployment, with all sorts of social tensions simmering just underneath. On Friday and Saturday nights the teenagers gather in the centre of town and there is nothing to do; there is one cinema, and the gym will be closed for the weekend. So they get roaring drunk. I went for an early-morning walk on Sunday in the wood near the park in Stornoway and saw evidence of the revelry the night before. Empty beer bottles and condoms lay all around, evidence of the bored, restless youth uneasily confronting the Puritan work ethic.

The Arain work ethic meets the Protestant work ethic

After an initial probing I discovered that the Muslim community were Arain from the Punjab in Pakistan (Ahmed 1986). The Arain have specific social characteristics. They are small farmers of low-income groups with agricultural and peasant backgrounds. They tend to be thrifty and austere and practise the work ethic that made the Calvinists such a force in the drive towards Western capitalism according to Max Weber's influential thesis, *The Protestant Ethic and the Spirit of Capitalism* (Weber 1962).

In Stornoway the Arain work ethic meets the Protestant work ethic and the result is the success story of the small Pakistani community. The success and the respectability are reflected in the neat, grey suits, white shirt, sober tie and clean-shaven appearance which the elders favour. Many of the young people go on to university. Education is another area where the two ethics are in harmony. The tradition of respect for learning in this part of Scotland matches the Arain emphasis on education.

General Zia ul-Haq was the most famous Arain of them all. During his time in the 1980s in Pakistan the Arains became prominent in politics, business and society as a whole. Dr Muhammad Afzal, the Education Minister, symbolized the Arain success story. He began life as a humble junior official at the creation of Pakistan and, some decades on, was in charge of education for the entire country. He was a man genuinely driven by a desire to educate and be educated.

The story of how the first member of the Muslim community arrived in Stornoway is itself worthy of legend. It was in the late 1930s when a

Pakistani traveller boarded a ferry on the mainland and turned up at Stornoway. He was a door-to-door salesman, and that is how the family began its business. Today the senior member owns the biggest car and the biggest store on the island. He employs more than a dozen Scots. None the less the store retains its original name, James Mackenzie, after the original owner. It signifies the extent of integration on the island.

I visited the cemetery where the first member who died on the island is buried. It is a peaceful site overlooking the harbour and stretches over some ten acres. Some Pakistanis have purchased a small plot in the midst of the restrained, characteristically Scottish Christian graves. The first person to die was also the first *haji* of the island. On his gravestone is the number '786' which does not make sense to anyone except Muslims who comprehend that according to Islamic numerology it translates as *Bismillah ar-Rahman ar-Rahim*, 'in the name of Allah the Beneficent, the Merciful'. Beneath the numbers is *ya Allah ya Muhammad* in Arabic calligraphy. The orthodox Muslim would object to the number 786 on the grave preferring the actual Quranic words.

Islamic revivalism in Stornoway

A nascent Islamic revivalism is discernible in the younger generation. The older generation did not build a mosque. Indeed they celebrate the religious festivals in a low-key manner by taking an evening off on Saturday; both the work ethic and local cultural sensibilities are thus satisfied.

But there are signs that the younger generation may want to assert itself in a more distinctly Islamic manner than the previous one. Rubina, a young woman who was studying for a PhD at Glasgow University, was emphatic about her religion and identity. She was prepared for an arranged marriage in Pakistan, and had no qualms about this or her role as a Muslim wife. It was strange to hear the affirmation of Muslim tradition in a strong Scottish accent.

Culture may have been subdued, but the sense of Muslimness is far from obliterated. The living room of one of the Pakistani household heads was full of Islamic symbolism, including photographs of Makkah and Madinah. But here in Stornoway that did not appear either threatening or disruptive. This Muslim community in Stornoway is an example of a minority that is almost invisible and well integrated.

THE GOLDEN ROAD TO SAMARKAND:
ISLAM'S FORGOTTEN FRONTIER IN CENTRAL ASIA

From Stornoway to Samarkand requires a leap of imagination. But by doing so we place in one frame two opposite Muslim minority experiences; one harmonious, the other tragic.

At the best of times, questions of identity are disturbing as they waken the ghosts from the past; in our modern times they are traumatic. Central Asia is experiencing one of the miracles of today: the revival of a culture frozen in time for a century. People are dispirited, dazed, emotionally drained. Questions of identity hang in the air: Who are we? What were we in the past? Who are the great figures of our history? What is our future?

It is well to recall that these areas were first colonized by the Russians in the last century and not, as commonly assumed, after the Russian Revolution. The Soviet colonization was in that sense a second one. Independence in the 1990s is therefore independence from two colonizations. But because of the deep nature of the colonization the response is slow. There is suspicion that this may just be a dream.

The anger has yet to come for the repellent actions that took place here; the rediscovery of a frozen culture has to begin in earnest. Up to a couple of years ago the people here were taught that their language, clothes and culture were backward, decadent and barbaric. They have to restructure, to reassemble the fragmented notions of identity. What we are seeing in Central Asia is an all-transforming moment in history; the point at which the quantum leap is taken.

Central Asia
The former Soviet Central Asian republics, traditionally called Turkistan, the land of the Turks, yielded five independent Muslim countries: Kazakhstan, Uzbekistan, Tajikistan, Kirghistan and Turkmenistan (another, Azerbaijan, is not in Central Asia). From the Caspian Sea to Mongolia, from the Siberian forests to the Hindu Kush, the total area is as large as western Europe. Its hub was the legendary silk road. Central Asia has about 50 to 60 million people. The majority are Sunni Muslims, but there are some Shias and Ismailis too. Central Asia is a cauldron of ethnic groups. The Uzbeks have the highest profile and they are the second largest Turkic group outside Turkey. In contrast the Tajiks are the oldest of all the Central Asian groups. In addition, the area contains large numbers of Russian settlers.

There are also ethnic tensions between the Uzbeks and the Turks in Farghana, between the Uzbeks and the Kirghiz, and so on. Poverty, unemployment, corruption, a desire to reorder the world in one or other ideological frame, all these add to the tension. The great journalistic din in the West about Islamic fundamentalism – shorthand for Iranian-style revolution – sweeping Central Asia may well be a self-fulfilling prophecy. Many people in Central Asia are becoming aware that something called Islamic fundamentalism is both an important and interesting phenomenon; that it is their birthright. However, it will be a few years before it assumes any real meaning.

Culture is eclectic – Mongol, Zoroastrian and Soviet influences mingling with Islamic ones. The graveyards testify to the eclecticism: the crudely drawn crescent to symbolize Islam – perhaps a word in Arabic; the horns on a pole representing the Central Asian nomadic tradition; and the Soviet cultural influence, a photograph, a picture or image of the deceased on the gravestone. Stories of candles and flames signifying Zoroastrianism are also told.

Economic prospects vary widely in Central Asia. Turkmenistan possesses gas reserves larger than Algeria's and, now that it no longer has its profits creamed off by Moscow, its tiny population could become as rich as any Gulf state. Kirghistan, by contrast, is poor and appears to face an uncertain economic future. The economic potential of Kazakhstan, which is five times the size of France, is promising. Beneath Kazakhstan's vast deserts and stony plateaux are rich deposits of uranium, diamonds, gold, coal, oil and gas. Wheat and meat are produced in the more fertile lands to the north. Most important from the international point of view, it is known to have a stock of nuclear warheads from the time of the Soviets. Its size, its position between Europe and Asia, and its natural wealth would guarantee it an important place in the future.

The ethnic balance is potentially explosive. Some 40 per cent of the 16 million inhabitants of Kazakhstan are Kazakh. Russians, Ukrainians, Germans, Greeks, Korean and other minorities who were moved there during and after the Second World War make up another 40 per cent. Many who are not Kazakh are now leaving. Foremost of those leaving are the Volga Germans, said to be leaving Kazakhstan at the rate of 150 000 a year. On the other hand, many Kazakhs abroad are beginning to find their way back home; 30 000 have already returned from Mongolia, many buying up houses which departing Germans are selling cheap. The crazy ethnic quilt is largely the work of one man, Stalin.

Stalin and Ibn Khaldun: binding societies

Stalin confronted the same problem that Ibn Khaldun faced some centuries earlier: what is the secret of *asabyah* or social cohesion that binds groups together? Ibn Khaldun explained the migratory cycle of groups, strong in *asabyah*, from mountains and deserts to cities, their eventual loss of *asabyah* and the weakening of bonds. It set the scene for more united and vigorous groups from the hills; the entire process took about three generations.

Stalin also understood the principles of *asabyah*. His aim was a simple one: to smash it. Stalin knew something about Muslims in Central Asia. He knew that at the core of their society are religion and tribalism that cement *asabyah*. The mosque was a central feature. It provided not only a religious function for Muslims but also an important social one. The holy book, the Quran, was another. Then there was Muslim *adab*: clothes, food, language, custom and architecture; all these provided cohesion in society.

The Soviet dictator therefore set about with hammer and sickle to destroy every vestige of these features in Muslim society. Mosques were closed and turned into prisons; elders were shot or deported; the Quran, or anything in Arabic, was burnt; local language and clothes were severely discouraged; and architecture came from Moscow: grey, grim, anonymous buildings that are so prominent in all the Central Asian cities.

The other cementing feature in Central Asia rests on tribalism. Tribes need to live according to their clan or sub-clan or lineage and in areas that correspond to these segments. Each area is demarcated for grazing, for herding and, where necessary, for agriculture. There is an almost mystical attachment to lineage bordering on ancestor worship. The mystique prevents the outside world from penetrating the tribe while it simultaneously prevents its disintegration.

Once before Central Asia had faced disruption on a massive scale. Led by Chenghiz Khan (meaning the great ruler), who lived from 1167 to 1227, the Golden Horde had devastated this area. The slaughter was unprecedented, and entire populations were wiped out. They came from the deserts like locusts, stripping and destroying everything before them.

On the outskirts of Samarkand lie the ruins of Afrasiab. The city existed before Samarkand in the thirteenth century. It was devastated by Chenghiz Khan. The ruins of the central mosque where people huddled in fear as the Mongols gathered outside can still be seen. The mosque and everyone inside it were burnt; nothing remained.

In time, although the Mongols destroyed the Turkish élite, they themselves became Muslim and eventually merged with the Turks. Taimur would be as proud of his Turkish ancestry as his Mongol one, the two cultures becoming one.

We may therefore identify several features forming identity in Central Asia: there is tribe (Turk or whatever), language (Turkish, Persian) and religion (Islam). Sometimes they overlap, at other times they collide. Babar repudiated his Mongol connections and prided himself on his Turkish ancestry. Yet he was keen to identify himself as a descendant of Taimur, and it was Taimur's pride in his descent from Chenghiz Khan himself that caused the term Mongol or Mughal to be attached to Babar's descendants.

Stalin appeared to have a good idea of the nature of all this. He was tampering with the core of tribal identity and was determined to shatter it. Through his understanding of *asabyah* Stalin destroyed the cycle by destroying the source. He drove the tribes from their mountains and deserts and resettled them. Within two generations they were no longer tribesmen. Entire tribes were uprooted and settled hundreds of miles from home. An Uzbek was likely to have a Tajik neighbour living next to him. Samarkand was the head, Tajikistan the body. Stalin decapitated it and created two separate republics. He had done what even Chenghiz Khan could not do: shatter *asabyah*. But he did not succeed entirely, and for the reasons we need to look more closely at Central Asian society.

The two poles of society: warrior and saint

To understand traditional Central Asian society we need to identify the two key poles that define it. They are formed by two extraordinary contemporary figures, both Muslims: Taimur, the warrior chief (d. 1405), and Bahauddin, the Sufi saint (d. 1389); one symbolizing imperial conquest, clan nationalism and grandeur, the other scholarship, tolerance and folk culture. One conquered by the sword, the other with love. One is feared in memory, and people increasingly speak of him again with awe; the other evokes affection, and people go to his tomb for solace.

To understand Central Asia we need look no further than these two poles. Society oscillates between them. They provide a contrast in Muslim leadership in this area. Indeed, for all his Islamic buildings and even some grudging respect for scholars, Taimur did not ever visit the saint.

The difference in the two poles is reflected in the nature of the two graves: the Gur-i-Amir at Samarkand, the grave of Taimur, intimidates the visitor with its scale and splendour; the saint's shrine at Bukhara welcomes the visitor with its simplicity. The blue tiles of the former and the brown mud of the latter offer another contrast.

For all his bloody conquests, Taimur remained a Muslim at heart. He is buried alongside his saint, Sheikh Umar. The hierarchy is maintained: the saint's grave is a foot higher than that of Taimur. According to local custom, there is a pole about twenty feet high at the head of the saint's grave with a horse's tail dangling from it. Here Mongol custom meets Islam.

The graves set the tone for the respective cities of Uzbekistan in which they are situated. Samarkand, the city of conquerors and merchants, strives to impress with its grand architecture; it overawes and dazzles. The buildings of Bukhara, the city of saints and scholars, are dignified and restrained; a quiet air pervades the streets. Avicenna came to study in Bukhara and claimed that it had the greatest library in the world. The *madrassah* and syllabus were a model for others. There are folk sayings claiming that although Samarkand is the greatest city in the world, its climate the best, its earth the richest, Bukhara is the 'strength' of Islam. Bukhara is the older city, seeing Samarkand as a parvenu.

Many noted figures in the Muslim world trace their links to Bukhara with pride. In India, Sayyed Abdullah Shah Bukhari (whose last name declares that link), the present Imam of the Juma mosque in Delhi and Nizamuddin Aulya, the great saint of Delhi, whose parents fled from Bukhara after the Mongol invasions, are two examples. The Imam's direct ascendant, twelve generations ago, was invited from Bukhara by Shah Jahan to head the new mosque he had built, the most important central mosque of India (the anthropological thirty years per generation would take us straight back to Shah Jahan's reign in India in the seventeenth century).

In Persian and Urdu literature Bukhara and Samarkand are legendary symbols of culture, science, learning, art and architecture. Yet today the West looks at this area of the world and thinks of it as a kind of Stone Age, a backwater.

During that long night of Soviet repression, when Central Asians could not fall back on their language or customs or religion, the memory of the greatness of Taimur's reign and the sayings and example of the saint sustained them. It is little wonder that in recent years these two have again dominated the cultural horizon. A few days before my arrival in Tashkent in June 1992 one of the main boulevards was renamed from Engels Avenue to Amir Taimur Avenue. ('Amir', a title meaning chief or ruler, is used with Taimur's name as a sign of respect.) Central Asians were restoring the great conqueror to his rightful place – unthinkable only a few years ago.

Stalin would have turned in his grave. Suddenly clans, tribes, rituals and religion were being restored. The name of Taimur was everywhere, and the saint's shrine was openly visited. Clearly this was an escape to a mythical past from the grim reality of the present. This emotion expressed itself in numerous ways in many people I talked to throughout Central Asia. It was a testament to the life, power and strength of a tradition that would not die.

Amir Taimur the warrior

The West knows Taimur as a dreaded name, Tamerlane, another Oriental conqueror, another Attila and, in a more modern context, another Hitler or Stalin. The image of Taimur was established with Marlowe's *Tamburlaine the Great* when it opened on the London stage in 1587. Its interpretation has always been understood in the political context of its time. The recent revival in London drew the inevitable comparisons in the British press: for the *Guardian* Taimur was 'a bulging-eyed monomaniac with a Hitlerian dream of world conquest' (3 September 1992); for the *Sunday Times* he was 'Stalin' (6 September 1992). In fact what Taimur represents in Central Asia is very different.

In Central Asia, Taimur is the colossus that overshadows all others, including recent conquerors like Stalin. Taimur was not only honoured in Central Asia but regarded in South Asia as the father of an entire dynasty. Although his ancestors were illiterate tribesmen, he was determined to compensate for them. He set out to make his capital Samarkand the intellectual and cultural centre of the Muslim world. Under Taimur and his successors Central Asia shone brightly as it had never done before and was not to do again.

From the accounts of Taimur that survive, he appears to have been a fierce warrior, a man of the sword, but not entirely indifferent to the great scholars of his time. His meetings with Ibn Khaldun, the Arab scholar, and his encounter with Hafiz, the Persian poet, were significant. Ibn Khaldun, always the practical scholar, wished to penetrate the recesses of the conqueror's mind to discover his military plans and then discourage him from attacking Damascus; Taimur wished to learn from Ibn Khaldun of the ways of the Arabs so he could add Cairo and North Africa to his conquests.

Taimur's meeting with Hafiz prompted a rebuke to the poet which is now part of legend. Hafiz had written these love lines:

For a mole on the cheek of my darling
Which the breezes of Shiraz have fanned
I would gladly surrender Bukhara
Or give back to its Khan Samarkand.

171

Taimur was not unaware of literary trends; in the world of *adab* the conqueror was meeting his match in the poet. 'You so easily give away my most prized cities Bukhara and Samarkand for the mole on your beloved's cheek,' said Taimur to the poet, displaying an ironic humour. Quick of wit and recalling Taimur's fierce reputation, Hafiz replied: 'It is the generosity of my heart, sir, that accounts for the poor condition you see me in.' Taimur was well pleased with the answer and favoured him. But the architect who was building his greatest architectural achievement, the Bibi Khanum mosque, one of the largest in the world, was not so fortunate. Legend has it that he insisted on kissing Taimur's wife on the cheek while Taimur was away on a campaign. The kiss is supposed to have left a mark and Taimur, suspecting something, traced it to the culprit. The man was killed. Women, henceforth, were ordered to veil themselves so as not to tempt men.

Taimur and his descendants were great patrons of the arts. Calligraphy, which derived from and reflected the Quran, was particularly prized. Quranic verses as decoration are found everywhere, on tombstones and textiles, on tiles and even on weapons. The calligraphy adorns buildings and books. The words of God reflect the spirit of the Quran and they beautify everything that a Muslim creates. 'Good writing', said the Prophet, 'makes the truth stand out.'

The spirit of inquiry took many directions. The observatory built by Taimur's grandson Uleg Beg, the scholar-king, is still preserved in Samarkand. He is said to have taught mathematics and astronomy in the college he also built there.

The design of monumental buildings around an open square was a feature of the age and it was copied later by the Safavids in Iran. Indeed Isfahan's glory, the great central square and its mosques, reflects the Registan in Samarkand. The blue-green tiles, the symmetry, the boldness of the buildings, the massive portal hiding the delicacy of the dome behind it, are all to be found in the great square in Isfahan. It reverses the common idea that everything on the periphery of Islam in the east came from Persia. Indeed it is obviously the other way round in this case.

Bahauddin Naqshband the saint
At the shrine of Bahauddin Naqshband in Bukhara there is a pervasive calm, a spiritual sense of wellbeing. Birds sing, pigeons gurgle, and the vines and the trees provide shelter to visitors. Sitting by the saint's grave I saw a stream of people enter the courtyard after kissing the entrance doors as a gesture of respect, although it is constantly emphasized that this is not Islamic. This

advice is even written on a board. People came with offerings which they placed beside the old man who sat near the grave reciting the Quran, without pause.

To the people of Bukhara, Bahauddin was their saint, their own local hero. The principles of the Naqshbandi Sufi order emphasized self-sufficiency, preferably in agriculture; eating only *halal* food – legitimate food untainted by corruption; staying away from government as much as possible; and, finally, learning to pray inside, in the heart. *Dhikr* (repeating and remembering God's name) would be the favoured method. These principles helped Muslims to survive the Soviet period.

Nasira, the official at the Intourist Hotel at Bukhara, had asked me to pray for her at the tomb of the shrine. She promised she would visit it soon, with proper offerings. From Bukhara herself, she was proud of the saint. Already the Soviet veneer was evaporating and people were reverting to tradition. As they were starved for Islam they were coming again and again. All had horror stories, all had deep feelings that had lain buried for generations.

The Imam of the shrine told me that if anyone was caught reading the Quran it could mean Siberia or even death. He pointed to the main prayer room and said, 'Many of the *ulema* were killed here. In class no student could mention the Prophet or any of the leaders of Central Asia, like Taimur or Babar.' Only Stalin, he said, was the *peghambar* (prophet).

Aged about sixty, gentle and scholarly, he was aware that he had been unexpectedly elevated to the helm of affairs of the saint's shrine at one of the most crucial moments of history. There was no anger in him, no hatred. He had clung to a kindly, compassionate understanding of Islam. His beloved shrine had only opened two or three years ago. Before then only tourists were allowed, and Muslims were strictly forbidden to visit the shrine. If a Muslim was caught here his membership of the Communist Party was stripped, and that led to all kinds of difficulties.

Already, the Imam said, there were so many Muslims visiting that the mosque overflowed with worshippers during prayers in the month of Ramadan. The Prime Minister of Pakistan was expected to come here in the next few weeks. The Imam has plans to open a Naqshbandi centre here. He even talked of a trade centre, a complex of shops and a festival. He pointed out proudly that this was the second holiest place for Central Asians after Makkah. Makkah, he said, can be visited once in a lifetime but people can come here all the time.

Seeing miracles

I prayed in the mosque when it was empty. The time was just before noon, before the formal time for prayer. Then abruptly the mosque started filling up with young and old men. I heard the voice of the young muezzin and I wondered when and how he learned the call to prayer. I came out feeling a sense of spiritual peace, of tranquillity. When I thought nothing could be more beautiful I heard a voice reciting the Quran.

I looked round to see a sight that filled my heart with an overpowering emotion of wonder. A boy sat in the midst of a group of elderly men, reciting the Quran. His poise and confidence were matched by his exquisite recital. The elders listened in silence. Women and young people sat around on the floor with rapt attention, many women sobbing uncontrollably. The evocative tableau appeared to be suspended in time.

I was witnessing a miracle. The recitation of the Quran had survived seventy years of the most brutal and savage repression, and here, like an orchid in the desert, it was in full bloom. Truly, the saint's blessings were in evidence.

The poignancy of the moment was heightened as I glanced at the old man sitting next to the boy. On his chest he wore numerous Soviet medals in red and gold and bearing the hammer and sickle. Many questions surfaced. Where and how did the boy learn this perfect rendering of the Quran when it was a crime to recite it? Was it at home? In secret? Was it from his mother? Or was it from a male elder? From the bemedalled gentleman, who turned out to be his grandfather, I learned later.

Architecture as a metaphor for society

For centuries the religious spirit remained strong in Central Asia and it was expressed in a strict Sunni orthodoxy. The *ulema* dominated and were supported by rich endowments; they supplied state administrators and judges from their number. Rulers respected the *ulema*. Both supported Islamic learning centres. The very concept of the *madrassah* or religious seminary as an institution separate from the mosque had developed here. So had the *pishtaq* or gateway, which glittered and shone with coloured tiles and was visible for miles over the rooftops of the towns. Perhaps the building plan itself, the four halls arranged around the courtyard, originated in the region's Buddhist monasteries. It symbolized the age of Islamic confidence. There was a concern for the maintenance and transmission of the central traditions of faith which was not diverted by the rise of Sufi influences. (The Naqshbandi played a crucial role in the conversion of the nomadic peoples.)

174

The *madrassahs* where the *ulema* learned the Islamic sciences were the typical buildings of their age. Rich endowment supported their work and many were built in the four leading centres of Bukhara, Samarkand, Khiva and Khokand. Students came from all over the Muslim world – India, Persia, the Arab lands. Bukhara had three great *madrassahs* in the sixteenth century and a fourth in the seventeenth century. It is said that in the 1790s there were 30 000 students in Bukhara, which had the atmosphere of a great university city with few equals in the world at that time.

From the seventeenth century onwards, the isolation from Iran began to tell. In the Ottoman and Mughal lands also there was a steady emergence of the local vernacular to compete with and eventually overwhelm Persian. By the seventeenth century, withdrawal and decline characterized these areas. There were still important Khanates, important areas sometimes producing a flicker of culture, but slowly the vitality in these societies was ending. It coincided with the rise of the great empires all along their borders; to the west the Ottomans, to the south-west the Safavids, to the south the Mughals. In the north the Russians, who would in the next century be making huge inroads into Central Asia, were also awakening. Simultaneously on all fronts Central Asia was gradually isolated. The trade along the old silk route between China and the West now died out. The Europeans were already discovering alternative routes by sea and the Russians were pioneering routes by land.

Khokand, the capital of the Khokand Khanate, was Turkistan's second important centre after Bukhara, with thirty-five *madrassahs* and 200 mosques. In the 1920s Stalin destroyed these. Only one mosque was allowed to remain.

Perhaps the best-known Central Asian monuments are at Samarkand in the Registan Square (Registan from the land of desert). The Registan preceded the great artistic achievements of the Ottomans, the Safavids and the Mughals by two centuries but it could match their best. Here were colleges that were contemporaneous to those at Oxford and Cambridge, containing spacious rooms for scholars and halls for classes. Looking at the Uleg Beg *madrassah* in the Registan, I thought to myself that here was a vibrant college, the first of its kind, built in the fifteenth century, equal in splendour to the glory of King's College in Cambridge. But by the seventeenth century the extravagance and the degeneration were visible. This is evident in the Registan.

The Registan, because of its breathtaking beauty, is seen as a piece, an integrated symbol of the architecture of the Taimur period. Yet it is also a commentary on the political and cultural fortunes of Central Asia, a metaphor for its society. The symmetry and scale of the buildings are impressive; each *madrassah* echoes the other. But they also tell us of the loss of vitality.

The original building here is Uleg Beg's *madrassah* in which the colour and calligraphy are restrained. The message is subdued, in need of subtle interpretation. There is a profusion of stars with their five points signifying the five pillars of Islam.

Opposite Uleg Beg's *madrassah* is another *madrassah* built two centuries later, the Sher Dar. We learn much about what was happening in the seventeenth century from the painting on the front of the portal, the *pishtaq*. The colours are extravagant: purple, gold and blue dazzle the eye. The foliage is equally scintillating. There are colourful animals, including two lions. Behind the lions are faces with pronounced Mongoloid features. A sort of sun, judging from the rays, rises from behind them. This is obviously the artist's attempt at imperial sycophancy. It is clearly not Islamic.

The Sher Dar *madrassah* is a mirror image of the original; it adds but does not create. It tells us of decline and reveals the cultural context of the seventeenth century. The Ottomans were at the height of their power, threatening Europe. The Safavids would be hostile to these people because of their animosity towards Sunnis, then the Mughals would overshadow them. Remember the Taj Mahal was a contemporary of this *madrassah*.

Here was the process by which one of the centres of Islam became a periphery of Islam. Once a model of excellence to others, it became marginalized and isolated. It was also a loss of curiosity, a loss of the desire to learn among Muslims. The world was moving on, and new forces and developments were emerging which would push these people out of the mainstream and into the margin.

Perhaps the most striking symbol of the total incongruity of the two cultures, Soviet and Muslim, appears in the Registan Square itself. Here, in the midst of the architectural grandeur, your eyes suddenly look in disbelief at the Soviet contribution to the Registan. At the main entrance to the square stands a gigantic ball with a hideous goblin-like face and thin hands on it. In spite of questioning I failed to discover its significance. Does it represent our globe? Is the demon a symbol of American capitalism? I could understand a Stalin or Lenin statue, as symbolic of the conqueror, but the ball left me bewildered.

Sitting in the Registan, looking at the weeping willows, the hills around and the majestic architecture of Islam, I was not surprised that Babar in India harked back to his ancestry with such pride. What were the young men, appearing slightly dazed and sitting for hours in the Registan, thinking about? Were they considering mundane matters – jobs and prices? Or were they wondering what directions to take, which paths to follow? Could they really believe that the long nightmare was over? On the surface, from their clothes, they looked like Soviets. It was when they walked that they gave a clue to their ancestry: they moved with the slow pace of nomadic people. This was not a lazy walk but a rhythmic one, conditioned by centuries of nomadic life.

Red star over Central Asia

The flight from Moscow to Dushanbe in Tajikistan takes a little longer than the one from Moscow to London. It is a move to different cultural and time zones, to an area close to South Asia and very far from Europe. The answer to the question in Moscow – how was Russia to control this far-flung region – was contained in two words: brute force.

By 1740 Kazakhstan was already threatened by Russia. The Central Asian states would fall like dominoes and by the early 1800s the Kazakh Khanates were abolished and Russian forts went up. In 1854 there were forts along the banks of the Syr Darya. Russian governor-generals were appointed in Tashkent, Bukhara and Khiva in the nineteenth century.

Azerbaijan, which is as big as Austria, fell to the Russians in 1806; before that it had been under the sway of the Turks, the Persians and, earlier on, the Arabs. The Tartars had already fallen to the Russians by the sixteenth century, the Caucasus and Central Asia by the nineteenth.

The Kazakhs fared badly because of their proximity to Russia. Their grazing lands were ploughed, and well before the Russian Revolution almost one million Russians had settled here. There were savage massacres on both sides and many Kazakhs flew to Xinjiang. In 1881, 20 000 people were massacred near Ashkabad and Gok-tepe in Turkmenia or Turkmenistan. But there was no escape from Russia. Russia consolidated its grip with the railway line which went to Samarkand in 1888 and Tashkent in 1905.

Throughout the nineteenth century both imperial Russia and imperial Britain played what the British called the Great Game in this region. The Russians called it 'the tournament of shadows'. The British had twice crossed the Indus into Afghanistan; both times there were wars and both times they were forced to evacuate Kabul. After the second Afghan war the Russians and the British signed an agreement. The Russians would not interfere in India and Afghanistan, the British would leave the Pamirs alone.

After the Russian Revolution a second colonization of this area began. The Soviet race to Central Asia is explained by the perception of those who led the Russian Revolution. The Soviets had an eye on India in order to defeat their great imperial enemy, the British, before going on to the rest of Asia (see Hopkirk 1986).

From Moscow it looked as if civilization had been brought to Central Asia. Material progress, science, secularism, all the shibboleths of modernity, were superimposed on Central Asia. Tribe, religion, custom and the past became dirty words, impediments to progress. Here were highways, electricity and schools. Here were tanks, buses and military transport trundling along the highways through the villages in what was now part of the Soviet Union. What no one ever mentioned was the cost to Central Asia, the sense of deprivation, of humiliation, of loss. Language, customs, culture, traditions, religion had been stripped away.

For Muslims Central Asia was no ordinary place. Samarkand had once been the centre of the world, the golden road to Samarkand itself a cliché, a dream of a way of life. What the Russians had brought, understood in this context, was tawdry, mean and shabby. What they had taken away was incalculable. Worse, what no one ever mentioned or acknowledged during the Soviet days was the fact that in their own right these Central Asian people had been the superpower of their time.

The Sovietization of Central Asia

Imagine what life would have been like for Muslims in a Central Asian town under the Soviets: the total breakdown of traditional social structures, the uprooting of the entire family, the arrangement of marriages outside the region which further break down family or tribal identity. The children encouraged to report on their parents, spouses on each other; the inability to telephone outside, indeed, the dangers of any kind of communication; all very Orwellian. The Soviet system had been designed to isolate the individual, to crush individual thinking, to obliterate any dissent.

The mosque shut, the holy books burnt, the elders killed. And on top of this the brutal imposition of an alien culture. The heroes from the past, Taimur and Bahauddin, dismissed with contempt and ridicule. The miracle is how anything survived. It was estimated that in the 1920s there were something like 26 000 mosques and *madrassahs*. The vast majority were closed. Some of these religious institutions with cruel irony were declared Museums of Atheism. Paradoxically, they provided a place in which to study religion for people who were interested in it but could not do so openly. I met many people of this kind whose knowledge of Islam was impressive because they kept it alive in these museums.

Joined with Sovietization was contempt for the local. The reasons for Soviet brutality here are not hard to find. There was the racial hatred of the 'Orientals', as European Russians looked down on them. There was the historical idea of revenge for the rule of the Tartars, and there was finally the ideological need to suppress all religions – Judaism, Christianity, Islam – under the blanket of Sovietization.

Contempt and ignorance for things Central Asian marked the Soviets. They Russified all Muslim names; even Bahauddin, the saint of Bukhara, became Bogoutdin. The mosque at his shrine is described inaccurately in the literature as 'a Mohammedan temple'. Local place names were changed. Dushanbe, meaning Monday in Tajik, was a small village before the Russian Revolution. In 1929 it was made the capital of the republic of Tajikistan and called Stalinabad; it was later renamed by Khrushchev. Lenin's statues in the streets, the names of the mountain peaks (two of the highest in USSR), one called Piklenina and the other Pikcommunizma, testify to the communist past.

The Soviets had contributed to local culture by casting giant, grey statues of Uleg Beg, Avicenna, Khayyam and Sadi in market squares, as in Dushanbe. The physiques of these statues suggested Greek athletes: broad shoulders, slim waists and sharp features. The selection emphasized the more unorthodox Muslims. Taimur and Bahauddin were severely discouraged, since one symbolized tribal pride and the other spiritual awareness. Both challenged notions of the centralized Soviet state.

Soviet artistic genius was also exhibited in the form of a gigantic statue of Mullah Nasruddin and his donkey outside the hotel at Samarkand. The Russians either did not realize that statues in themselves are an anathema to Muslims, who do not believe in physical images, or did not care. Besides, the Mullah's book contained the Cyrillic, not the Persian script, and would have been incomprehensible not only to the donkey but to the good Mullah himself.

Modern Samarkand is drab and mediocre; yet this was the legendary heart of Central Asia, the crossroads of the world. South Asia and China, the Middle East and Russia, Arabia and Persia all met here. In Dushanbe the Academy of Sciences, the opera, the theatre, the parliament building, with their Corinthian columns, French colours and European architecture, show not a hint of Islamic architecture.

As I travelled across the land from Dushanbe to Samarkand, a journey which took about ten hours by road, I did not see any camels or tents or men and women in traditional clothes. I saw no traditional mountain villages, no children playing, no village life. As we sped through the countryside I dreamed of horsemen galloping hard on their way to some conquest. I was driven through idyllic green valleys, over difficult passes, through desolate spaces. Small random houses, no people, no laughter – no noise, nothing of the chaos of the bazaar that I was so used to in South Asia. Everything was flattened under the grim, grey steamroller that was the Soviet Union.

'Islamic fundamentalism' in Central Asia

When Western journalists write of Islamic fundamentalism sweeping Central Asia, they understand the nature of neither Islam nor Central Asia. Here an entire culture shattered to pieces is now being rediscovered by Muslims. It is a painful rebirth that will take a generation before it assumes any coherent form. It is an attempt to rediscover language, history and culture. Although some people may be using the symbols of Islam it will be a long time before it means more than mere rhetoric.

Central Asia is rediscovering the two poles around which its society was formed for centuries. But Taimur's was a dangerous pole, for it evoked conquest and war, confrontation and tribal hatred. Bahauddin stood for universal peace, love and tolerance. Now a third pole has been added, the so-called Islamic fundamentalist pole. This is ill defined and weak. It is represented by angry young men who have lost patience with the two traditional poles and want to move much more quickly, more aggressively, along the Islamic path. They find the Sufi pole too otherworldly, too soft, too mystical and too universal in its call for 'peace with all'. Some look to Iran for inspiration, others to Pakistan.

On the surface there are signs of Islamic activity in Central Asia. Saudi Arabia was the first country to set up a foreign bank in the Kazakh capital, Alma-Ata, where the Al-Barqa Bank will also open an office. The Central Asian republics enjoy observer status at the Islamic Conference Organization. Statistics show that ten mosques are opening every day. Three years ago there were only 1160; now there are well over 5000. It is said that a million copies of the Quran have been sent here from abroad. *Eid* prayers in Dushanbe attracted a crowd of 15 000 in 1992. New national flags, like the Uzbek one, refer straight back to Islam with a crescent and stars.

The Islamic Renaissance Party (IRP) wants a unified Central Asian Islamic state but it is banned in all the republics except Tajikistan. In Kazakhstan there is already an Islamic movement called Alash. It wants Russians to go home and advocates a revival of Islam. However, Alash has not been allowed to register as a political party. Some leading members are in jail awaiting trial. But they have already made attempts to assert their power-base through the mosque in Alma–Ata.

Another contentious issue is the alphabet. Until they were absorbed by the Soviet Union, Central Asians used the Arabic script. Stalin first forced the Roman alphabet on them. He was following Kemal Ataturk, who wanted to safeguard Turkey's future as a secular state by denying them the language of the Quran. Later, to bind them further to the Soviet Union, Stalin ordered the change to Cyrillic.

Now the question of language is back on the agenda. Some observers see it as the vital pointer to whether the region will follow the secular Turkish model or revert to Islamic culture. The Tajik government has already decided to convert to Arabic from 1995 and the other governments are debating the issue. The council of religious leaders of Central Asia, meeting in Tashkent in the summer of 1992, called on the governments to revert to Arabic. Tajiks make clear that one reason for the change to Arabic is to get away from Turkish influence. Tajiks have bitter memories of the Turks.

It is in Tajikistan where there is the greatest chance of an Islamic government. The reasons are simple. It is outside the cultural zone and influence of Taimur's pole. The Tajiks are an Indo-European, ethnic island in a sea of Turks. Both are Sunnis, and that is what prevents the Tajiks from looking too closely to Iran for inspiration, but they speak Persian and that is a powerful cultural factor. The Farghana valley, the land of Babar, was self-consciously Islamic. The Namangan area had been renamed Islamabad. The heroes in Tajikistan are Muhammad Abduh, Afghani and Iqbal, all universal pan-Islamic figures. Indeed one of the poems of Iqbal is the opposition's choice for the national poem if it comes to power. Iqbal's relevance today in the Muslim world is a comment on the resilience of his ideas and their emotional content.

Tajikistan has the highest birth-rate and the lowest income per capita of the former Soviet republics. It is also the least organized, with 70 per cent of the people still living in the rural areas. Its Islamic Renaissance Party, which is rumoured to be linked to groups in Afghanistan, demands an Islamic order. Once the Quran was banned here because the Soviets saw it as 'ideologically harmful literature'. These are the ingredients for an explosion and it was not long in coming after independence. In February 1990 for a few days the capital Dushanbe was torn by ethnic rioting which left some fifty people dead. Russians were attacked, and so were Westernized Tajiks.

The Tajiks respond quite positively to Pakistan. They see it as 'pragmatic and economically progressive'. Although Iran is culturally close to the Tajiks it does not really strike a deep chord. The Turks are too secular and too modern – and for these very reasons are popular in the other republics. Pakistan, Iran and Turkey have created the Economic Co-operation Organization, which the Central Asian republics have agreed to join.

Turkey is putting its diplomacy into high gear. Turgut Ozal is the only foreign head of state who has toured the region. Embassies are opening in every capital, and Turkish businessmen are on the move everywhere. It is significant that President Karimov of Uzbekistan made his first trip abroad to Turkey, although both Pakistan and Iran were vying for this honour. To the Uzbek intellectual, Turkey offers perhaps the most attractive model, with 'Quran in one hand, computer in the other'. It is a two-way love affair. In describing the sudden emergence of the Central Asian states, Nur Veergin, Professor of Sociology in Istanbul, felt a sense of 'intoxication':

> In Turkey, we feel a little bit intoxicated. All of a sudden something happened and we didn't do anything for it to happen. It happened in spite of us. All of a sudden we discovered five or six republics, people who have the same kind of language as us, who have the same religion, who have the same names, who look like us, who have the same body language, who eat the same thing, they have the same cuisine. It's a marvel, it's an intoxication. These are our relatives that we finally have found, discovered. And of course that gives us, very selfishly, at least it does to me, a sense of, well, we're not alone any more.

Uzbekistan's population of 25 million and relative economic stability make it one of the important areas in Central Asia. Together with Tajikistan it was at the heart of the great Central Asian kingdoms centred at Bukhara and Samarkand.

The processes of Islamization

The Central Asian sitting next to me on the flight from Tashkent to Moscow said a prayer in Arabic as the plane taxied for take-off. Then, when the Aeroflot meal, a cellophane bag of inedible edibles, was offered to the passengers, he ate two slices of ham without a thought. He had discovered a part of his Muslimness but still had to discover other parts of it. At Bukhara airport the only food available was tinned ham and the only liquid to drink was vodka. I remained hungry and thirsty. And this in the city famed for centuries as the pillar of Islam.

Wearing the Pakistani dress, the *shalwar-kameez*, enabled me to see how others saw me in Central Asia. Throughout the region I was accosted by friendly people who noticed my Pakistani clothes, asked if I was a Muslim and were obviously pleased when I said yes. Japanese tourists asked me to pose with them in the Registan because they assumed I was a native of Central Asia, a bit of local colour for their cameras. No doubt to them all Muslims looked alike.

Many of the Muslims I talked to were not aware of Islamic injunctions and customs. In Bukhara, in the main square I ate lunch next to a slightly inebriated group of local officials (another legacy of the Soviets, the officials tending to drink from lunchtime onwards). Becoming friendly, perhaps because of my Pakistani dress, one lurched forward with a bottle of vodka and said, 'Muslim brother, we must drink.' When told that I could not drink because I was a Muslim, the official was indignant: 'What do you mean? We are Muslims too!'

The driver on the long and tiring journey from Dushanbe to Samarkand was a Muslim, a fact he announced proudly. It was confirmed by the word 'Allah' stuck in front of him. It was probably all that prevented a serious accident, considering the reckless way in which he drove. Badges with 'Allah' on them were visible throughout Central Asia, as was the skull-cap, another symbol of Islam until recently discouraged. There is a thriving business selling Islamic books and pamphlets at all the major shrines – unthinkable a year or two ago.

Not everyone wishes to travel the Islamic path. In the Office of Religious Affairs in Bukhara there was no sign of Islam in the literature that lay around. The official in charge of religion there had survived the last decades and was a typical Soviet bureaucrat. A Tartar, but born in Bukhara, he had a Muslim name which was Russified as Ismailovic Amirof. Arguing against Islam, he reeled off the well-rehearsed arguments. Women would be hidden behind veils and not be allowed to work; everything would revert to the dark ages. The trends did not make him happy. He confirmed that, almost overnight, about sixty mosques opened in Bukhara. He also pointed out the increase in the number of students at the Bukhara *madrassah*, the only one Stalin allowed: there were eighty in the Soviet times, the number fixed and unchanging; then, 200 last year and 400 this year.

I chatted with a group of people for the better part of a day outside the Uleg Beg observatory in Samarkand. Children's names were Fatimah and Umar, classic Islamic names. These men and women complained that for the Russians they all looked alike; they were all Orientals. Yet there were obvious differences between them in terms of tribes, peoples and cultures.

In the group there was a policeman in Soviet-style uniform who looked distinctly Mongolian. They teased him, saying he was the son of Chenghiz Khan. He was indignant. He told them he was descended from Taimur, wishing to assert a more Muslim identity. They called him a Mongol. I said the Mongols in India were known to have produced the Mughal dynasty and the great Mughal Badshahs (kings). They then teased him in a good-natured way all afternoon, calling him 'Mughal Badshah'.

Nadir Beg, the guide at the Uleg Beg observatory, summed up the past and the present for me. He said that in his heart he believed in Allah. He did not believe in Gorbachev or Lenin, only the Prophet. But interestingly Nadir did not see a contradiction between communism and Islam. For him the ideal virtues of communism – brotherhood, hard work, truth and honesty – were the virtues of Islam and they were not incompatible.

Into the future

The countries of Central Asia have arrived at independence without a freedom struggle. This makes the process simple but it creates all kinds of major problems for the future. It means that there is no ideological or administrative structure in place for the new situation. The old leadership can no longer cope with the new reality. Its reflexes, its thinking and its values are embedded in times that are now suddenly irrelevant. It also means that the sacrifices that forge new nations do not exist. It means that leaders who have spent time in jails, under arrest and suffered loss do not exist. Above all, it means there is no firm set of objectives, no moral or ideological underpinning, no coherent frame of reference for the new nation.

For the nation in search of a hero there is no Jinnah, Nehru or Gandhi, no venerated founding fathers tested on the anvil of the freedom struggle. The present leaders, still dazed, are grey and bureaucratic from their conditioning in the Soviet system. They will need not only a sharper wit but a sharper intellect to steer their countries through the difficult and turbulent waters into which they find it plunged. It all came too easily, not because of what they had done or said but because of events taking place hundreds of miles away, events that had nothing to do with them, events taking place in Moscow and Washington.

The men of straw heading the new Muslim republics, who will stay for a short time in place because of the steel structures of a rigid, centralized administration which are not easy to change overnight, cannot comprehend the scale of the change (a few weeks after my visit in the summer of 1992 the president of Tajikistan fell after a violent struggle). Their responses are arthritic. The anger and resentment from underneath will continue to build.

It cannot be held back by the Soviet-style cadres and the Soviet-style ideas. The genuine original, omnipotent Stalin was one thing; an imitation local version is quite another.

The old guard are terrified of the glacier that is visibly melting beneath them. That is why they continued to support Gorbachev in his attempts to preserve the Soviet Union. These men did not have even the imagination to realize what independence meant for their area. Indeed, independence came in spite of their wishes, not because of them. We will be hearing much more of the resurgence in Central Asia, the quest for identity, the phase that many post-colonial societies went through half a century ago.

In the next few years a younger generation will come of age, one that has shaken off the communist past, one that will be exploring its history to discover it own identity. That generation will inevitably find Islam, if we are to go by what is happening in the rest of the Muslim world. It may well be that, as in the past when new groups from this area gave Islam a fresh breeze, these Central Asians will also revitalize Islam. But many factors will determine the future of Central Asia, not least the influence of a post-Soviet Russia.

THE MUSLIMS OF INDIA: A PEOPLE IN SEARCH OF A DESTINY

In 1947 the Muslim leadership and middle classes in India disintegrated as people fled to Pakistan and others tumbled from their high social positions (as we saw in chapter 4). The next decades were traumatic; Muslims remained dazed while attempting to regroup. But they did not really succeed. A generation later some individuals have struggled heroically up the social ladder and have established names for themselves, but the community as a whole is in a long, slow and sad fall, an almost inevitable trajectory of decline. The events and dates are clearly etched in the Muslim mind: the uprisings of 1857–8, the Partition of 1947 and now, in the 1990s, the dramatic rise of communal violence.

Muslims in India may be around 110 million in number (census enumerations are estimates and approximations at best). But all they have to cling to now is the memory of past greatness. This memory does not reside in books, because few of them are able to mount serious intellectual arguments, but is to be found in those splendid monuments that lie scattered over the landscape – the Taj Mahal, the Red Fort, the Juma mosque, the Qutub Minar. And it is precisely at this point where they are most threatened, for there is a growing movement among Hindus who claim that these monuments were built not by Muslims but by Hindus themselves (see Ahmed 1993).

Different kinds of Muslim society

The Muslims of India appear to be divided into three loose categories often at odds with each other. First there are the Muslims who form a thin layer of the establishment. On the surface there is nothing to distinguish them from other successful Indians. You will meet them at cocktail or dinner parties, holding a glass of whisky, alongside a non–Muslim wife, often making cruel jokes about the illiteracy, backwardness and obduracy of their own community. Among this group are the Muslims who wish to be cremated and not die like other Muslims and be buried. They call their daughters and sons by Hindu names. They have consciously distanced themselves from their fellow Muslims. They wish to survive as individuals and do not want to be involved with the community.

The second category, again small in number, consists of those who are prepared to speak up for the community and are often branded as communalists by the press. They include people like Imam Bukhari, the Imam of the Juma mosque in Delhi, and Sayyed Shahabudin, the MP – although the two are very different in style and background. They are courageous in their attempts to take on the far superior odds and represent their people. The third kind consists of those bewildered, confused and uncertain millions and millions of numberless, faceless people spread all over India.

The Muslim malaise

The Muslims are desperate to cling on to some sort of identity in the face of the massive cultural and media onslaught. It is this desperation that partly explains their rallying behind the three major cases which they saw as Muslim causes in the 1980s but which led to deaths and further alienated them from the majority: the Shah Bano case, in which Muslims succeeded in overturning a Supreme Court decision granting better financial rights to Shah Bano than provided by her husband who had divorced her under Muslim personal law; the banning of *The Satanic Verses* in India; and the Babri mosque controversy in Ayodhya.

So as they cling to their identity they are further castigated for being isolationist, backward and marginal; the accusations of a ghetto mentality create the ghetto and reinforce it. It is a cycle in which they are trapped and from which for the time being there seems no escape.

Poor leadership, poor economic chances, poor literacy figures and an uncertain sense of direction have created in this community a feeling of despair and doom. The fact that they are spread all over India and not concentrated in certain towns and districts further divides them and detracts from their strength.

Muslims are being squeezed out of the villages, they are refused accommodation, and good jobs are rarely available to them. One of the saddest comments was made by a young lecturer at the Aligarh Muslim University who said there was no hope, no future. Perhaps even sadder was the statement made to me by a distinguished and successful Muslim about his community, the Afridi Pukhtuns. The greatest ambition of the young men, he said, was to become a bus driver or a truck driver. They were illiterate, quarrelsome and with no clear objective in life.

It is a long way from the Khyber Pass which the Afridis have controlled since the time they harried Alexander the Great to the time they destroyed the armies of the Mughal emperor Aurangzeb. Tribalism has not translated successfully here. Gone is the tribal panache, confidence and honour; in its place is emptiness and despair. Driving a truck is what Muslims who once ruled over India aspire to today; this is the dénouement of the Muslim drama in India.

The developments in media and communication technology help create an all-India perception of national issues, including the Muslim community. A generally hostile attitude towards Muslim matters has developed over the last few years among journalists and politicians. The Muslims provide an explanation for almost anything that goes wrong in India. From family planning (Muslims have too many children), to economic poverty (Muslims are always poor and backward), to illiteracy (Muslims do not wish to learn to read and write), to national issues such as law and order (Muslims are not to be trusted, because in Kashmir they are fifth columnists, at heart they are Pakistanis and they support the 'enemy'). Muslims now are the cheap and easy targets.

Ayodhya feeds into the political culture of India today on every level and everywhere. The media do not allow it to be forgotten. Again and again the theme is repeated that Muslim invaders arrived in India to destroy temples and build mosques in their places. The Muslim argument is that the destruction of the mosque at Ayodhya will be the prelude to the destruction of the 3000 other mosques on the list prepared by the extremists. The impact on Muslims of its demolition by violent mobs in December 1992 has been devastating (the PAC, the Provincial Armed Constabulary, true to form, stood idly by during the ten hours it took to accomplish the deed).

As it is, Muslims are on the defensive, isolated and depressed. They are falling behind in education and a vicious circle is building up: because they are uneducated they cannot compete; because they do not compete they do not get the good jobs or good businesses. In turn they are seen as backward and illiterate and not trying hard enough. The Hindu majority is mostly indifferent to them and blames them for their poverty, for their large population. Many feel Muslims have been pampered enough. Then there is the BJP, with over 200 MPs, which is actively hostile, seeing Muslims as a source of all that is wrong in a purified Hindu India. The subtext is that if they are prepared to give up Islam and become Hindus again all would be forgiven. And this indeed is happening. It is little reported, but through the *shudi* – or purification – ceremonies Muslims are being reconverted to Hinduism and reincorporated into the caste that they once perhaps belonged to.

Imam Bukhari, the Imam of the Juma mosque in Delhi, shaking with rage, told me in late September 1992 that 'a sword was hanging over the heads of the Muslims'. He recounted an incident that had taken place on the very morning we met. In the early hours in his neighbourhood some drunken Hindu policemen (there are never Muslim policemen, and the police are accused by everyone, including Hindus, of being communal in their attitude against the Muslims) rushed into a mosque and then a Muslim home and placed their guns at the heads of the sleeping women, insisting that they hand over the young men. Alcohol, inebriation, the violation of the mosque, the honour of women – all these would cause offence to Muslims anywhere in the world.

The Imam described numerous incidents when Hindus opened fire into Muslim gatherings after peaceful *eid* prayers. He repeated that although not all Hindus were communalists – and there were many decent Hindus supporting Muslims in the attempt to maintain some sanity in the land – there were parties who were determined to wipe out the Muslims and who were using physical force to do so.

But this must not create the wrong picture. Many Muslims see these pressures as a test of their faith, and this has created a renewed fervour. In their poverty and loneliness they are also confident that it is their faith that sustains them in these hard times: 'We are better than our brother Muslims in Pakistan. Our faith is purer as it is tested more often.'

The great debate in the press is itself a healthy sign. Rather than let it poison the system it comes out in this fashion; it is a tribute to the free press of India. The true enemies of India are the poverty, the illiteracy, the intolerance and the communal hatred – not one community or the other. Until this dawns upon all communities, India will not have peace, and as long as India does not have peace there will be confrontation in South Asia. This will divert desperately needed resources into the kind of futile and inconsequential wars that have taken place between India and Pakistan every decade or so, destroying further and further the uniqueness of the South Asian cultural legacy of synthesis and harmony.

The Hindu response

The Hindu response may be broadly divided into three. First, there are academics and intellectuals, the pious and the saintly, those who represent the best of Hindu character and can rise above caste and communal differences to be fair and sensible. The work of Rajmohan Gandhi or Krishna Iyer on the Muslims is a testimony that this strain remains in the Hindu character. As a grandson of Mahatma Gandhi, who was often politically opposed to Mr Jinnah, Rajmohan Gandhi is to be especially commended, for he has risen magnificently above communal and national prejudices. There are thousands of citizens like these two who want a movement towards harmony. Then there are the journalists and writers who a generation ago would have been prepared to call themselves secular and kept away from the conflict between the two communities but now have thrown their weight behind their own community. Finally, there are the open and declared communalists. These focus on the Muslims and say loudly and clearly that the Muslims of India are traitors and their only recourse is to pack up and leave the land or accept Ram Raj, the Lord Ram. There is no other choice. They are offering the Muslims of India the same choice that the Christians in Spain offered them after their victory in the fifteenth century.

Pakistan is never far from the minds of both Muslims and Hindus in India. Many Hindus see the Muslims in India even now, almost half a century later, as sympathizers of Pakistan. But after the 1971 war, when Pakistan split into two countries, the idea of migrating there some day or supporting it is unreal. Pakistan, with its eternal internal political and ethnic problems, has ceased to be a source of pride and attraction. Muslims say they are Indian; now they will live and die in India. They wish to be accepted in India.

The Hindu ideal of a gentle, accommodating and tolerant religion is an attractive one, and most Hindus are indeed gentle, accommodating and tolerant, but Hinduism is being transformed through all sorts of complex processes into an aggressive force in India today. This is the dilemma that faces many pious Hindus and they are worried. The Muslim response is

189

uncertainty and confusion. Everything they appear to do seems to be counter-productive. They have lost their language, Urdu; they have lost their culture; and the PAC is their worst enemy, which singles them out every time there is a crisis (see Akbar 1988).

Many Hindus, in turn, feel threatened by Islamic revivalism. They imagine hordes of Muslims massed on the borders of Pakistan on one side of India and Bangladesh on the other, and, behind Pakistan, in Iran and Afghanistan. They see Muslims everywhere; in Indonesia and in Malaysia. Yet what they do not see is that many of these countries have been fighting or hostile to each other for decades – Iran and Iraq, Afghanistan and Pakistan, and so on.

It would be as incorrect to convey an impression of a monolithic Hinduism as it is to talk of a monolithic Islam. Hinduism is riven with tensions which can erupt into clashes between the lower castes against the upper castes, one region against the other, and those who speak one language against those who speak another language. Political parties also divide loyalties. Similarly, sectarian, regional and linguistic differences can pit Muslims against Muslims. However, in the broader context of Hindu and Muslim rivalry, people usually side with their own community.

India, the land of contrasts

India is a land of dramatic and often bewildering contrasts: the sophisticated philosophy of its academics and thinkers and the primitive passions of the bazaar; the satellites in the skies and the beggars in the cities; the ideas of tolerance and non-violence and the children and women burnt alive during the riots.

In India we do not see the traditional four castes but two castes: the fat people who sit in expensive air-conditioned restaurants in Delhi, Bombay and Calcutta; and those with matchstick-thin limbs, one step from starvation, running after you for a few rupees. There are no Hindu and Muslim distinctions in the latter; they are God's special children in a Gandhian sense.

But there is also that unique synthesis in India. The best recent book on the Urdu poet Mirza Ghalib was produced not by a Muslim but by Pavan Varma, a bright young Indian diplomat who is a Hindu (and currently press secretary to the president). It is a well-written, sensitive and balanced account (see Varma 1989). But it hints at two things in contemporary India: that the strand of synthesis survives and is valued; but perhaps also that Muslims have lost the capacity even to represent their own great figures.

On my first night in Delhi in September 1992 I sat in a modern restaurant in Connaught Circus attempting to explain to my English friends the complex relationship between India and Pakistan. They imagined it was only one of hatred and confrontation. The Englishmen were asking me how I felt in Delhi. Did I feel threatened and vulnerable in an enemy country? I replied that this was partly correct but I also tried to explain the thousand years of genuine cultural synthesis that had taken place. I talked of the saint at Ajmer whose shrine attracted Muslims and non-Muslims alike. I talked of the food; indeed the food that we were eating, the tikkas and nans, were Muslim in origin. I talked of the architecture, the Taj Mahal and the Red Fort, which were now the symbols of modern India, and I talked of the poetry. But I was finding it difficult to explain the synthesis. Then I slowly became aware of the most hauntingly evocative Urdu love poem (*ghazal*) which was being played in the restaurant. The melancholy words came floating through the din of the noisy customers. It was Mehdi Hasan, one of Pakistan's most famous *ghazal* singers, singing a *ghazal* of Mirza Ghalib. I paused in my explanation and triumphantly declared that this summed up my argument: here in an Indian restaurant was one of Pakistan's top singers performing a song written by an Urdu poet from Delhi.

On a personal level, even as a Pakistani, a Muslim and a visitor, I was shown an abundance of human warmth, cultural synthesis and intellectual reaching-out. Some very distinguished writers, all Hindu, most of whom I was meeting for the first time, presented me with copies of their books. Rajmohan Gandhi signed his (1986) 'in admiration and friendship'; Pavan Varma (1989) 'For Akbar *Bhai* [elder brother], next to whose canvas of learning I stand completely dwarfed – with much affection'. Similar expressions of warmth and respect were inscribed in books by Dr Suhash Chakravarty (1991) and Dr L. M. Singhvi, the Indian High Commissioner in London (1991). Krishna Iyer, one of India's most respected intellectuals and an ex-Supreme Court judge, reviewed an earlier book of mine (Ahmed 1991) thus: 'Discovering Akbar Ahmed through his brilliant book *Discovering Islam* was my first experience. . . . Ahmed is, above all, human and so is his book. I am in love with both' (Iyer 1992). Aftab Seth, a distinguished scholar-diplomat, was equally supportive and generous in his reviews. I quote these remarks not for the purpose of self-congratulation, but simply to illustrate the mutual affection and understanding that so often occurs between Muslims and Hindus – the synthesis that is possible.

The misuse of history

Of the many historical monuments created by the Muslims probably the most famous are the Taj Mahal in Agra and, in Delhi, the Qutub Minar, the

Red Fort and the Juma mosque. The Muslim inspiration and source of their creation has never been in doubt. But extremist groups are claiming that the first two, with a long list of other Muslim monuments, are of Hindu origin. The Muslims, these Hindu groups say, forcefully appropriated them, adding Quranic verses and calligraphy to give them an Islamic character; it is time to restore them to their Hindu character (Ahmed 1993).

Although few serious Indian historians, whether Hindu or Muslim, give credit to these arguments, they have some support (Oak 1965). They are also beginning to gather a popular bazaar following. On my visit to India I saw evidence of how the process works.

At the Taj Mahal in my presence Hindu priests, with shaven heads and wearing loincloths, placed a flame on the grave of Shah Jahan and began to chant Sanskritic verses. This may have been the famous cultural synthesis of India, the blurring of religious boundaries, it may have been, as the Muslim guide with Ayodhya on his mind claimed, the declaration that this was a Hindu temple and would once again be a place of Hindu worship. In the blurring of reality and rumour in South Asia it was difficult to tell.

History is never far from the surface in contemporary India. Newspaper articles and letters constantly cite Aurangzeb as a hero among some Muslims but a villain for most Hindus. Few mention that on the whole Muslims were sensitive to their Hindu compatriots. From the start Babar abolished cow slaughter; and up to the last Mughal emperor it was banned in Delhi as a gesture towards the Hindus. Sir Sayyed did the same at Aligarh. The contribution to Hindu culture of figures like Akbar and Dara Shikoh is forgotten.

Bazaar sociology does not stop with the past; it feeds into the writing and perception of modern history also. In India, if Muslim rulers are depicted in the stereotype as alien invaders, mainly drunk and destroying temples, in Pakistan the Hindu past simply does not exist. Hindus too are dismissed as stereotypes, as cowardly and mean. For Muslims there, history only begins in the seventh century after the advent of Islam and the Muslim invasion of Sind shortly afterwards; the great pre-Islamic civilizations of Moenjodaro, Harrapa and Taxila are hastily brushed over or altogether ignored.

In the communal hatred something has been lost, something has been destroyed – something valuable and precious; something uniquely South Asian. And that something is the sense of tolerance and harmony, a tradition as old as Indian history. In conclusion, the problem of Muslims living as a minority, and not only in India, will be a major one as we enter the next century.

ISLAM IN THE AGE OF THE WESTERN MEDIA

———————————— ● ————————————

By the end of the 1980s the world had changed dramatically. And the causes of change crept on us quietly, almost without our noticing. The main developments concern widespread use of the audio-visual media. These include the video, the fax machine and satellite communications technology. In the context of the global political situation, in which the USA has emerged as the master of the age, these developments assume a special cultural significance.

ISLAM AND THE WEST: CONFRONTATION OR CONSENSUS?

In the 1990s America and its cultural allies (like the countries of Europe) appear to dominate the world. They do so through the media. That is why the media are seen as hostile by the Muslim world. Anything from the West is regarded as potentially threatening; this creates neurosis and suspicion. Anyone associating with the West is seen as an agent, a representative of the CIA. It is the gut reaction, the bazaar response, of a people repeatedly humiliated and let down by the West. It is not the response of Islamic civilization which has survived over a millennium and produced some of the most enduring cultural systems ever seen.

The West, dominated by North America and Western Europe but also including countries such as Japan, is the driving force in the new global culture. The standards of living of many of their citizens have never been so high in history. But they have little to offer those outside their borders. Indeed, they would close their borders to outsiders. The notions of 'fortress USA' and 'fortress Europe' are just beginning to develop and will certainly grow in the coming time.

Strong notions of race and social superiority are embedded in these countries and can very easily translate into dangerous political philosophies. We see the Nazi salute and ideology openly displayed in Germany once again. This was unthinkable even a few years ago. Once again the cries against Jews and foreigners are thick in the air, as crude racism re-emerges in Europe, including France and Britain. Once again immigration laws are debated and are being made stricter. So into the next millennium the dominant Western nations will wish to maintain a tightly run island of prosperity to be protected from the hordes of the hungry and restless wishing to join them.

Then there is the Islamic world. In its population and its resources it is potentially capable of forming a major world presence. Its politics, however, remain volatile. Its leadership still requires vision and stability. Its own thinkers still require clarity. It is for this reason that Western journalists find it easy to label groups of Muslim countries as an arc of crisis, or an Islamic crescent of crisis, and dismiss them. They take some Muslim countries and connect them across Asia or Africa; so Central Asia, Afghanistan, Iran, Iraq and Turkey form a crescent. This is a journalistic cliché.

Correctly or not, Muslims perceive the Western media as hostile. Many factors explain this sense of discomfort. The general attitude of hostility is largely true. Western programmes about Muslims are often slanted to suggest negative images of Muslims. Many carry messages of political instability and the poor treatment of women – the two notorious Orientalist prejudices against Islam.

The restless generation coming of age in Muslim societies is another factor. It has grown up with the media and feels familiar with American culture. It is ambiguous about what it sees: it cannot live by the American standards it observes, yet paradoxically it wants them. It also feels contempt for much of what it sees on television (particularly sex and violence) and believes it to be representative of American society. Frustrated, it finds its only legitimate sense of identity in its own traditional civilization, which is Islam. This generation therefore emphasizes its Islamic identity by rejecting the West.

As we know, Islam is not the only religion experiencing a resurgence. There has been a rise of religious revivalism throughout the world. This has often taken new expressions, sometimes aggressive ones. Whether evangelical Christianity in the USA or Hinduism in India, this phenomenon of revivalism is peculiar to our age. Notions of the secular, of progress and of science which many took for granted a generation ago are being challenged.

194

Another factor is that Muslim societies appear to be experiencing problems with the contemporary world and its ethos based on speed, cynicism and disbelief. Islam recommends balance and steady pace. There is also the noise and dazzle of the media. Again, Islam emphasizes quiet, meditation and simplicity. The family itself is under attack in today's world. Islam emphasizes the family as the key unit of society and would safeguard it at all costs. Most important, Muslims believe in God in an age dominated by materialism and agnosticism or atheism.

Further, people have already been predicting that after the collapse of communism the West's next enemy would be Islam. Now that there are no more powerful enemies for the West to conquer since the break-up of its main adversary, the USSR, Islam alone remains in its path, preventing final world supremacy. There is a growing feeling among writers and commentators that the world is heading for a final show-down, a final crusade, between Islam and the West.

Because there is so much anger and frustration, there is little analytic or objective thought around Islam; there is little sense of working out solutions, of pondering on problems, in a global context. There is sometimes despair and at other times a wild attempt at striking at the enemy. Not unnaturally, this prevents understanding, analysis or communication.

The Muslim failure with the media

Anyone today with access to a television, radio or newspaper will have been recently inundated with negative images of Muslims. The controversy regarding *The Satanic Verses*, the Gulf War and the collapse of the BCCI are three examples of the media focusing attention on Muslims and causing heated argument. Through the drama that surrounded the author and the novel, the way the Gulf War developed and was fought, and the story of the bank, Muslims all over the world were forced to engage in a debate with non-Muslims and indeed with other Muslims. With media descriptions of a 'criminal culture', to many in the West Islam appeared to be a force for anarchy and disorder.

Some of the main questions in the media about Muslims that related to the above examples were: Is the burning of books a standard Muslim response to literature they don't approve of? Does this mean Muslims do not prize knowledge and learning? Are Muslim leaders merely dictators who invade and occupy smaller neighbours forcibly? Are Muslim businessmen only capable of fraud? What are Muslims really like?

Muslims themselves were angry and bewildered by the extent and intensity of the criticism. While they did not approve of *The Satanic Verses*, most did not wish to kill the author; while many did not support the invasion of Kuwait by Iraq, they felt it was high time someone challenged the bullying attitude of the West; and while they were shocked at the extent of corruption in the BCCI, and many lost their deposits, they nevertheless felt that the manner of its public exposure was partly motivated by a deliberate attempt to humiliate Islam.

In the age of the media, of the sound bite, of television images, Muslims have not yet found a way of expressing themselves adequately. Their leaders – whether Gaddafi or Saddam – rely too much on mob oratory and controlled television appearances which appear artificial and ineffective in the West. Besides, the vernacular translates poorly. Hyperbole may be thought appropriate for the mob gathered in the Muslim city – wiping the enemy from the face of the earth, the mother of battles which would claim thousands of lives, and so on – but it translates badly in the international press. Muslim leaders either appear as military dictators ordering the chopping of hands and the whipping of the poor (Zia in Pakistan and Nimeiri in Sudan) or as tribal tyrants (Arab rulers) or as socialist dictators (Saddam in Iraq and Assad in Syria).

There seem to be two distinct Muslim responses to the Western media in the 1990s. I will give two examples from Pakistan. One response is mimicry, to accept Western culture, indeed to reflect and further it, often unthinkingly. The weekly paper, *Friday Times* (Lahore), and the monthly magazine, *Herald* (Karachi), both in English, are edited by Oxbridge/London University journalists who provide useful and often penetrating political commentary. But they also faithfully echo Western jargon and ideas. Even the word 'fundamentalist' is used, without a trace of self-consciousness, to describe fellow Pakistanis; indeed it is often abbreviated to 'fundo'. Both carry detailed and regular commentary on the latest videos and pop songs coming from America. Pop stars like Madonna are frequently featured.

The other response, also from Pakistan, is that of the Jamaat-i-Islami political party. A member announced in public that if Madonna or Michael Jackson were to be invited to Pakistan the party would not only agitate against the government for allowing the invitations but ensure that the functions were disrupted. More zealous members promised to break the legs of those who participated.

While one reaction was to absorb without thought what was coming from the West, the other was total rejection. (They were echoing the two separate streams of education I pointed out in chapter 4.) But are these really well-thought, balanced and serious responses? Will they be long-term? Do they solve anything? Do they help us to understand better the relationship between Islam and the West?

Muslims have yet to discover how to use the media to project ideas and images of their own culture and civilization. A perfect example comes from Muslim Spain. Although the King of Spain has dutifully apologized to Jews for what his ancestors did to them in the fifteenth century with the fall of Granada, he has not apologized to Muslims. It is known that he is keen to build bridges but still awaits a Muslim initiative on the matter. From this it appears that Muslims who are so acutely aware of the loss of Andalusia in their popular literary culture find it difficult to translate this into realpolitik and international diplomacy. The failure to do so has cost them heavy. They are always lagging behind in the world, and the injustices inflicted on them are barely mentioned.

Another example comes from Afghanistan. We have discussed the *mujahid* as the equivalent of a Muslim Zorro figure. But in the Western media the word means different things in different times and places. *Mujahid* in the Middle Eastern context is a young man with a Kalashnikov wearing battle fatigues, his face covered by a Palestinian scarf, taking a Western hostage. A *mujahid* in Afghanistan was a heroic tribesman fighting the Soviets. There were thus different interpretations, different responses to the same person fighting for the same cause: the right to self-determination and dignity.

But the media are fickle. Once hailed as the giantkillers, those that successfully fought a superpower, the Afghan *mujahidin* in the wake of the new world order find themselves discarded. The Americans now see little need for them. Afghanistan is still in a state of turmoil, one-third of the population wiped out and the remaining scarred physically and mentally by one of the most savage confrontations in modern times. The Afghans find themselves at a loss.

The Gulf War and the media

When they came out of the Arabian desert in the seventh century, Muslims had little besides horses and faith. It was this faith that scattered the more established and powerful armies before them. It was a time when faith could sweep all before it, and that lesson was never forgotten.

In 1991 in the Gulf War we saw how things had changed. The Iraqis could not even come near the enemy as death rained down from the skies thousands of feet above. It was impossible even to hold one's own against a superior technological force. It was a pitiful spectacle, a massacre.

It is a truism that the media are used as a weapon in today's world. I was in Britain during the war and I watched television and read the newspapers closely. In the first few days there was a complete blackout of news reported from the Arab side. Television channels broadcast a number of discussion programmes with some very distinguished participants. Because the Western media had built up the war as a major conflict between two largely balanced forces it was difficult to separate reality from illusion. Saddam's army (the fourth largest in the world), Saddam's nuclear potential, Saddam's Scud missiles and Saddam's supergun were constantly paraded before us. It was going to be a bloody and prolonged fight.

The reality was totally different. Some of the most powerful nations in the world had combined their forces to lure, fight and destroy a Third World power. And at best Iraq was nothing more than a Third World power. Its armies had not even succeeded in penetrating beyond the borders into Iran in the long war in the 1980s. This was in spite of the full backing of the West and indeed the Arabs who wished to prevent the Iranian revolution from spilling into their areas.

However, watching the war on television one had the impression that this was going to be a repeat of the Second World War. Saddam had been elevated to the rank of a Hitler – indeed the word was commonly bandied around. Then there was the completely onesided nature of the commentary and analysis. No brown or black faces were to be seen on the discussion panels in the early days. Furthermore, not only Iraqis but Arabs by extension became the enemy. It became the war of the white man against the brown one, the European and American against the Arab. By further extension it soon became the war of the West against Muslims.

This equation, looking back coldly now, appears astonishing. And yet it happened and is true. Because of this identification of Muslims as the enemy, numerous incidents were reported of Muslims being taunted, beaten and abused in the UK. The irony of picking on a Bangladeshi in the London Underground, a man who had nothing to do with Saddam and his politics or indeed the Middle East, did not strike those who vented their anger against Muslims. Even Indians were not spared. The further irony of an Indian – perhaps a Hindu – being taunted as a Saddam supporter strikes us as ludicrous now but created an uncomfortable atmosphere during the war.

I was aware of the seriousness of the situation because I was one of a group of Muslims invited to call on the junior Foreign Minister, Douglas Hogg, at the Foreign Office. The delegation conveyed some of the apprehensions of the beleaguered Muslim community in the UK at the height of the war. A long list of incidents that had taken place over the last few days was presented to the minister. This included women being spat at, pushed and abused because they were easily identified as Muslim (wearing a *hijab* or *shalwar-kameez*). In the public mind anyone who even looked remotely Muslim was supposed to be a supporter of Saddam.

This atmosphere created a siege mentality within the Muslim community. Muslims began to feel their loyalty was on test. Many opposed Saddam and his policies, but there were many others who did not necessarily approve of him yet saw in him a man who had the courage to stand up to the West.

The television discussion programmes in the West at first did not allow the opposite point of view. Not only were there very few speakers who could represent the Muslim point of view but they were rarely given a chance. Those that did appear sympathetic to Muslims were dismissed as the loony left or romantics who knew nothing of political reality. In one such British television programme in which I appeared the distinguished panellists virtually dismissed Victoria Brittain simply because she expressed pro-Arab sentiments and wrote for the *Guardian* newspaper (although the latter probably created greater animosity than her support for the Arabs in some of the conservative panellists – particularly since the *Guardian* consistently opposed the Gulf War). There was no doubt that the Muslim point of view was not only marginalized but was not allowed to be represented.

On Channel 4's *Midnight Special* programme I found that positions were often firmly taken before discussions and then firmly held. There was little attempt at exchange of ideas or even dialogue; and these were extremely distinguished people: MPs, air marshals and experts. However, I also found that some of the famous names showed unexpected sympathy for the suffering of the Iraqi people. Harold Pinter, for example, spoke strongly in support of the underdog. He was, of course, roundly attacked by most members of the panel.

It was quite clear that whoever controlled the media could project *how* the war was being fought. More important, they could project *why* the war was being fought. The other side was simply not given a chance. Even untrue stories could be cooked up or true stories be presented in a manner that blurred reality. We were shown the savage bombing of a building in Baghdad that killed hundreds of civilians in the basement. We were not sure what happened. We were told that this was a military target. It was only through the emotional voice and the disturbed eyes of the British television reporter who went in and saw the carnage that we were aware that something terrible had happened. Hospitals, bridges, homes – the very fabric of society was being demolished. For each news item we had to use a method of calculation, to make adjustments, to arrive at the truth.

But there were other extraordinary developments in the Muslim world itself that needed to be explained. Although many Muslim goverments supported the West against Saddam, the people were with him. It was a strange phenomenon, this support for Saddam. Muslims were aware that he was far from the ideal Muslim ruler – that, in fact, he was a tyrant created by the West and supported in the 1980s to stem Iran's Islamic revolution. Yet in Pakistan and Egypt, although the governments sided with the Western allies, the people took to the streets in support of Saddam. The Supreme Council of British Muslims met in Bradford and unanimously supported Saddam. His posters became the most popular item throughout the Muslim world. Suddenly Saddam was being seen as another Nasser, even another Saladin, who stood up to the West. Although Saddam was neither of these, he had assumed an almost mythical status. So intense was the sense of humiliation and anger among Muslims that they would even rally behind the devil himself if he stood up to the West. This is not only a disturbing explanation but an uncomfortable reality.

Media encouragement of Muslim orthodoxy

There is a causal relationship between the Western media and the orthodox position in Islam. Ironically, the media encourage what they set out to deflate. Let me explain. Until the availability of modern technology which would link distant parts of the world, Muslim societies were culturally diverse. The Quran and the *shariah* provided guidelines but local practice often varied. So the most colourful syntheses of cultures are recorded from one end of the Muslim world to the other. In due course these became part of Islamic observance. Unchallenged, they were accepted as custom.

Today, however, nothing can go unchallenged because everything is public. Within minutes, accounts of the behaviour of a Muslim group in one part of the world can be flashed to another. This has given the main centres of orthodoxy unimaginable power and has allowed them to act and behave as the guardians of orthodoxy in a manner unthinkable and practically impossible only a few years ago.

Looking at South Asian Muslim customs, we observe that many of them are derived from Islam's close contact with Hinduism. Over the centuries these have become part of Muslim custom. But their absorption into Islam alarmed Muslim scholars. In the eighteenth century the Muslim scholar and reformer, Shah Waliullah, emphasized the need for Muslims to reject these customs. But his voice, although powerful and respected, was none the less a single voice. His following and his writing had an impact but it was limited to the literate. Today the power of the media is such that any custom which is deemed to be abhorrent or unorthodox can be exposed to literally millions of people through the media. It is therefore much more difficult to practise something that is not officially sanctioned or accepted by the orthodox.

Sufism provides an interesting example. It is increasingly under attack by the orthodox. The media images of Sufism as a corrupt, decadent cult attracting hippy figures do not help. Sufism has already been under attack over the last century by modernizing Muslims who absorbed Western scientific and enlightenment concepts. Arab leaders with socialist ideas, like Nasser, have also attempted to suppress it.

Although Sufism in its purest forms is traced directly to the Prophet himself, and some of the greatest Muslim figures have been inclined towards Sufism, the more distorted forms attracted much contemporary criticism. Tomb worship, saint worship and stories of miraculous powers have contributed to the disrepute that Sufism now seems to have fallen into. However, this does not mean that Sufism is to be rejected in its entirety. It is one of the most endearing faces of Islam. Its philosophy of universal love, of universal peace, *sulh-i-kul*, is one of the most powerful and attractive messages it has for our age. Besides, its orthodoxy cannot be challenged. The Sufi's first task is to master the *shariah*; a Sufi must first be orthodox before he can go on to the stage of mystical achievement.

Yet Sufism stands as a discredited force particularly among the younger generation. This is for several reasons. The strictly orthodox Wahabis of Saudi Arabia believe that much of Sufism is little more than mumbo-jumbo, a deviance from the straight path. They are especially critical of the notion of intermediaries between man and God. They believe that power attaches to God alone and not to human beings. Not even the holy Prophet has any special status apart from the fact that he is the last messenger of God. Some extreme sections of the Wahabis would even go as far as discouraging visitors to the tomb of the Prophet because it attracts worshippers who in turn begin to worship the tomb rather than God.

This is logical and correct. But, like all philosophies carried to an extreme, it can create problems on the ground. It produces a rigidity which does not allow for alternative explanations. Backed by the power of scholarship, funding and propaganda, it can easily convince the younger generation that anyone accused of being a Sufi is little short of indulging in *shirk*, attributing a partner to God, one of the most serious crimes in Islam. I have heard accusations against some of the most respected and saintly figures in contemporary Islam who were suspected of having Sufistic leanings. These people would in turn chuckle and say, 'May God give Muslims better understanding.'

The media play their part in discouraging Sufism. It is not easy to convey the Sufistic message in the media. The hidden meanings of the saints, mystical powers and esoteric images do not translate easily. The image is far more powerful than the message. A Sufi is easily reduced to a Hollywood caricature.

The other Muslim position, the more formal and orthodox, is paradoxically enough boosted by the Western media. Images of crowds yelling anti-Western slogans and pictures of militant young men capturing embassies or blowing up planes do not discourage other young Muslims. On the contrary they attract them. It gives them a sense of identity, a pride in their cause. They are striking a blow for Islam, for the glory of their religion. They are prepared to make any kind of sacrifice and indeed it is on the news all over the world. This is acknowledgement. So the media play a role in assisting one form of Islam as against another, however unwittingly.

The Western bogeyman: Islamic fundamentalism

What is this so-called Islamic fundamentalism? Why is it becoming such a force in world politics today? Islamic fundamentalism is an imprecise and elusive term which attempts to convey contemporary Islamic revivalism and resurgence. Certain features of this phenomenon can be identified. There is a belief that Islam is a comprehensive way of life, that it includes society, politics and economics. There is also a belief that the failure of Muslims is due to their departure from the straight path of Islam and their infatuation with Western secularism and its materialist ideology. Then it is felt that the renewal of society necessitates a return to Islam, which draws its inspiration directly from the Quran and the Prophet. Many Muslims also believe that, in order to create a truly Islamic order, the present Western-inspired civil and criminal codes must be replaced by more Islamic ones. Westernization is condemned but modernization is not; science and technology are therefore accepted but they need to be subordinated to Islamic belief. The process of Islamization itself requires organization and association of dedicated and trained Muslims who will struggle in *jihad* against corruption and social injustice. However, some go beyond this set of beliefs. They see the West as continuing the Crusades against Muslims with the Crusader mentality. They reject even their own Muslim governments because they are not inspired by the *shariah*. While accepting that the Christians and Jews are people of the Book, their links with Western colonialism and Zionism make them unbelievers.

Many factors feed into this Islamic revivalism. Most significant are the rapid developments in communications which link up Bradford with Islamabad, Washington with Cairo, connecting Muslims living in the West to their own societies. There are also visiting scholars, diplomats and travellers. This is why when the explosion took place around *The Satanic Verses* in Bradford a movement developed rapidly among Muslims all over the world. In Bombay and in Islamabad Muslims were killed protesting against the book. Benazir Bhutto, who had just assumed the office of Prime Minister, said, 'Salman Rushdie almost sank me.' Never before in history could the problems of an author living across the world have had such an effect on the politics of a country like Pakistan.

There is also a sociological factor. We note a polarization in Muslim society which often leads to conflict. Neither extreme is desirable: neither integration, for it implies the blurring of borders which would in the end deny a separate Muslim identity; nor isolation, for Islam is not and cannot be isolationist with its emphasis on the universal and the global. But the tensions of the times have created the crisis of polarization, and the lack of leadership among Muslims has allowed it to grow to the point of mutual incomprehension.

World politics have also contributed to the growth of the phenomenon. From the Muslim perspective it is important to understand that during the Cold War both the USA and the USSR were equally suspect in their dealings with the Muslim world. The Muslim perspective was best summed up by Khomeini's dictum *na sharq na gharb*, neither East nor West.

During the 1950s and 1960s the USSR threatened Muslims. One of my memories as a young undergraduate in Pakistan is Khrushchev's drawing a circle around Peshawar in Pakistan threatening to wipe it out with a nuclear attack. Syria and Iraq fell to a local variant of communism and the results were disastrous. It was feared that if the USA removed its protection many other Muslim countries would fall to the Soviet Union. Then, in the 1970s, things began to change.

When the Soviets invaded Afghanistan in 1979, it was expected that like so many dominoes the surrounding states of Iran and Pakistan would be the next to fall. But the Afghans stood their ground, and eventually the USSR packed up and went home. This was followed by the complete break-up of the USSR, which in turn led to the emergence of six new Muslim states. Not unnaturally, this sequence of events was linked by Muslims to their own vision of Islamic destiny. For Muslims it was the triumph of their faith against Godless Russia; the inevitable victory of good over evil.

With the collapse of the USSR, Muslims believed that the USA alone remained as the major force hostile to Muslims. However, we must emphasize that not all Muslims accept conflict with the USA as inevitable. Many nations have close ties with the USA, including Egypt, Saudi Arabia and Pakistan.

In considering why Islam is becoming more of a world force today, we need to explain what is happening to make countries like Algeria – once firmly secular – turn to Islam. Algeria itself is an interesting example because it was one of the first Muslim countries to achieve independence from a European colonial power. After a heroic struggle which cost millions of lives, it then set itself on the path to secular democracy. Having rid itself of the French it would try to become as far as possible French. The paradox was not resolved. It was simply frozen.

All this, however, did not meet the economic and political aspirations of the ordinary Algerian. A generation later Algeria seemed to have got nowhere. Worse: in the process it began to lose its own sense of identity. Horror stories of the treatment of Arabs in France further alienated Algerians from the French model. Questions were raised: if we are to be totally French and yet the French despise us there must be something wrong? Where do we look for another identity? Is the answer in our own culture and religion? The alternative source of identity was, of course, Islam. It was always there. Earlier it had simply been assumed. Now the present generation of Algerian leaders began to examine it seriously and discovered in the process that there were many Algerians thinking along these lines.

'Islamic revivalism', 'Islamic resurgence', 'Islamic movement' – we imagine these are new and peculiar to our age. We think we are understanding something happening in the world by labelling Muslim expressions thus. In fact these very terms are as old as Islam itself. Islam is nothing short of an endless revolution, the eternal quest to reach out to God. It is the universal desire of human beings to pose the eternal questions and attempt their answers in our brief span here on earth.

CONCLUDING THOUGHTS

A hundred years ago Muslim lands were under the European colonial powers. Muslim capitals such as Algiers and Cairo were occupied. Those that were not, like Kabul and Tehran, were under the influence of one or other power. It was the nadir of Muslim political fortunes. Today, a hundred years later, there are about fifty Muslim states, almost a billion Muslims in the world (with, significantly, about ten million Muslims in the West).

Islamic symbolism remains high among Muslims. Constitutions are declared Islamic and flags bear an Islamic star or crescent. Airlines like Pakistan International and Gulf Air say a prayer before the flight when announcing take-off. Major hotels indicate the direction of Makkah for those of the faithful who wish to pray in the rooms.

Perhaps because of the global Islamic position that is forming, there is also a feeling among non-Muslims that Islam is a threat. Throughout the world there is confrontation between Muslims and people of other religions: in South Asia between Hindus and Muslims (India and Pakistan), in the Middle East between Jews and Muslims (Israel and the Arabs), in Africa between Christians and Muslims (Nigeria and Sudan). Even the disintegration of the communist states shows how deep-rooted these divisions are in history. In Bosnia Muslims once again confront Christians, and in Azerbaijan Azeri Muslims fight it out with Christian Armenians.

The Andalus syndrome is never far from the Muslim mind. The sense of injustice, of loss, of the cruelty of the world is sharp. It is captured by a South Asian Muslim character in an Urdu novel commenting on Muslim losses which fuse in his mind and cause confusion:

> The bearded man tried hard to recollect: after a while, he said, 'all I can remember is that as I was leaving Granada . . .'
>
> 'Granada!' the rest looked up at the bearded man with a start . . . And the poor old bearded man, already shocked at their mocking disbelief, felt utterly distraught at the laughter . . . 'I've been uprooted,' he remarked dolefully, 'and that's what matters. What difference does it make now for me to remember whether it's Granada that I've been thrown out of, or Bait-al-Muqaddis [Jerusalem], or Jahanabad, or Kashmir . . .?'
>
> The depth of sadness in his voice had an intensely melancholy impact on all the men. They drifted into silence. After a while the bearded man said tearfully, 'Friends, we left behind all that was once ours, and now it seems we've even left behind our memories.'
> (Husain 1973: 93)

Andalusia, Kashmir, Jerusalem and now Bosnia – the list of Muslim losses is long. It brings together the past and the present. It acts as an open wound.

Political injustices, deep-rooted hatreds, disintegrating empires and over-zealous reformers explain some of the confrontation between Muslims and non-Muslims today. But it is also to be explained by the ethnic and religious revivalism all over the world. It is a revivalism that is still to be understood in its present global context. We must therefore attempt to explain the differences that exist between Muslims and non-Muslims. By doing so we will make some sense of our different positions. By avoiding it we will perpetuate the stereotypes and misunderstandings. There is no reason to assume that differences in themselves set different civilizations on a collision course. Indeed, in the plural world that we live in the differences must be not only tolerated but also understood.

Understanding Islam

The confrontation between Islam and the West can be one of great stimulation to both sides. Or it can be debilitating and violent, adding to the list of those unpleasant incidents at airports and embassies that we are so familiar with in the last decades. Only this time, with the world increasingly shrunk, all of us will be involved and not only through the television in living rooms but in far more direct ways than we can imagine. It is time for the people of vision to transcend their positions and aim to build bridges towards each other into the next millennium.

The study of Islam is complicated in the West. Many of the prejudices of writers and intellectuals which are rooted in the secular tradition are transferred to Islam. This transposition allows mistakes and assumptions. The most common are misogyny and negative ideas of the priesthood which are imposed on Islam. It is through this filter that people look on religion. They see Islam as licentious (which it is not); they see it as misogynist (which it is not) and as plagued with a priesthood (there is no priesthood in Islam).

There is also an urgent need to move beyond the important but now well-understood debate about Orientalism. We accept that many of the distinguished Orientalist scholars were sometimes writing with a racial and colonial bias – so forcefully brought to our notice by Edward Said. We agree that Orientalism still influences scholars and media commentators on Islam.

But it is time to move ahead. We are living in changing times. The globe has shrunk dramatically. We need to understand the other dispassionately, with a view to living together as good neighbours. The instant images in the media depicting Islam as a monolithic, violent and aggressive religion – the 'rage of Islam' genre – do not help. Fortunately some of the present generation of Western scholars have risen above national, sectarian or religious prejudices. Indeed their scholarship finds an echo among Muslims. Their method is to go to the source, to rely upon Muslim voices. This allows non-Muslims to see how Muslims construct and interpret reality. The work of Professors John Esposito and Michael Fischer in the USA and Professor Francis Robinson and Dr Hastings Donnan in the UK symbolizes this trend.

Church and state are separated in most of the West, and this is what most Western people prefer. They see in Islam a religion which would bring back the church into their lives. This is not true. All Muslims carry the church within them.

It is also important to keep in mind that unlike the ideal Christian (turning the other cheek) or Buddhist (the world as a place to be renounced), however different they may be in real life, ideal Muslims are prepared to fight for justice and for their rights. They do not believe in turning the other cheek. They are commanded to challenge what they see as injustice or what is tyrannical. It is this that makes Muslims sometimes argumentative. They cannot be passive. A good Muslim is a committed citizen.

Ignorance and misunderstanding of Islam exists among both Muslims and non-Muslims. Non-Muslims, ignorant and misunderstanding Islam, fear it. They imagine that it threatens their most basic values. Fantasy, conjecture and stereotypes take the place of fact and reality. Similarly Muslims have their own misconceptions. They too, reacting to the hate and fear of non-Muslims, create a kind of defensive posture within their societies and a combative climate based on militant rhetoric which blames outside conspiracies.

In this heat and misunderstanding the voices of the quiet men and women, those leading ordinary lives, those dedicated to the ideas of peace and tolerance, are drowned. They are still there but they are seldom heard. They are seldom heard because it not in the nature of the media to allow such voices. The media prefer the people with the loudest voices, and it is those people who appear to be setting the agenda; to be provoking controversy and debate among both Muslims and non-Muslims. Good Muslims cannot escape their destiny. The holy Quran has tied them down again and again. It tells them not to use loud voices. The loudest voice, it says, making a sharp point, is that of the donkey.

Muslims wish to convey their message to the world. They believe they have something good, decent and helpful to offer in the way people live. This is not unique to them by any means. Most religions have a strong missionary aspect. We know that Christianity, Buddhism and Hinduism are also experiencing a similar surge of the desire to convince and convert.

Conversion, however, is often seen as provoking violence and brutality. Lines are drawn around one's own group. If you are not with us you are against us. If you are not a friend you are an enemy. If you are not welcome then you are to be shot at. It is this simplified vision of relationships that is causing so much bloodshed and hatred in large parts of the world whether in Europe (Yugoslavia) or South Asia (India) or indeed Africa (Nigeria, where religions engage in almost medieval confrontations). If there has to be convincing and conversion on any scale, if there has to be triumph in proving the superiority of one's own position, it must be based on debate and discussion. No other method will suffice in today's world. This must be noted by all the practitioners of religion and all those involved in the debate whether directly or indirectly.

The voices of Islam: at the crossroads
Each of the main forms of Islam is influenced to a large degree by its cultural and geographical context. Each claims to be as true as the next. Each traces its origin and interpretation directly to the central tenets of Islam, to the Quran and the life of the Prophet.

Mainstream Sunni Islam is possibly the most broad-based, tolerant form and certainly the one with the largest number of followers – almost 90 per cent of Muslims are Sunnis. However, the Wahabi school within the Sunnis believes in a strictly literal interpretation of the Quran. It dominates Saudi Arabia, which has a small population of about ten million but huge influence because of its oil revenues and as guardian of the holy cities of Makkah and Madinah. This school would interpret everything in the Quran literally: thus the chopping off of hands, death for adultery, and so on. Underlining the uniqueness of God, they would even play down the Prophet as simply a human messenger and no more. Wahabis are acknowledged as the most orthodox and authentic school by many Sunnis.

But Sunni Islam displays a wide spectrum. At the opposite end to the Wahabis are advocates of what is called moderate Islam in the West. In the revivalism in Turkey Muslims are conscious of their Islamic heritage but they wish to live in the world today. Islam here is confident and looks forward to playing its role in the international community in the future.

Types of Muslim organizations among the Sunnis include the religious parties which are self-consciously Islamic, like the Muslim Brotherhood in the Middle East and the Jamaat-i-Islami in South Asia. The Muslim Brothers and the Jamaat-i-Islami are two of the most prominent and organized parties in the Muslim world. Their dedicated cadres, the sophistication of their literature and their readiness to engage in modern political discourse make them a potent force. However, they have not proved a success at the polls either in Egypt or in Pakistan, the two countries in which they command a substantial following. Their members have often been persecuted at home, and they have had a bad press in the West. They are labelled 'Islamic fundamentalists', although many of them are everyday professionals such as doctors and engineers who simply want to lead better and more moral lives.

Also worthy of mention is the Tablighi Jamaat which began in Delhi early this century. Many would say it is the most popular reform movement in the Muslim world. Members believe in inculcating the missionary spirit, spreading Islam and working in mutual love and harmony. They scrupulously avoid politics.

In the present age the Shia form of Islam, with its base in Iran, implies religious fervour and revolutionary ideals. It sees the West as the primary enemy both culturally and politically, as propping up corrupt Muslim rulers for purposes of exploiting their lands, whether for oil or politics. With the emergence of Imam Khomeini this form of Islam gained its greatest influence, becoming identified in the Western media with Islam itself. But it is well to remember that the Shias constitute only about 10 per cent of the total number of Muslims in the world.

Sufism, which both Sunnis and Shias share, is considered by many urban-based intellectuals and young people to have died and to be no longer valid. For most Wahabis it is anathema, reeking of saint- and shrine-worship. But, as we saw, there has always been a vigorous interest in the study and practice of Sufism throughout the world. For those who feel that Sufism is now an outdated system with little to offer in our world, the fact is that Sufism sustained Muslims in the dark Soviet days in Central Asia (as described in chapter 5).

Then there is the Muslim youth, often cutting across sectarian boundaries. An increasingly large section of the Muslim population is young. Many have grown to adulthood in a largely secular world. But the problems of their society – unemployment, breakdown of civic facilities, collapse of law and order – have pushed them towards looking for alternative ways of ordering their lives. Islam is ready and at hand for them. It is a fresh, energetic and promising method of approaching life. The young are thus approaching Islam directly, not through learned tomes or established scholars, but returning to the Quran and the life of the Prophet. This is the one great difference between the past and the present.

More than the scholars, more than the political leaders, more than the religious figures, it is the ordinary young Muslims who provide the force in the Islamic revival; they provide the hope for the future. In a crucial sense they are starting from the beginning; they are rejecting what their fathers stood for and what their elders spoke of. They have the confidence and commitment to reject. But their anger and passion must not allow them to lose sight of Islamic balance and compassion. Each generation must now rediscover Islam for itself.

The question for the world is which form of Islam will prevail. It is an important question for non-Muslims as well as Muslims, for it will determine the course of the relationship between Islam and the West in the next century. The answer is not easy to provide, considering the complexity and diversity of the Muslim world. But the responses of the West and the resolution of outstanding Muslim problems will to a large measure determine the answer.

Building bridges
There are many steps that can be taken to help understanding between Islam and the West. The effort needs to come from both sides. First, the media need to take a more balanced and more understanding position. They need to resist the temptation to pass judgement, to slip into old-style Orientalist prejudices. They must also avoid the trap of using loaded words like fundamentalism which cloud judgement and create prejudice. The Western media must look at Islam objectively, even with some empathy, and not respond to events in Muslim areas with constant aggression and hostility. It is also crucial that they should not impose their own intellectual frame on Islam.

It is necessary for the West to rid itself of the colonial and racial dimensions of its attitudes towards Islam. It is too easy to look at development projects – whether schools or roads – in Muslim countries and dismiss them as backward. It is well to remember that until a generation or two ago most Muslim societies were ruled by European colonial powers, that many of these societies were deprived of the basic modern amenities. Most areas were without electricity, without roads, without drinking water. These are difficult hurdles but they have to be cleared by Muslims. So it is imperative for the West to look on Muslims as equals, on their own terms, not look down on them as some inferior species.

Second, more Muslims need to be visible in the Western media – in films, on discussion programmes, on the radio and so on. It would allow them to project their point of view as well as to counter their exotic and alien image. As the West dominates the world media the initiative must come from it. Third, more conferences and seminars for the general public need to be organized to explain Islam in the West. There is a great demand but not enough is done in this field. Similarly, an exercise in the opposite direction is needed to explain the West to Muslim societies. Too often in the rhetoric there is the implication that because the Muslim ideal is such a fine and noble one everything else is to be sneered at and rejected.

Fourth, a basic knowledge of Islam could be taught in Western schools so that children do not grow in ignorance of it; ignorance breeds fear and prejudice. Conversely, Western values, like democracy, need to be explained in Muslim schools; also that the West has more to offer them than just sex and violence, the Muslim stereotypes of the West. The major literary works could be translated and made available to each other. Reading about each other would de-demonize the demon that symbolizes the opposing side.

Finally, the major problems that cause so much anger and distress among Muslims need to be addressed: those of the Bosnians in Europe, the Palestinians in the Middle East and the Kashmiris in South Asia, for examples. The routine beatings, torture and killing must stop. Life has become hell on earth for these Muslims. The West must illustrate to the Muslims that justice will be done in these cases; that the United Nations does not act only to hammer its enemies (as in the case of Iraq). In turn Muslims must convince the world that the media images of them as law-breaking and violent people are not true, that foreign embassies, diplomats, travellers and non-Muslims are safe in their countries. These acts are one way of capturing the headlines but they are not Islamic in content or spirit. The fight against injustice and oppression must continue but must take other forms.

The above points will assist understanding and tolerance. It is in this hope that I worked on this book. 'What comes from the lips reaches the ears. What comes from the heart reaches the heart,' says an Arab proverb. I hope that this book will reach the heart.

Glossary

adab: Muslim manners, proper behaviour (Arabia/Iran/South Asia); also called *riwaj* or custom in Afghanistan and Pakistan

adl: equilibrium, balance (important Quranic concept)

alim: religious scholar; plural *ulema*

Ashurah: the tenth day of the Muslim month of Muharram, when Shias commemorate the martyrdom of Imam Hussain at Karbala

ayatollah: 'sign of God', title of a high-ranking Shia religious leader; Ayatollah al-Uzma is the chief ayatollah

bida: innovation, deviation from Islamic tradition

caliph: from *Khalifa*, successor (originally to the Prophet); ruler of Islam

chador: traditional garment, worn in public, covering a woman from head to foot (also see *pardah* and *hijab*)

dawah: 'call to Islam', propagation of the faith; more broadly, social welfare and missionary activities

dhikr: 'remembrance', Sufi practice of repeating or remembering God's name to become more conscious of God's presence

din: religion, life of piety – see *dunya* as opposite concept

dunya: world, life of the world; the here and now – see *din* as opposite concept

Eid al-Adha: Festival of Sacrifice, the last day of the *haj*

Eid al-Fitr: Festival of Charity or festival of the breaking of the fast, the end of the month of fasting, Ramadan

fana: annihilation, Sufi concept of merging with God

faqih: legal expert; jurisprudent

faqir: beggar, recluse; a follower of Sufism who has embraced poverty or detachment from worldly goods

fatwa: formal legal opinion or decision of *ulema* on a matter of Islamic law

hadd: *(pl. hudood)*: 'limit'; Quranically prescribed penalty or punishment for theft, adultery, fornication, false witness, drinking intoxicants

hadith: sayings – and doings – of the Prophet, his traditions

haj: (fifth pillar of Islam): the annual pilgrimage to Makkah required of all Muslims at least once in their lifetime. After *haj* the pilgrim is given the title *haji*

halal: permitted, lawful activities (e.g. *halal* food)

haram: prohibited, unlawful activities

hijab: veil or head covering worn by Muslim women in public (also see *chador* and *pardah*)

hijra: departure, emigration; from the Prophet's *hijra* in AD 622 across the desert to Madinah; this also marks the start of the Muslim calendar

hizbullah: party of God

ihsan: compassion, kindness (important Quranic concept)

ijma: consensus or agreement of the community, a source of Islamic law

ijtihad: independent judgement or interpretation of Islamic law; innovation within Islamic law

ilm: knowledge

insaf: justice

insan-i-kamil: the perfect person; used for the Prophet

Islam: submission or surrender to the will of God

Ithna Ashari: twelve Imam Shiism; resting on the belief in the twelve Imams; dominant in Iran

Jahiliyya: state of ignorance; time before coming of Islam

jihad: striving, effort, struggle; striving spiritually or physically against evil; colloquial: religious war

kafir: disbeliever, one who does not believe in God

kalima: statement of faith; see also *shahada*

khutba: sermon delivered in a mosque; the Friday *khutba* at the congregational prayer is an important yardstick of Muslim thinking

madrassah: religious college or university, seminary

miraj: the Prophet's night journey to Jerusalem and ascent to heaven

muezzin: the person who calls people to prayer at the mosque

Muharram: first Islamic month in which Imam Hussain was martyred at Karbala

mujahid (pl. *mujahidin*): solider of God

mujtahid: one who practises *ijtihad* or interprets Islamic law

mullahs: Muslim functionaries usually appointed to take care of the mosque

muruwwa: notion of manhood, code of honour, in Arab tradition

Muslim: from Islam; one who submits to God's will

nasab: ancestry, lineage

pardah: veil; could be in the form of scarf or sheet in order to maintain modesty (also see *chador* and *hijab*)

pir: Sufi master

qawali: Muslim devotional music from South Asia

Rahman, Rahim: Beneficent, Merciful – names of God

Ramadan: the month of fasting

salaam: peace; colloquial: greetings. Hence Islam as religion of peace

salat (second pillar of Islam): five daily prayers; prayer in general

sawm (fourth pillar of Islam): fasting; abstention from food and drink from dawn to sunset during the month of Ramadan

Sayyeds: descendants of the Prophet; also called Sharif and Shah

shahada (first pillar of Islam): declaration of faith that there is no god but Allah and Muhammad is His Prophet/Messenger.

shariah: law based on the Quran and the *sunnah*; literally: the path to be followed

Shia: 'party or faction' of Ali, those Muslims who believe that the Prophet designated Ali and his rightful descendants as the true leaders of the Muslim community

shura: consultation; colloquial: consultative body

sulh-i-kul: peace with all; Sufi saying and motto

sultan: ruler/military commander in medieval Islamic states

sunnah: custom of the Prophet; hence Sunnis – from *ahle-sunnah* or followers of the *sunnah*

tariqah: 'way or path', the teachings and devotional practice of mystical brotherhoods; also used to refer to Sufi brotherhoods

tasawwuf: Sufi way or path

tauhid: central unity of God; monotheism; God's sovereignty over the universe

ulema: traditional religious scholars or clergy

ummah: Islamic community, brotherhood

vilayat-i-faqih: guardianship or government by an expert in Islamic law; the office commands enormous prestige in Iran

zakat (third pillar of Islam): annual alms tax or tithe of 2.5 per cent levied on wealth and distributed to the poor

References

Quotations from the Quran are taken from the following editions:

Ali, A. Yusuf (trans.) (1989) *The Holy Quran: Text, Translation and Commentary*, new revised edition, Amana Corporation, Brentwood, Maryland, USA.

Pickthall, Marmaduke (trans. and intro.) (1988) *The Meaning of the Glorious Quran*, Taha Publishers, London. Originally published 1930.

Ahmad, Khurshid (1974) *Family Life in Islam*, The Islamic Foundation, Leicester.

Ahmed, Akbar S. (1980) *Pukhtun Economy and Society: Traditional Structure and Economic Development in a Tribal Society*, Routledge, London.

Ahmed, Akbar S. (1986) *Pakistan Society: Islam, Ethnicity and Leadership in South Asia*, Oxford University Press, Karachi.

Ahmed, Akbar S. (1988) *Discovering Islam: Making Sense of Muslim History and Society*, Routledge, London.

Ahmed, Akbar S. (1991) *Resistance and Control in Pakistan*, Routledge, London.

Ahmed, Akbar S. (1992) *Postmodernism and Islam: Predicament and Promise*, Routledge, London.

Ahmed, Akbar S. (1993) 'The History – Thieves: Stealing the Muslim Past?', *History Today*, vol. 43 (January), London.

Ahmed, Akbar S. and David Hart (ed.) (1984) *From The Atlas to the Indus: The Tribes of Islam*, Routledge, London.

Akbar, M. J. (1988) *Riot after Riot*, Penguin, New Delhi.

Anand, Mulk Raj (1967) 'Fatehpur Sikri', *MARG: A Magazine of the Arts*, vol. XX, no. 4 (September), Bombay.

Ashraf, Syed Ali (1988) *Islam: Teacher's Manual*, Westhill Project R.E. 5–16, Mary Glasgow Publications, London.

Azzam, Leila and Aisha Gouverneur (1985) *The Life of the Prophet Muhammad*, Islamic Texts Society, London.

Babar, Zahiruddin (1922) *The Babur-Namah* (Memoirs of Babar), trans. and ed. A. S. Beveridge, London; repr. Luzac, London, 1969.

Boase, Roger (1989a) 'The Disputed Heritage: Europe's Cultural Debt to the Arabs', *Bulletin of Hispanic Studies*, vol. LXVI, London.

Boase, Roger (1989b) Foreword to Ibn Said al-Maghribi, *The Banners of the Champions: An Anthology of Medieval Arabic Poetry from Andalusia and Beyond*, selected and trans. James A. Bellamy and Patricia Owen Steiner, Hispanic Seminary of Medieval Studies, Madison, Wisc.

Boase, Roger (unpublished) 'Arab Influences on European Love-Poetry', unpublished paper.

Chakravarty, Suhash (1991) *The Raj Syndrome: A Study in Imperial Perceptions*, Penguin, New Delhi.

Chaudhuri, Nirad (1990) *Thy Hand Great Anarch! India 1921–1952*, Hogarth Press, London.

Danziger, Nick (1987) *Danziger's Travels: Beyond Forbidden Frontiers*, Paladin, London.

Dehlvi, Sadia (1992) 'In Praise of the *Shariat*', *Friday Times*, 26 March, Lahore.

Edwards, John (1992) 'A Conquistador Society? The Spain Columbus Left', *History Today*, vol. 42 (May), London.

Efe, Ahmet (1987) *Hagia Sophia*, Efe Tourism, Istanbul.

Esposito, John L. (1991) *Islam: The Straight Path*, expanded edition, Oxford University Press, New York.

Fischer, Michael M. J. (1980) *Iran: From Religious Dispute to Revolution*, Harvard University Press, Cambridge, Mass.

Fischer, Michael M. J. and Mehdi Abedi (1990) *Debating Muslims: Cultural Dialogues in Postmodernity and Tradition*, University of Wisconsin Press, Wisc.

Friedman, Thomas (1990) *From Beirut to Jerusalem*, Fontana, London.

Gabrieli, Francesco (1977) *Muhammad and the Conquests of Islam*, Italy.

Gandhi, Rajmohan (1986) *Eight Lives: A Study of the Hindu–Muslim Encounter*, State University of New York Press, Albany, NY.

Haggard, Rider (1904) *The Brethren*, Cassell & Co., London.

Halliday, Fred (1992) *Arabs in Exile: Yemeni Migrants in Urban Britain*, I. B. Tauris, London and New York.

Hawking, Stephen (1988) *A Brief History of Time: From the Big Bang to Black Holes*, Bantam Press, London.

Haykal, Muhammad Husayn (1976) *The Life of Muhammad*, trans. from the 8th edition by Ismail Ragi A. al Faruqi, North American Trust Publications, USA.

Heikal, Mohamed (1992) *Illusions of Triumph: An Arab View of the Gulf War*, HarperCollins, London.

Hill, Christopher (1991) 'The End of History?', *History Today*, 40th anniversary issue, vol. 41 (April), London.

Hopkirk, Peter (1986) *Setting the East Ablaze: Lenin's Dream of an Empire in Asia*, Oxford University Press, Oxford.

Hourani, Albert (1991) *A History of the Arab Peoples*, Faber & Faber, London.

Husain, Intizar (1973) 'The Lost Ones': English translation of '*Woh jo kho'e ga'e*' (from Intizar Husain's collection of short stories, *Shahr-e Afsos* Maktaba-e Karwan, Lahore, pp. 9–28), in *Pakistani Literature*, ed. Ghulam Rabbani A. Agro, vol. 1, no. 1, Pakistan Academy of Letters, Islamabad, 1992.

Ibn Arabi, Muhyi d-Din (1974) *Tarjuman al-ashwaq*, Murcia, 1165–1240, in *Hispano-Arabic Poetry: A Student Anthology*, ed. James Monroe, University of California Press, Berkeley.

Irving, W. (1990) *Tales of the Alhambra*, GREFOL, SA, La Fuensanta, Mostoles, Madrid.

Iyer, Krishna (1992) Review of Ahmed (1991), *Front Line*, 28 February, Madras.

Maududi, Abul A'la (1978) 'What Islam Stands For', in *The Challenge of Islam*, ed. Altaf Gauhar, Islamic Council of Europe, London.

Menocal, Maria Rosa (1987) *The Arabic Role in Medieval Literary History: A Forgotten Heritage*, University of Pennsylvania Press, Philadelphia.

Nielsen, J. S. (1992) *Muslims in Western Europe*, Edinburgh University Press, Edinburgh.

Oak, P. N. (1965) *Taj Mahal Was a Rajput Palace*, Asiatic Printers, Delhi.

Ozal, Turgut (1984) in 'Turkish Islam and the Secular State' by Nicholas Ludington, in *The Muslim World Today*, Occasional Paper no. 1, American Institute for Islamic Affairs, Washington, DC.

Pal, Pratapaditya, Janice Leoshko, Joseph Dye and Stephen Markel (1989) *Romance of the Taj Mahal*, Thames & Hudson, London.

Poston, Larry (1991) 'The Future of Da'wah in North America', *The American Journal of Islamic Social Sciences*, vol. 8, no. 3, Herndon, VA.

Rispler-chaim, Vardit (1992) 'The *Siwak*: A Medieval Islamic Contribution to Dental Care', *Journal of the Royal Asiatic Society*, 3rd series, vol. 2, part 1 (April), London.

Robinson, Francis (1982) *Atlas of the Islamic World since 1500*, Phaidon, produced by Equinox, Oxford.

Rushdie, Salman (1988) *The Satanic Verses*, Viking Penguin, London and New York.

Schuon, Frithjof (1976) *Understanding Islam*, Mandala Unwin Paperbacks, London.

Shah, Idries (1990) *The Way of the Sufi*, Arkana/Penguin, London.

Siddiqi, Dr Muzammil H. (1991) 'Muslims in a Non-Muslim Society', *Brighton Islamic Centre Bulletin*, vol. 15, no. 3 (July–September), pp. 12–13, Brighton.

Singh, Khushwant (1988) *Train to Pakistan*, Ravi Dayal, New Delhi.

Singhvi, Dr L. M. (1991) *Freedom on Trial*, Vikas Publishing House Pvt, New Delhi.

Varma, Pavan K. (1989) *Ghalib: The Man, The Times*, Penguin, New Delhi.

Watson, Helen (1992) *The City of the Dead*, Hurst & Co., London.

Watt, William Montgomery (1991) 'Perceptions of the Crusades', *Yad-Nama*, vol. 1, Islamistica, Università di Roma, La Sapienza, Studi Orientali, vol. X, pp. 513–24, Rome.

Weber, Max (1962) *The Protestant Ethic and the Spirit of Capitalism*, Allen & Unwin, London.

Picture credits

Index

Welfare Party 99, 102
women, position of:
  in harem 77–8
  in Iran 113, 147
  in Islam 140, 143–7
  outside Islam 22, 61

Yazid, caliph 49–50, 111

Yugoslavia, former state 12,
  66, 151, 208

Zafar, emperor 118
Zaidi sect 49, 53
Zainab, daughter of the
  Prophet 24
zakat 40–1

Zauq, Sheikh Ibrahim 118
Zia, Begum 92, 147
Zia ul-Haq, General 94, 123,
  129–30, 135, 157, 164, 196
Zionism 47, 128–9, 203
Zoroastrianism 167